NEVER FEAR

NEVER FEAR

RELIVING THE LIFE OF
SIR FRANCIS CHICHESTER

IAN STRATHCARRON

UNICORN

First published 2016 by Unicorn, an imprint of Unicorn Publishing Group
101, Wardour Street,
London,
W1F 0UG

A catalogue record for this book is available from the British Library

ISBN is 978-1-910787-16-8

Edited by Johanna Stephenson
Designed by Baseline Arts Ltd, Oxford
Index by Elizabeth Wise
Printed in India by Imprint Press

CONTENTS

Dedicated to Evie and Arlo, and Little and Patch

ACKNOWLEDGMENTS

Thank you to all who helped make the book come true:

Adrian Clark for help with Gipsy Moth V
Alexander and Lucy Rhind from the Old
   Rectory, Shirwell
Andrew Simpson at the RAF Museum in
   Hendon.
Anne, Lady Chichester for her memories of
   Sheila and Sir John
Barry Pickthall at PPL for help with images
Belinda, Lady Montagu for the '60s memories
Bob Gibson for Gipsy Moth flying instruction.
Chris Chapman in Wellington, New Zealand
David Gibbons of the National Trust at
   Arlington Court
David Martin for his family memories
Edward, Lord Montagu for family help
Ewen Southby-Tailyour for his briefing on
   Blondie Hasler
Giles Chichester for his connections
Gordon Wilson in Peacehaven, New Zealand
Gregor Halsey of the London Model Yacht
   Club
Ian Hutton and Jessy Lawrence at the Lord
   Howe Island Museum
Jamie Chichester, Sir, for his family
   explanations
Janelle Blucher and Gaye Evans at the Norfolk
   Island Museum
Janet Grosvenor of the Royal Ocean Racing
   Club
Jeremy Goodwin in Auckland, New Zealand
John Delaney at the Imperial War Museum
   Duxford
John Roome of the Royal Ocean Racing Yacht
   Club

Ken Robinson for his Beaulieu recollections
Lance Chapple of the Royal Sydney Yacht
   Squadron
Lyndsay Tooley from Norfolk Island
Manu and Snah Patel from Devon
Marty Montagu-Scott for help with Buckler's
   Hard research
Neil Waterson in Upper Hutt, New Zealand
Neville Cullingford, Squadron Administrator
   at RAF Hullavington
Nick Blake, Squadron Adjutant Flight
   Lieutenant at RAF Hullavington
Norah Perkins at Curtis Brown for their
   generosity with permissions
Peter Bradford of the Royal Sydney Yacht
   Squadron
Peter Bruce for his insights
Peter Bugge of the Guild of Air Pilots and
   Navigators
Philip Clifford of the Brooklands Museum
Piers and Silvie Le Marchant with Gipsy Moth
   III in Corfu
Ralph Goodwin in Peacehaven, New Zealand
Ralph, Lord Montagu for help with Beaulieu
   research
Richard Baggett of the UK Sailing Academy
Rob Thompson and Eileen Skinner of Gipsy
   Moth Trust
Roy Palmer for the use of his Gipsy Moth
Rt Revd Alan Winstanley at St Peters, Shirwell
Sarah Hustler at the Poole History Society
Sebastian Cox, Head of Air Historical Branch
   at RAF Northolt

FOREWORD

I am delighted to be writing the foreword to this book as in many ways Francis's life was like the foreword to my own.

Unlike him I took to the water early in life, already a seaman when joining the Merchant Navy at seventeen. Francis was in his mid-fifties when he first raced a yacht, and that was as crew. Yet, as Ian points out in this excellent account of his triumphs and tribulations, twelve years later he was one of the most famous men on the planet and certainly by far the most famous yachtsman.

In fact it was at his moment of greatest celebration that the first seeds of long distance record breaking stirred in my soul. I was sailing my boat *Suhaili* back from India when I first heard of Francis's circumnavigation and thought at the time that it left just one record left unclaimed. Francis had circumnavigated solo, albeit with a one month pit stop in Sydney. Surely the next challenge, the last unadventured adventure, was to circumnavigate solo without a pit stop at all?

Fascinating to me, reading Ian's *Never Fear*, is how much long distance sailing has changed in the years between Francis's and my circumnavigations to those who would attempt to circumnavigate today. The hard skills remain: seamanship of course, plus dealing with fear and loneliness. It is the soft skills that have made racing easier yet more demanding; likewise, safer yet riskier. Whereas we now know to within a few metres where we are all the time, in those days we had to wait for a sun sight, often for several days. Yet this knowing of position itself demands greater performance to reach the next position. And so with safety: satellite technology has made being rescued far more likely than before – it was more or less unthought of in our day – so the sailor's danger signals that were red are now merely yellow. The higher the bar, the higher the jump. Likewise with the weather: now we can see live on screen what is going to happen where and when; in the 1960s we had a barometer and a weather eye on the clouds and wind direction to judge the portents for what might be approaching.

It follows that Francis's greatest skill, that of a master navigator, is a redundant skill in today's world. Like Ian piloting the tanker up the Mississippi, an iPhone with the right app is all you really need if close to land – and offshore, satellites take over where mobile signals fade.

But what are not redundant are his qualities as a man. I recall two Francises. Francis I was the record breaker: a monomaniac on a mission, totally determined, focused to the point of what seemed rudeness, fearless, fatalistic, the mountain mover. Francis II was the Francis ashore: charming, patient, civilised, generous and cultured, the family man, easy with friends and courteous to strangers. What Francis I and Francis II shared was a man happy in his skin, whichever skin was on him at the time.

Francis could only ever have been an Englishman, in fact he was the caricature of a foreigner's view of the ideal Englishman: understated yet heroic when needed, calm but not to be bossed around, disliking of anything to do with a 'fuss', especially a media fuss, even more a medical fuss, amusing in conversation, self-depreciating, loyal to friends, without obvious foes, magnanimous, wry, easily humoured and easily humorous.

Francis was the example I followed, in fact we joked about me finding out what record he would attempt next so that I could prepare to break it later. And he did; and I did. I am so pleased his memory will live on through this excellent biography and I am sure the reader will enjoy reading it as much as the author clearly enjoyed writing it.

ROBIN KNOX-JOHNSTON

It's extraordinary how you feel the world should be run after being alone for so long.

CHAPTER 1

Arise, Sir Francis

I T WAS, EVERYONE AGREED, a wonderful occasion: mid-morning summer sunny, with Union flags, royal standards and naval ensigns ruffling in a lazy westerly breeze, Old Father Thames resting at high tide, banks brimming with crowds, all anticipation and excitement, waiting for their Queen, surrounded by her pageantry, to knight their hero.

Ashore lay Wren and Vanbrugh's seventeenth-century baroque masterpiece, Greenwich's Royal Naval College, emblem of empire, its twin-domed wings haughty over their matching Solomonesque palaces reaching down to the river around the Grand Quadrangle. On the square's lawn naval cadets sat cross-legged on the grass, behind them junior ratings and officers, a set of blue and white on green, and behind them the Chichester family and friends in suits and tweeds, pearls and summer hats, smiles and laughter.

On the ground floor of King Charles II's original Greenwich Palace, in the Wren Room overlooking the river, Her Majesty the Queen and the Duke of Edinburgh, attended by their host, Admiral President Vice-Admiral Sir Horace Lyddon and their aide-de-camp, Captain Hedley Kett, were briefed on the morning's schedule by the Queen's long-serving Private Secretary, Sir Michael Adeane. It was 9.45 am. As usual the Royal Household's organisation was impeccable. *Gipsy Moth IV* would berth in precisely thirty minutes and cast off precisely sixty minutes after that. In the meantime there was a public ceremony to perform and a tour to be made, all finely timed and executed.

In the adjoining Hawksmoor Room Lord Plunket, Equerry to the Queen and godson of Her Majesty Queen Elizabeth the Queen Mother and Buckingham Palace Press Officer Sir Richard Colville unsheathed the ceremonial sword and knelt on the ceremonial stool, double-double-checking the tools of the ceremony. The knighting sword was the very one with which, in 1581, an earlier Elizabeth, Queen Elizabeth I, had knighted an earlier Sir Francis, Sir Francis Drake, for an earlier circumnavigation on board *Golden Hind* a few cables upstream at Deptford.[1] On that occasion, as Sir Horace scarcely needed reminding, the bridge connecting the ship to the shore collapsed 'and upwards of One Hundred Persons did fall into the River'. On this occasion, Lord Plunket scarcely needed reminding, the ceremony would be held in public, a worldwide televised public too, in a late change from the planned private knighting. About the gold-painted and crimson-cushioned knighting stool Colville could be more relaxed: it had no provenance and, as yet, no mishaps to its name.

At 10 am the Queen's close friend, letter-writer and lady-in-waiting, the Hon. Mrs Mary Morrison, entered the Wren Room for the Queen's and Prince Philip's final look in the full-length mirror that the Royal Household ensures precedes them on all occasions. The Queen was forty-one years old, five feet six inches tall in her raised John Lobb cream shoes. Entitled to wear the full naval uniform of her rank, Lord High Admiral of the Royal Navy, she chose to let the celebration outrank her and wore a Norman Hartnell off-white two-piece suit with royal blue cuffs and collar and matching hat. She looked admirably nautical, just right for the day. Prince Philip, five years older and six inches taller in his Church derby shoes, forswore his rank's uniform too, that of Admiral of the Fleet, and wore a dark grey double-breasted suit from Gieves & Hawkes of Savile Row. At 10.10

am Colville and Plunket re-joined them in the Wren Room. With five minutes to go the royal party was complete and chit-chatting in practiced serenity.

———∞∞∞———

Serenity was in short supply aboard *Gipsy Moth IV*. The whole voyage from Plymouth to London, which should have been the triumphant homecoming climax to Francis's circumnavigation, had been bedevilled from its inception; and now yesterday a new spanner had been chucked into the works, a royal spanner that could hardly be gainsaid.

Francis had first heard of his knighting on his last night in Sydney, five months ago, when he and his wife, Sheila, had been awoken in the early hours by an excited Commissioner, Sir Charles Johnson, with the hot news from the Palace. The next morning, as he was casting off to finish his voyage around the rest of the world, the Governor-General, Lord Casey, handed him a confirming telegram from the Queen. From then onwards the Royal Household and Sheila had been watching his progress home and keeping a number of days from mid-June to mid-July free for the formal knighting ceremony. By the time he was in the Bay of Biscay, firm dates from the Queen's diary were being floated to Sheila and they settled on 13 June for a private knighting in Greenwich, home of the longitude meridian with which he had reckoned a thousand fixes and symbol of Britannia's seaborne empire, followed by a public reception and lunch given by the Lord Mayor at Mansion House for a homecoming Londoner.

Working backwards from Greenwich on 13 June, Sheila and the Palace agreed on a week for Francis, their son Giles and her crew to sail *Gipsy Moth IV* from Plymouth to London, so leaving Drake's old Devon port no later than 6 June. At that stage Francis was estimated to arrive in Plymouth around 1 June, so leaving the best part of a week for celebrations and recovery there – more than enough time, it would seem. Sheila had no option but to assume that all would be well, which she knew really meant Francis's frail health would be well, but she must have known deep down what all sailors know from experience: sailing schedules and landlubber timetables seldom rub along too well together.

Francis actually arrived back a few days earlier than anticipated, on 28 May, after a gloriously fast and calm passage up through the Western Approaches. Plymouth was there to greet him: half a million souls thronged the Hoe and shorelines to see him arrive in a beautiful sunset. The world's media were there to greet him too: photographers and camera crew had hired more or less anything that would float to capture the moment. Francis was overwhelmed but grinned back through clenched teeth. He hated 'a fuss' at the best of times but after five months of living at peace with himself, this hysterical floating fandango crowding in on him and *Gipsy Moth IV* was the very opposite of the quiet reunion with Sheila and Giles for which he had hoped.

On 30 May the Lord Mayor of Plymouth laid on a Thanksgiving Service followed by a fully functioned civic reception and dinner. Next day the Royal Western Yacht Club hosted him. Press conference followed press conference. Everyone wanted a piece of Francis and after five months of sharing himself only with himself, he now had to share himself with the world. Everyone now seemed to have known him for years, everyone was now his old friend from way back, everyone was a well-wisher who had always known he would do it, everyone wanted to slap his back. After a week the constant, unwanted, unnatural adulation was wearing him pale and gaunt. The sea of people and their agendas was proving harder to weather than the sea itself. Sheila urged him to cancel the last great occasion, another formal dinner, this time given in his honour by the naval Commander-in-Chief of Plymouth. She and Giles were ready to sail for Greenwich the next morning. Francis said he couldn't cancel; during dinner he collapsed and was admitted to the Royal Naval Hospital. They diagnosed a burst duodenal ulcer and exhaustion, nervous and physical. They confined him to his hospital bed so his body might recover.[2]

Buckingham Palace then suggested a new date: 7 July. Sheila called on their old family – and Royal Family – friend, Commander Erroll Bruce, to be the Sailing Master for the voyage. Francis would have the three weeks' rest that the hospital demanded and then a week as a passenger on *Gipsy Moth IV* for the journey to London.

1967 was the summer of sun as well as the summer of love and the good weather shone for their cruise along the south coast. They stopped just once, at Newhaven, and were promptly mobbed by more jubilant well-wishers, who nearly capsized the pontoons. As they passed Dover the Warden of the Cinque Ports greeted them and another flotilla of press launches – or as Francis called them, 'press hooligans' – descended on them; aboard *Gipsy Moth IV* they smiled and waved like royalty and sailed on. Erroll Bruce reported that while Francis was happy to smile and wave, the effort tired him; he was clearly still unwell. On 5 July they found a lovely, peaceful anchorage, as used by the old clipper ships, at the mouth of the Thames under North Foreland and enjoyed their last peaceful evening aboard together; they knew that for the next forty-eight hours they would be swept along by a Force 8 gale of public expectations.

On 6 July the celebrations along the Thames began with gun blasts at Southend and continued with vast cheering crowds lining the narrowing river. From every creek and inlet local boats came out to wave or join the flotilla. While waiting for the tide to change off Gravesend they were entertained to lunch on board the training ship HMS *Worcester*. Towards the end of lunch they saw an official launch speeding towards them. On board was the same royal press officer, Sir Richard Colville, who was now waiting to greet them ashore.

A Gipsy Moth biplane flies past Gipsy Moth IV en route from Plymouth to Greenwich

On board the *Worcester* Colville now became the royal spanner in the works. The Queen had changed her mind. Instead of a private ceremony in the Hawksmoor Room at the Admiral President's Palace, there would now be a public ceremony in the Great Quadrangle. She had been told about the sword; she could sense the public joy; the weather was perfect; the world was watching; she was the Queen; and the Queen had changed her mind.

On board *Gipsy Moth IV* they protested as best they could: all their clothes for the ceremony had been sent ahead from Plymouth to Greenwich; in the lockers to hand they only had crew kit. Sheila's least scruffy outfit was a bright red trouser suit; she had no shoes but only sandals; the boys just had reefer jackets. No problem, Sir Richard smoothed, giving Francis his own tie and rustling up some others from the *Worcester*'s mess room, it's quite acceptable to step ashore in crew clothes, it adds to the atmosphere. 'And Lady Chichester too, in crew clothes?' asked the future Lady Chichester. Colville replied haughtily: 'It is Her Majesty's wish that Sir Francis should be honoured as he comes ashore, and what could be more suitable than for you all to be dressed for sailing as you come ashore?'

Now Francis objected: he was not well, and how embarrassing it would be for the Queen if he wobbled or fainted in front of her. Colville replied: 'Commander Bruce will give you a sip of brandy beforehand.' Francis replied that he would not breathe brandy on his Queen. All protest seemed in vain. The nonchalant Colville shrugged and left. The crew braced themselves for this new and very public development.

And thus they awoke on board *Gipsy Moth IV* at first light on 7 July. The setting didn't help lift their nerves. A special mooring had been prepared for them at Woolwich just three miles, or half an hour, upstream from Greenwich. Situated where the Thames Flood Barrier now lies, the mooring was in a thoroughly industrial setting, just downwind of the droning Woolwich power station with its foul fumes and dust layer, in the days before London's air and river had been cleaned up.

At 9.40 am, with a loose flotilla of fifty boats jostling behind them, Erroll Bruce asked Giles to slip the mooring lines and off they cast. *Gipsy Moth IV* looked her very best: garlanded with signal

Arriving in Greenwich (British Pathé)

Sheila in that red trouser suit and those sandals (British Pathé)

flags and burgees, an Australian Ensign off her jib shroud, her mizzen topped with a Royal Yacht Squadron White Ensign, she was suitably weather-scarred and thoroughly scrubbed. The Thames here is only 400 yards wide and on board they could see and hear the waving and cheering from an East End long since redeveloped and now no longer even particularly British, let alone Cockney.

By 10 am they had rounded the loop where the Millennium Folly now sits and could see the domes and flags of Greenwich waiting for them a mile ahead. Behind them the pleasure armada whooped their klaxons and blasted their foghorns; some let off rescue flares. Erroll slowed her down; timing was everything. Down below, *Gipsy Moth IV* only had one mirror, a foot square, pitted affair in the main heads. Sheila and Francis did their best in front of it. Giles was on deck with the mooring lines. At exactly 10.15 am Erroll turned her into tide, throttled back and pulled up alongside: a perfect landing.

On the pier naval cadets scrambled the mooring lines fast while the silver trumpets of the Royal Marines struck up a nautical fanfare echoing from the roof of the Painted Hall. On this cue, the Royal Standard and the flag of the Lord

High Admiral were broken and the Queen's Bargemaster, the
stout and whiskery Albert Barry of the Royal Victorian Order,
resplendent in scarlet court coat and waistcoat with gold sash
and trimmings, long white socks and black brogues and cap,
stepped on to the jetty and offered a welcoming hand to Sheila,
then to Francis, Giles and Erroll. As they assembled ashore, legs
not too wobbly, a guard of honour of Royal Watermen, more
scarlet and gold brocade, garters and shining medals, formed to
usher them up the crimson-carpeted ramp.

*From Francis
to Sir Francis
(British
Pathé)*

⸻ ⚮ ⸻

The silver trumpet fanfare was also the cue for the royal party to
leave the Admiral President's suite and make its way across the
lower end of the Grand Quadrangle towards the pontoon. The
crowd now took up the fanfare, cheering and clapping the Queen
and Prince Philip. Vice-Admiral Lyddon and Sir Richard Colville
followed a few paces behind, both in full naval pomp, followed
by Mrs Morrison, Captain Kett and Sir Michael Adeane. Off-
scene, Lord Plunket escorted two officers with the knighting
sword and knighting stool respectively to their positions.

As the Chichester party walked through the Watergate, all black wrought iron and gold tridents, they found the Queen waiting for them. Francis, in his reefer jacket, was first to be received, taking off his cap and shaking her hand in a deep bow. Behind him Sheila, noticeably bigger-boned than her husband, in the bright red trouser suit, dark pink spotted scarf-cap and sandals, curtsied and waved forward Giles and Erroll, looking very much like younger and older versions respectively of Francis.

The royal convoy now walked quickly towards Plunket, who was standing on a plaque announcing the 'BIRTHPLACE OF KING HENRY VIII IN 1491 AND HIS DAUGHTERS QUEEN MARY IN 1516 AND QUEEN ELIZABETH I IN 1533'. Francis rather uncertainly put his left knee on the stool and bowed his head. Plunket gave the Queen the historic sword and in one movement she dubbed his starboard then his port shoulder, saying: 'I beg you to bestow the Honour of Knighthood and to be a Knight Commander for individual achievements and sustained endeavour in the navigation and seamanship of small craft.' Sir Francis stood and bent his head forward so the Queen could place around his neck the pink and grey riband of a Knight Commander of the Order of the British Empire and pinned the star to his reefer jacket. She then moved down the line to shake hands with Lady Sheila, while Sir Francis could be seen looking up and smiling, almost to himself, at the Royal Observatory building on the hill overlooking them, the home of the navigators' meridian.

The two parties now walked back towards the Watergate, the Queen alongside Sir Francis, Prince Philip alongside Lady Sheila and the others more loosely following behind. 'Wave to them,' the Queen told Sir Francis, 'it's your day.' The Royal Watermen bristled to attention as they passed, and the Queen's Bargemaster led the royal procession down the ramp towards *Gipsy Moth IV*.

At this stage the scene is lost from all our sources: the BBC, Pathé and Movietone news clips, not to mention my friend, neighbour and eyewitness to the day, Sir Jamie Chichester, the twelfth baronet, on a day's leave from Eton. So we rely on Erroll Bruce's account, kindly given to me by another friend and neighbour, his son Peter, an equally distinguished yachtsman:

> *The ceremony over, every item as precise as the Royal Household always makes such affairs, Sir Francis invited the royal couple to visit* Gipsy Moth, *and he told me to dig up a bottle of champagne that sailed around the world with him. When I struggled to open it, Prince Philip, who knew me quite well, relaxed the atmosphere by warning me 'Look out, Erroll you'll squirt champagne at Her Majesty' and he duly earned a wifely reprimand. Francis gave the Queen and Duke each a small bale of the finest merino wool from the people of Australia. The whole great occasion over, I took the yacht off from Greenwich Palace Pier, then under Tower Bridge to berth on Tower Pier, where Sir Francis was welcomed by the Lord Mayor of London as the formal ending of a Londoner's voyage.*

If the reception from the Thames had been rather restrained and respectful of the royal moment, once clear of Greenwich all formality was forgotten as *Gipsy Moth IV* sailed on. The downstream flotilla had now been joined by their upstream sisters and as they passed under the huge raised arms of Tower Bridge, the Port of London fireboats let whoosh giant plumes of spray towards the sky, while the River Thames Police launches couldn't resist whipping up celebratory doughnuts in the water. Every siren and klaxon and foghorn joined in the cacophony. Surrounded by such tribute, *Gipsy Moth IV* now looked tiny, almost frail, and on board the Chichesters tinier still, making

Francis's achievement seem all the more extraordinary. Ashore tens of thousands of well-wishers lined the river, waving and cheering in the sunshine from wharves and piers, warehouses and offices, embankments and bridges.

At exactly 12.20 pm Erroll Bruce made his second perfect landing of the day. On Tower Pier the Chichesters were greeted by the Lord Mayor of London, Sir Robert Bellinger, in full mayoral robes and chains, and Lady Bellinger in a brilliant lime-coloured suit and sporty bobble hat in blue, pink and white. It was hardly fair on red trouser suited Lady Sheila – but Lady Bellinger was Belgian and possibly didn't understand. At least everyone at Greenwich knew that her outfit had been scuppered by the late royal change of plan; here, the press especially thought that Sheila wore a bright red trouser suit, spotty swimming cap and sandals to a banquet through choice. She was never to hear the end of it.

The Chichesters spent ten minutes on the pier, shaking hands with the great and the good of the City of London Corporation, posing for photographs and waving to the crowds. In the footage we can see Lady Sheila looking around for someone; then she waves to a small, elderly figure, a clergyman, on the edge of the pier; she tugs on Sir Francis's jacket and they walk over to hug the famous and charismatic Revd 'Tubby' Clayton, the Chichester family spiritual exemplar and founder of the Toc H Christian charity for the wounded of war.

The procession now left the pier and the Chichesters were shown into a white 1964 Mulliner Park Ward Rolls Royce Silver Cloud III drophead coupé, with Sir Francis sitting high on the cabrio cover and Lady Sheila and Giles in the rear seats below. The Metropolitan Police had laid on two grey horses and four white-faired motorcycles as outriders, and off they all cast, up the hill past the Tower of London, turning left past All Hallows Church, where the ancient bells pealed out in greeting, along Eastcheap and into Cannon Street.

All along the route office workers in shirtsleeves and blouses leaned out of the windows, waving and cheering. Sir Francis looked up left and right and waved back. The pavements too were full of cheering and clapping well-wishers in their lunch hour and by the time they reached St Paul's Cathedral and doubled back up Cheapside and Poultry to Mansion House, Sir Francis had both port and starboard arms waving back to the crowds, high up to the open windows and low down to the brimming pavements.

Now the Chichesters had to make their last great public appearance of the day. From a specially made balcony between the Corinthian columns of Mansion House, they looked down on a crowd of 5,000 packed into Mansion House Street and Poultry. (In all, according to the Police, 250,000 Londoners turned out that day to pay tribute to Sir Francis.) Raising his hands to stop the cheering, the Lord Mayor said: 'You personify all that is best in Britain – the spirit of initiative, adventure and determination. In the past eighteen months you commanded not only the attention but also the respect of the world. Your voyage has shown the world that Britons still have something which everyone needs – courage and resolution in the face of seemingly insurmountable odds.' Then, to renewed cheering, the Lord Mayor gave Sir Francis a silver table decoration as a gift from the people of London. Inspired by a similar gift presented by an earlier Lord Mayor, James Harvye, to the earlier circumnavigating Sir Francis, Chichester's orb, like Drake's, had the waypoints of the voyage picked out in glowing rubies.

With a final wave the Chichesters entered Mansion House, descended the magnificent marble staircase and took their places at the top table in the Egyptian Hall. Sheila noted that, 'The banquet was like a fairy tale; beautiful lifebuoys made of red and white carnations, the Royal Yacht Squadron colours – everything so exciting and so right'. They were clapped in to lunch with 'Gaily Thro' the World' played by the Orchestra of

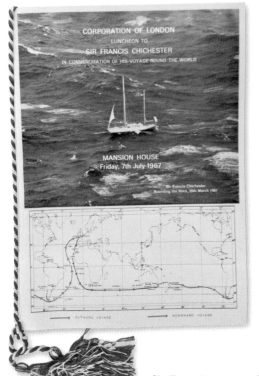

Her Majesty's Royal Marines. Full silver service luncheon was served.

After lunch the Lord Mayor gave a welcoming home speech, quoting Milton, Tennyson and, inevitably, Masefield:[3]

I must go down to the seas again,
to the lonely sea and the sky,[4]
And all I ask is a tall ship and a
star to steer her by;
And the wheel's kick and the
wind's song and the white sail's
shaking,
And a grey mist on the sea's face,
and a grey dawn breaking.

Sir Francis, responding after a long-standing ovation, said that he was deeply moved. He gave thanks to the assembled company, and especially to Sheila for her encouragement and flair for understanding him and his quest. He said, *inter alia*:

'Being so many months alone, I have seen what is valuable in my own life with brutal clarity, and also what is valuable on the national and international scene. It's extraordinary how you feel the world should be run after being alone for so long.

I don't think there is any truth in the rumour that Mr Wilson,[5] after seeing Mr Heath[6] in a yacht two weeks ago, is presenting Mr Brown[7] with a yacht to sail around the world alone. I seem to realise that the terrific welcome I have received is not merely for me. It is a kind of symbol. This voyage of mine represents an independent effort – a private enterprise of the sort that appeals to the British mentality. It

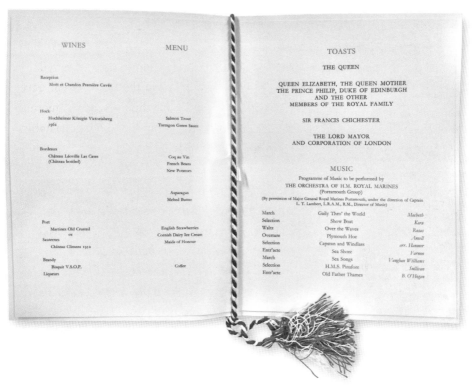

is not really suitable for his temperament to have a state or someone else to nurse him financially, physically, morally or anything else from the cradle to the grave.'

After lunch they clapped the family out as the orchestra played 'Old Father Thames'. Outside, Francis put his sailing cap back on – with some relief, it appears – and waved to the few hundred well-wishers who were still waiting for him.

'Are you contemplating a career in politics, sir?', a journalist shouted.

'Tell me if you hear of a good vacancy', Sir Francis grinned back.

From the crowd a spontaneous round of 'For He's a Jolly Good Fellow' sprang up, followed by a young ringleader in bright shorts shouting:

'Three cheers for Sir Francis Chichester. Hip-hip!'

'Hooray!'

'Hip-hip!!'

'Hooray!!'

'Hip-hip-hip!!!'

'HOORAY!!!'

With a final wave, the Chichesters settled into the back of a
black mayoral Daimler Sovereign for the short ride back home.
We don't know if they were expecting another street celebration
but as they turned left off St James's Street into their own St
James's Place, that is exactly what they found. Francis's friend
and fellow sailor – and owner of the adjacent Duke's Hotel –
Harold Rapp, had teamed up with the Royal Ocean Racing
Club, also on St James's Place, and decked the street out in
bunting. Residents and members lined the pavement, clapping
and cheering. And there, waiting for them on the doorstep of no.
9, was Erroll Bruce, back from positioning *Gipsy Moth IV* in St
Katherine's Docks.

For the Chichesters this homecoming was the most emotional
part of an intense and overwhelming day. Inside they flopped,
drained yet elated. Among the many presents waiting for them
were half a dozen bottles of J&B Rare Scotch Whisky from
Justerini & Brooks just round the corner in St James's Street.
Erroll did the honours and four crystal clinks were met with
four loud 'Cheers!' as laughter and relief filled the first-floor
drawing room. It had been, everyone agreed, a most wonderful
and triumphant day.

NOTES:

1. The sword is now on display in the wardroom at HMNB Devonport.
2. Francis loved the medical officer's report: if Francis had been in the Navy he would be invalided out straightaway; on the other hand, a civilian doctor would probably prescribe a long sea voyage!
3. John Masefield had been the Poet Laureate of the United Kingdom from 1930 until his death two months before this reading.
4. Francis chose 'The Lonely Sea and the Sky' as the title for his 1963 autobiography.
5. British Labour Party prime minister at the time.
6. Conservative Party opposition leader at the time, a middling racing yachtsman, who became the worst prime minister of all time from 1970 to 1974.
7. George Brown, Wilson's useless, drunkard deputy and rival.

If anything terrifies me, I must try to conquer it.

CHAPTER 2

Frying Pans and Fires

IT WAS NOT ALWAYS THUS. Sixty years earlier, when Francis was seven, his father thought it best to let professional bullies beat him instead; he sent Francis to boarding school. They chose a local Devonshire penal colony, then called Ellerslie House, later renamed Belmont House, about 10 miles away from his home village of Shirwell and just to the west of Barnstaple in the village of Bickington.

It would have been hell anyway but he had the misfortune of having his elder brother, John, there as a Senior Boy. John, five years older at twelve, had seven years of sibling vengeance to unload and now, with a gang behind him and their mother far away, he set about bullying young Francis relentlessly. Almost immediately a bit of prank in the showers backfired on Francis and John arranged for him to be sent to Coventry[8] for three weeks. No boy dared, or even wanted, to speak to him. For Francis it was an inexplicable and unforgettable experience: 'It seems hard to believe that senior boys would do such a thing to a 7-year-old new boy, just because of a stupid joke that went wrong.'

Worse was to come. Ellerslie had started off with good intentions as a parish school built in the grounds of a Bickington church. In 1899 it was enlarged and a very handsome two-storey neo-Georgian mansion built in its extensive grounds. The grounds were made into playing fields and the whole enlarged enterprise handed over to the Exeter diocese, which appointed a particularly nasty piece of work, Revd Douglas Martin Hogg, to be headmaster.

This pervert took an instant dislike to Francis's independent spirit. Maybe he sensed that a bullied boy would be more fun to bully further. In his autobiography, written fifty-seven years later, Francis recalls that Hogg's technique was to send the boys up to their dormitory to wait for their beatings there. In the dorm the boy would be left trembling with fear while Hogg trembled with anticipation below:

> *My first term I was up for a beating seven times. The headmaster, who was a big, powerful man, sent one up to the dormitory at a fixed time. Here, one waited beside one's bed. Being kept waiting was the worst part, and I couldn't stop myself from trembling. He made us strip off our trousers, and beat us on the bare bottom. But not always. Sometimes he made us strip off and bend over, and then he didn't beat us…*

Ellerslie School

Nowadays social media would expose the perverts almost immediately, but until recently unsupervised, remote boys' boarding schools were a magnet for sadists and child molesters, especially those of the frocked variety. They could, and knew they could, act out their most bizarre sado-sexual fantasies with complete impunity. Hogg obviously had his own weird fantasies, such as not beating boys but rather admiring their taut bare buttocks and trembling legs. (Of course it happened in girls schools too. My elderly neighbour was sent to a convent in Cumbria where she and the other girls were repeatedly whipped on their bare bottoms by the Mother Superior.)

To save money, Francis's father – another horrid vicar – had his son board weekly at Ellerslie. Early every Monday morning the family's groom-gardener, Wilkie, would rig up the horse and trap and deliver Francis to Hogg's deprivations; every Friday afternoon he would collect him and deliver him to his father's strictures. How Francis must have dreaded those journeys between fire and frying pan: seven years old and beaten by a martinet vicar at home and by a sadist vicar at school; subjected to his brother's bullying all week and his father's damnation liturgy every weekend.

Thankfully, his misery at Ellerslie only lasted a year as his parents changed schools, not because of the penal conditions but, as he noted rather sardonically, 'Only because I was always ill there, which was a nuisance'.

I must say I felt chilled reading Francis's account. It reminded me of the penal colony in Berkshire to which my parents sent me at a similar age, a particularly grim experience called Horris Hill. If Ellerslie was run by a single sadist, Horris Hill had three, all brothers, called Stow or Stowe.

Luckily the Ellerslie House story has a happy ending: it was demolished. The playing fields are now full of detached white stucco houses, also mock Georgian, funnily enough, and the top field now has a new Ellerslie House, the delightful rambling home with a view belonging to Manu and Snah Patel, who have been very helpful with my research and very hospitable on my visits.

Francis
aged 3

Francis's home was the Old Rectory at Shirwell, five uphill-and-down-again hedgerowed miles north-east of Barnstaple, where his father was the vicar at St Peter's. That part of North Devon is remote now; it would have been remoter still a hundred years ago, not so much the middle of nowhere as the end of nowhere. It is steeply undulant, verdant English countryside and a paradise of nature in which to grow up.

It was also Chichester-shire, a county within the county of North Devon. The Chichesters had prospered and multiplied there for 650 years after a middling squire from outside Wessex, a certain John Chichester, married the heiress Thomasine

Raleigh; through her side the family can be traced back to the West Wessex of Anglo-Saxon times. The first knighthood was bestowed on the family by King Edward III for services rendered during the Siege of Calais and the Battle of Poitiers in 1346 and 1356 respectively.

Although North Devon was packed full of Chichester cousins, and although they intermarried determinedly, there was very little danger of inbreeding due to the sheer abundance of Chichesters extant. Of a dozen Chichester stately homes and parkland estates in the area, Francis's branch of the family was centred on two: Youlston Park and Arlington Court. The former, after a recent chequered career as a 'country house experience' and film location, is now once more a rather gloomy private house set in a woody hollow, and the latter is a beautiful National Trust attraction. Luckily Arlington Court is run by the Chichester historian David Gibbons and to his wise offices I quickly repair.

'It all seems so eccentric by today's standards', says David, a skinny 46-year-old enthusiast with jet-black hair. He looks up from pouring the tea, 'but a hundred and fifty years ago it was only natural for the Chichester widower of Youlston Park to marry the Chichester widow of Arlington Court, which is exactly what happened. Sir Arthur of Youlston Park married Sir Bruce's widow Rosalie Amelia from Arlington Court. Lady Chichester of Arlington Court remained Lady Chichester of Arlington Court, she kept her title, name and home, only she gained a new husband.'

Later, Francis's great-niece Angela Chichester gives me a memoir from Ann Laramy, the granddaughter of Youlston Park's butler, from which:

Sir Arthur was a widower for several years. Then Lady Bruce of Arlington Court became a widow and they decided to get married; but they never lived together.

Each evening Sir Arthur and my grandfather would leave Youlston for Arlington, have dinner and then leave at 10.00 pm for home. On Sunday Lady Chichester and daughter Miss Rosalie joined Sir Arthur's family for lunch at Youlston and then leave at 4.00 pm for home. This went on until Sir Arthur's death.

'So take me through Francis's immediate ancestors', I ask David.

'Francis had a very powerful grandfather, Sir Arthur, the eighth baronet. Powerful in the sense of being a big man with a big personality. A big love of life. A great white hunter.'

'And Francis's grandmother?'

'Well, to put it kindly, in those days Chichester women were expected to be sausage machines and not much else, and she was both. She bore him fourteen children. Eleven survived, about average for the time, I suspect. And of course she herself died early from it, bearing the fifteenth. But then they did, mothers died from the constant rearing.'

'And where did Francis's mother or father fit in to the pack?'

'Father. His mother, unusually enough, wasn't a far-flung Chichester. Far-flung meaning somewhere else in North Devon. No, it was his father. Shall we take a look at the tree?'

We walk along what would have been Arlington Court's servants' quarters and through a door into the family part of the house. Visitors are being shown around by guides in each room; all is gentle and orderly, respectful of property, polished parquets, muffling carpets, fading tapestries, maturing refinement. The National Trust as we know it. We walk into a small withdrawing room that has been made into the Chichester travels memorabilia room. Occupying most of one wall is a family tree rendered in beautiful calligraphy, tracing family lines back to the Restoration.[9] By the time we see Francis's father we are on the bottom right-hand twig of the tree.

'So here we are', says David. 'Francis's father was Charles. So he was one, two, three, four, five, six, seven, eight, nine, the ninth of eleven. The sixth out of seven sons, which is a more relevant way of looking at it.'

'And Charles's brothers, Francis's uncles, how did they fare?'

'The eldest, Arthur – he would have been groomed to take over Youlston and the estate – died before having an heir, so the title passed to Sir Edward. The usual arrangement was that the eldest son took over all the estate, which is why many of our big estates have survived. Our famous primogeniture. The second and third sons joined either the Army or Navy and the fourth or fifth sons either the Church or politics.'

'And any interesting uncles?'

'Well yes, this Sir Edward, the ninth baronet, was certainly one. He went on to become an admiral. They say he kept the German and American fleets from going to war in Manila in 1898 during the Spanish American War. He won the CMG[10] for that.

'The other interesting one was the next son, Henry, who left to seek a fresh fortune in California, where he was promptly shot dead.'

'Then we have Charles, Francis's father. What do we know about him?'

'He went to Oxford, to Brasenose College. Then when another cousin, Revd John Chichester, died his father arranged for Charles to step right into his shoes. He became the local vicar in one of the family parishes, Shirwell. There's nothing to suggest that he was ever remotely religious. But then why would he be?'

'And what's that?' I ask, looking up at a large wooden relief.

'That the family crest,' replies David, 'a heron catching an eel.'

'Looks rather pleased with himself,' I say, 'the heron.'

'That would be right,' agrees David, 'a good Chichester heron, that.'

Francis's father, the martinet Rev. Charles

Later, back in his office for more tea, this time with chocolate digestives, I dig out my bashed-up copy of Francis's autobiography *The Lonely Sea and The Sky*. Here's what Francis remembered about his father:

> *I have been told that he was ordered by my grandfather to enter the Church on the old principle of one son each for the Army, the Navy and the Church, but my father told me that he had wanted to enter the Church. I think, however, that he was unsuited for it, and that if he had been in some other profession, he would have made his mark. He was continuously fighting against his possibly*

unconscious wishes and using up his nervous energy in
a tremendous effort to do the right thing. In the end he
became a Puritan of the severest kind.

In the house he seemed to be disapproving of everything I
did, and waiting to quash any enthusiasm.

Great-niece Angela remembers how her father used to go to the
Old Rectory for supper on Sunday after services and how strict
it was there, while Ann Laramy wrote:

We often went to the Rectory to see them and to have tea,
and it was here I met Francis on one of his rare occasions
home. After Grace, you were not allowed to speak, and
ate your tea in silence until the Rector thanked God for
tea and friends.

Another visitor to the Old Rectory was Ruth May, granddaughter
of another Youlston Park butler and daughter of the local seed
merchant. She dreaded delivery trips to the Chichesters:

My mother was always invited to tea on these occasions,
as a result of her connection with the family, and when I
was about five I was also invited. I hated it because after
Grace you were not allowed to speak until the Rector had
finished his tea.

Back in the public rooms, we are standing in front of the Sir
Francis Chichester showcase in one of Arlington Court's halls. 'It's
a funny thing', says David, 'but most of the visitors' first questions
are about Francis, although his connection here was quite remote,
only through his spinster aunt, Rosalie, thirty-five years his elder.
That's his mother there.' We look at a black and white family
portrait taken outside the Old Rectory. Francis is about seven and

the next in line, his sister Barbara, about two. Between them stands their mother, Emily, looking very prim and trim in long white lace with a thick, dark waistband and flower-trimmed bonnet. She is petite and pretty. Quite how and why she became involved with the Chichesters is unclear, as she came from a middle-class, musical London family and not the usual Chichester distant cousin marrying pool. I can only presume they met at Oxford. Francis's father sits in a reclining chair, formally dressed in black, a thick-set, not unattractive-looking man, considerably larger than his wife.

'Do you know he doesn't mention his mother once in his autobiography?' I ask David.

'That's rather unusual.'

'Unique,' I reply, 'I can't think of another autobiography when the mother isn't even mentioned. We know she was the organist at the Shirwell church and she gave music lessons.'

Ann Laramy remembers her thus:

Starting at the age of 2, I was taken to Shirwell Church for the Easter morning service. We went out from Barnstaple with horse and carriage. On arriving at church, the Rev.

Charles Chichester and his wife stood each side of the font to welcome the congregation in, Mrs Chichester holding her prayer book in both hands.

I was puzzled that my mother curtsied; I had never seen this before, and wondered why. I was told you always did this when you met either the Rector or his wife in the village. As I got older I wondered what with would happen if I did not curtsey, and tried it out. Never again! Mrs Chichester's prayer book crashed on top of my head, never to be forgotten.

Miserable family: Barbara, Emily, Francis and Charles Chichester

In fact it was Aunt Rosalie, the chatelaine of Arlington Court, who was to be Francis's proxy mother, in much the same way as Francis was the childless Rosalie's proxy son. Among other letters in his archive, David has a very affectionate 1937 Christmas card sent from Francis and Sheila in New Zealand to Aunt Rosalie, with a photograph showing 'some of the one million trees we have planted since 1927'. Planting trees and land conservation were by then Rosalie's passion: by then she had made Arlington Court into a nature reserve, before bequeathing it all to the National Trust.

Arlington Court

David gives me his biographical notes about this true British eccentric, from which:

> *She inherited Arlington Court when she was sixteen.... Possibly because of her geographical isolation, but also undoubtedly because of her deep and abiding love of her home, Miss Chichester never married but instead remained at Arlington Court. Hers was not the life of a lonely recluse, though: she had a lively interest in many fields including art, music, inventions, astronomy and politics.*
>
> *She won prizes for photographs that she developed and printed herself and wrote regularly for the Daily Sketch. She also personified the archetypal inquisitive Victorian, amassing huge collections of shells, model ships, pewter, stuffed animals, greeting cards and objets d'art in a private museum.*

Miss Chichester loved to travel ... The National Parks she visited on her two world cruises and 1921 visit to Australia and New Zealand inspired her to open Arlington Court to the public.

Unusually for the time, she was vehemently opposed to hunting and had a fence built around the estate to preserve the deer. She became a successful breeder of Jacob's sheep and Exmoor ponies ... Polly – her late father's parrot – flew freely about the house and peacocks were permitted to walk unhindered into the house itself.

To get some idea of Francis's home life we turn to Bill Wilkie, son of the family retainer. He was one year older than Francis and both were cut off in a remote corner of the Devon countryside. They only had each other to play with. Even so, Bill had to call Francis 'Master Francis' and Francis had to call Bill 'Wilkie'. Bill himself grew up to have a distinguished career and to become Mayor of Barnstaple. When Sir Francis was granted the Freedom of the Borough of Barnstaple in October 1967, it was his only childhood playmate, Bill Wilkie, who made the presentation. The mayor opened his speech by saying: 'Today is a great day in the life of Sir Francis. It is a great day also in the life of the borough of Barnstaple, for we are presenting Sir Francis with the greatest gift we have to offer.

'I say with great humility that the little I have done in my life is small indeed compared with the great achievements of Sir Francis.'

He then went on to recall some childhood memories: 'He was very much an individual. At times he was very badly behaved and always very determined. At times his nanny had great trouble to restrain him.... We used to play with his airgun and if he could not hit the target he would get in the devil of a temper – he was always striving for the best.... He particularly disliked his elder brother John. They we remarkably dissimilar and used to fight like cats.

'Most of his free time he spent in the fields around Shirwell, usually armed with a butterfly net to catch moths and butterflies or collecting birds eggs, frogs or lizards. Every autumn he used to help my father and his workmates cut up logs for the winter fires. He loved being outdoors, hated being indoors.'

Elsewhere, Bill recalled how Emily was a 'dutiful wife' but there was never any affection shown in the house; Bill remembered the emotional temperature as 'being like a refrigerator'. There were four children: John, five years older, then Francis, then Barbara, five years younger and then Cecily, three years younger still. By the standards of the fast-breeding local Chichesters Emily was a slow burner, presumably held back by lack of visiting rights.

Bill also recalled: 'When Francis came back from New Zealand after ten years in 1929 he arrived in his own plane, a Gipsy Moth, at Youlston Park. He took my father and my wife up for a ride. He hadn't seen his father for ten years. He caught a sleeve on a wing and said quietly "Oh damn", or some such, mild. Then he saw his father nearby and immediately said, "So sorry, sir", before shaking him formally by the hand.'

Bill doesn't mention if Emily was there or not; probably not.

I am lucky enough to be shown around Francis's home, the Old Rectory, by the current occupiers, the Rhind family. Alexander and Lucy, both in their mid-twenties and in the media in London, down for the weekend, are my gracious guides. After a full tour we chat over Earl Grey tea and just-made chocolate cake. The rambling old house is handsome and heavy, solid, late-Georgian in style although early Victorian in date. It had already been divided in two by the time Alexander's grandmother bought it forty years ago and now the Wilkies' old quarters have been converted into three flats. The garage is now the office of Jonathan Rhind Conservation Architects and the old stable is now an annexed house. In Francis's day the rectory had eleven bedrooms and even now the Rhind's half of the grounds are big enough to host their drove of donkeys, led by the un-Eeyore-like Sunshine. The Old Rectory has finally become a happy hamlet.

———— ⚬⚬⚬ ————

Even if Francis grew up with no affection and considerable cruelty, he didn't lack for space inside or out. But as Bill Wilkie remembered, it was the space outside the forbidding walls that Francis loved. The house, with its deep Georgian windows, looks out over particularly beautiful, rolling, expansive countryside, with sheep and mixed herds scattered among the rolling pastures, as indeed Ellerslie must have done a hundred years ago. In the abundance of North Devon Francis found an escape from home and school that would later come to define him:

> I made no friends at school and had none of home. I had two sisters, but the older, Barbara, was five years younger than me and we hadn't much in common in the way of adventure. I gradually drifted into the habit of setting off on my own into an escape world of excitement and adventure.

———— ⚬⚬⚬ ————

No Francis research in Devon would be complete without a visit to St Peter's Church in Shirwell, just up the hill from the Old Rectory, which played such a large part in his family's life. The church itself remains unchanged from his earliest impressions of it, and may well be little changed since it was founded in 1267. From the plaques we learn that the first Chichester to be rector here was in 1513 and that there has been a steady stream of presumably willing and unwilling third-, fourth- or fifth-born Chichesters, such as Charles, in residence at St Peter's and its various rectories until the present day.

I visit at Harvest Festival and try to imagine myself as young Francis, sitting on the hard front-row pew, listening to his father droning on about hell and damnation and watching his mother summon up the netherworld on the organ. It proves impossible: the current rector, Rt Revd Alan Winstanley, is a twenty-first century man – and not even from these parts. Youngish and dapperish, he arrived in Shirwell from a twelve-year missionary stint in Peru and originally hails from Leigh in Lancashire. The accent remains, Lancastrian not Peruvian, and the liturgy is light-hearted and breezy, with the words of the hymns and readings displayed on a big screen via PowerPoint. Of course, there's the usual hugging and kissing you have to embrace these days too; the only surprise, after all the glad-handing and bonhomie, is Alan's insistently creationist message, as if the Bible was meant to be understood literally and not as it was written, metaphorically. Hey ho.

At the end of the service Alan is kind enough to introduce me to the congregation and invites volunteers with memories of Francis to join me at the Harvest buffet. Over lemon drizzle cake and cup of builder's tea I meet David Friend, who was one of the bearers at Francis's funeral. He tells me that all the bearers had to be 'yeomen of the parish. Yeoman, not a word you hear much these days.' It's not, and he looks like you would like a yeoman to look: big and hearty, ruddy and stout. Later, near Francis's grave, he points to a field across the lane: 'I'm the only person here who has worked that field with a horse and plough.'

Walking along the buffet to the Bakewell tart I meet John Conibear, who was one of the bell-ringers seen that funeral night. Francis was so famous it was on the BBC News. I ask how come. 'When Sir Francis returned safely to Plymouth in '67, bells were rung across the country. The BBC News filmed it here in Shirwell. The Nine O'Clock News. Richard Baker it was, the newsreader back then. Of course I was only a nipper.' Then pointing to a Sunday-best-dressed woman near the tea urn, he says, 'That's who you want to talk to, she's a proper Chichester.'

And that's how I meet Francis's great-niece Angela. Among many other snippets I learn about Francis's brother, John.

'Johnny married his best friend's widowed mother. She was about thirty years older than him. Francis and Johnny never got on with each other. Francis wrote to Johnny when he was dying and said he would like to see John before he died. John said he was much too busy in the garden to see him. Very sad.'

———— ✺ ————

But there was at least a term-time respite between the Ellerslie fire and the Shirwell frying pan: his five years, 1909–14, at a prep school, The Old Ride School. He remembered:

> *By the time I was transferred (from Ellerslie) to another preparatory school, The Old Ride, at Branksome, Bournemouth, I must have been a thorough savage, a rebel against everybody, including my parents.*
>
> *But I loved The Old Ride. I liked the boys, I liked the masters and I liked the place itself with its strong pine smell, and the sandy soil covered with pine needles. Somehow, by the time I left, I became captain of the cricket XI, although really I was never much good at cricket; I was also captain of the school.*
>
> *One of my friends was a junior at The Old Ride at that time. He told me recently that he had been entered in a swimming race, and that I said to him, 'You have got to win – or else…' and that he was so frightened that he went ahead and won. I expect I was still somewhat of a bully, and wonder if my experiences at Ellerslie were any excuse.*

Like Ellerslie House, The Old Ride has disappeared with time. Thanks to help from Sarah Hustler at the Poole History Society, we know that the ownership and name of the school changed from The Old Ride School to The Old School to Oratory Preparatory School. In 1973 Oratory Preparatory School succumbed to the bulldozer and became the large detached houses around Oratory

Gardens in the semi-exclusive Martello Park suburb of Poole. Francis's 'strong pine smell, and the sandy soil covered with pine needles' remain but the houses in the suburb are hidden and shaded by the pine trees behind the ubiquitous boxwood evergreen hedges. From Sarah's historic maps and plans we can make out where The Old Ride School and grounds were – and the new houses are – but it takes a good snoop on Google Earth to reveal the extent of the swimming pools and tennis courts sprawling round the bungalows in the old school grounds today.

One episode from Francis's time at The Old Ride School will ring a bell with prep school boarders. It is notorious that school staff send pupils to bed long before they are ready to sleep in order that they, the teachers, might have a more extended evening. This was the rigorous regime known as 'lights out', after

The Old Ride School, happier days

which no talking was allowed. In my penal colony one of the weird brothers Stow or Stowe would often wait outside and at the first whisper from the still-wide-awake boys would burst in and lay waste to any bottom to hand. As a result the boys would crawl into each other's beds and under the sheets so as not to be overheard; later it would be to listen to Radio Luxemburg.[11] If a master burst in he would have presumed he had just busted a Dionysian orgy. Luckily for us, it never happened; unluckily for Francis, it did:

> Once our dormitory was caught after Lights Out with everybody visiting some other boy in his bed. There was the most frightful hullabaloo about this. We were told we were very lucky not to get the sack, and I believe that if we had not all been involved, we would have. No one mentioned the word 'homosexuality', and I would not have known what it meant if it had been mentioned. And as we used to visit every other bed in turn, I am quite sure that I must have known if any of the boys were interested in this vice. I don't think any of them knew anything about it, and that we merely used to go and swop yarns, and the whole spice of the matter was that it was forbidden to talk after Lights Out.
>
> In the event we were brought up for questioning one at a time for week after week, and finally all flogged.

The flogging continued apace at his next school, Marlborough College, where he was immured during the First World War years. Nowadays butter wouldn't melt in its Marlburian mouth: like all twenty-first-century public schools it resembles more a co-educational holiday camp than the toughening-up school of Empire it once was.

First, there was the food:

> The food, was terrible. We used to say that the roast meat was horseflesh; the reek of it turned one's stomach. However, we felt half-starved, and would have eaten anything. This feeling of starvation was certainly due to vitamin deficiency. From one term to the next we never had any fresh

fruit or uncooked salad, or vegetables. It was no wonder that we had a general outbreak of boils.

Then there was the cold:

Marlborough Downs are exceptionally cold. There was some heating in the form rooms, but none in the dormitories. The huge upper schoolroom, where 200 senior boys lived during the day when they weren't in actual classes, had only two open fires. Only the biggest boys were allowed to warm themselves at these fires. I decided that the occasional periods of warm-up available during the day only made one suffer more, so I wore nothing but a cotton shirt under my coat, discarded my waistcoat, and slept under only a single sheet at night. I aimed to get used to the conditions like the Tierra del Fuegan natives of a century ago, except that I didn't sleep inside a dead whale I was eating.

And then, of course, the constant beatings:

The usual punishment was a beating. Most of the discipline was in the hands of the senior boys. Their sole form of punishment was beating, and this was so copiously applied for any infringement of an extensive and complicated social code that it amounted to licensed bullying.

Upper School was ruled by four prefects, who sat in state at a table in front of the fire, the only source of warmth, known as Big Fire. One of them would carry notes round to the boys he was going to beat; this was during prep when we were all at our desks, and as soon as prep finished, all the 200 boys made a wild rush to encircle the prefect's desk. The chairs were pushed away, the victim bent over the desk, and he was beaten as hard

as the prefect could possibly manage by taking a running
jump and using a very long cane.

All of this brings to mind John Betjeman's verse autobiography, *Summoned by Bells*. Recalling his time at Marlborough five years after Francis, he wrote:

> Upper School captains had the power to beat:
> Maximum six strokes, usually three.
> Swift after prep all raced towards 'Big Fire',
> Giving the captain space to swing his cane:
> '*One!*' they would shout and downward came the blow;
> '*Two!*' rather louder; then, exultant, '*Three!*'
> And some in ecstasy would bellow '*Four!*'?

Well, it's a changed old world and that we know, but not much can have changed as much as Marlborough College. I am lucky enough to be shown around by the official school historian and ex-deputy headmaster, Terry Rogers, a very sprightly and thoroughly dapper 75 year-old. 'Of course back in young Chichester's day it was all pretty Spartan, mostly because it was set up eighty years before him specifically for sons of the clergy. Like Francis himself. There wasn't much in the way of fees and everything was cut to the bone, heating, food, all the things he complained about. But funnily enough the boys took a certain pride in being able to withstand the infamous toughness.'

'Useful in war and empire', I say. 'And the endless beatings'.

'Indeed. Look at these, the Beatings Books.' Terry hands me some notebooks. Each term the four prefect/beaters had to keep records of whom they beat, with how many strokes, when they beat them and what for. There were about three or four a day, an average of three strokes a pop and the offences ranged from 'Unflush Desk' to 'Whispering' to 'Unkempt Dress' to the most frequent, the catch-all 'Caught Out'. Caught Out at what history doesn't reveal, Terry suspects geographical rather than excuserial misdemeanours. At the end of the term the Beatings Books were signed by all four prefects: one term ended with the triumphant, '203 Beatings. A Record!'.

'Now there are no punishments of any kind,' Terry says rather wistfully. 'It's almost laughable. Detention, maybe, but that's useless.'

'And no cold?' We had been talking about Betjeman and Terry read out:

It is the winter that remains with me,
Black as our college suits, as cold and thin.
Doom! Shivering doom! Clutching a leather grip
Containing things for the first night of term –
House slippers, sponge bag, pyjamas and Common Prayer.

Then Terry tells me this story about Francis's first head boy in 1914. 'The head boy was called Harold Roseveare, he was *jeunesse dorée* really – wealthy family, blond, wonderful at sports, a scholar, he'd got his place at Cambridge, a scholarship there. He left at the end of the summer term fully expecting to take up his place at Cambridge and a glittering life ahead. Except the war broke out and he found himself in the trenches. His last job here was to hand over to his successor, Sidney Woodruff. Roseveare was dead by the start of the autumn term two months later and there in the school magazine is his obituary, written by the new head boy, Sidney Woodruff. End of that term, December 1914, Sidney Woodruff in turn leaves Marlborough, and Francis would certainly have known him too, and is dead by the summer term with a posthumous VC. And not only Sidney Woodruff but later his two brothers, both Marlburian prefects, both of them killed. This was the fate of the prefects in the four war years Chichester was here. Born a year earlier and Chichester might well have gone the same way.'

Terry has been kind enough to dig out some F.C. Chichester records before I arrive and after lunch we look at photographs of him aged seventeen and eighteen in the school rugby and hockey teams. We see a young man always at the edge of the rows and even then leaning away from the group, not exactly plump but not yet wiry as he was to become, defiant and hostile to the camera. In the notes written by the School Captain we find him described as: 'A hard and keen worker in the scrum but somewhat disadvantaged in the matter of eyesight. He is not heavy enough at present but could be useful in the future.' Then a year later: 'He has more than justified last year's expectations. He always goes extremely hard and although hindered by his bad eyesight goes through an enormous amount of work.'

In his autobiography fifty years later Francis reflected:

There was something mean and niggardly about our existence at Marlborough; we seemed to be mentally, morally and physically constipated. The whole emphasis was on what you must not do, and I consider that I

A 1917 Marlborough house hockey team. Francis is top left

am only now beginning to shake off the deeply-rooted inhibitions which had gripped me by the time I left.

One instance of the effect of this is that until recently I would shake with fear if I had to get up and speak to more than half a dozen people, because the terror of doing or saying anything which would not be approved of by a mob code was so rooted in me.

I looked round one day at the ten boys above me, most of who were far cleverer than I was, or could ever hope to be. I thought to myself, "What a knock-kneed, pigeon-breasted, anaemic, bespectacled, weedy crowd they are! There must be something wrong with this set-up. Real life is flowing past, and leaving me behind." I told my housemaster that I was leaving at the end of term.

That was the last term of 1918, and the college caught the Spanish influenza epidemic. There were so many boys down with it that we were lying in rows on the floor of the sanatorium. I think most of us were pretty ill, but only a few died.

When I got home and told my father that I had left Marlborough, he was furious – justifiably so. I had treated him badly, and I do not know why I had not asked his permission to leave. Perhaps I wanted to be absolutely certain of leaving, and felt that he would not consent. I was due to go to the university and stay there until I was twenty-five, preparing for the Indian Civil Service. I felt that this was all wrong, and that I would not be living a proper life.

And so with his unhappy, hemmed-in childhood behind him, young F.C.C. set about leading his proper life. He emigrated to New Zealand.

NOTES:

8. A British English expression: not to be acknowledged in any way.

9. The restoration of the English monarchy after the Civil War in 1660.

10. The Most Distinguished Order of St Michael and St George (Companion)

11. The only radio station to play pop music in the 1950s and early '60s, using a powerful offshore transmitter on 208AM to get round the BBC's monopoly on broadcasting and disapproval of popular culture.

I like trees too, so we got cracking.

CHAPTER 3

Making Hay

IT'S EASY TO SEE WHY FRANCIS NEEDED TO make the break from England. The First World War and his Marlborough years had ended at the same time; for Francis, Marlborough had seemed like his own world war. The military career option, which his Chichester connections could readily have arranged, was clearly out of the question for the institutionally averse Francis. The clergy career choice was the last one on earth he wanted after his religiously maniacal upbringing. Staying in Devon didn't appeal either; his was a poor branch of the county-wide Chichester clan, without land, title or reputation. In any case, his was a free spirit that couldn't take any more hemming in. He began making plans to spread his wings and seek his fortune. Australia seemed the natural choice – wide open with opportunities, the other side of the world from Shirwell, yet still home in an Empire sense.

One day out pheasant shooting at Youlston he met a sergeant in the New Zealand Army back home on leave. Francis told him of his plans to emigrate to Australia; the sergeant, Ned Holmes, recommended New Zealand instead. Francis was won over by having at least one person he knew there in the shape of Ned, whereas in Australia he knew no-one. He now turned his energies into securing a working or steerage passage to New Zealand.

In 1919 all Francis had to sell the world was his body – and the type of can-do attitude that young men of Empire seeking their fortune carried with them. He left England with £10 in gold sovereigns from his father in his pocket and he determined not to return until he had turned that into £20,000, about £900,000 in buying power today. In that, as we shall see, he succeeded – at least in property and on paper.

And so he set his body and spirit to work. Over the next two and a half years he worked his passage in the boiler room of a steamer to New Zealand, shovelled shit on a farm near Wellington, got sacked from there and sheered and herded sheep on the farm next door, reaped and sowed on yet another farm, crossed over to the South Island to become a lumberjack, mined for coal, fossicked for gold – and hired himself out to pretty much every opportunity that came up in between.

His decision to change from manual to mental labour came after an all-night drinking session in a mining camp miles from anywhere on the South Island. All around him were men who made good money and spent it all on bad whisky. Through the haze of his hangover he 'looked at one of my comrades who was dead drunk, and said to myself, "My God! That's me in twenty years' time". I depended entirely on what I could earn, and although this mining was well paid I could not save. There was the constant drinking for one thing, and sometimes five gambling schools would be in full swing at the same time. I decided that I must make a break.'

His first thought was to be the opposite of a manual labourer, a writer of fine fiction. He fancied himself as 'a mixture of Conrad, Kipling and Somerset Maugham'. He bought a book on 'How to Write a Masterpiece', or similar. But it was no good; as he himself admitted, 'I knew nothing of life and nothing of writing'.

He headed back to the North Island and met a man who knew a man who wanted someone to sell subscriptions door-to-door for the local rag, the *Weekly Press*, in Wellington. They reneged on his commission, so he quit – but he had learned a useful lesson: he could sell. Next he found a job selling a book-keeping system, the *Farmers Register*, to farmers. He soon reckoned on two sales out of every five visits, so in order to increase the visits he bought a motorcycle, which 'had a clutch but no gearbox, and could be started only by running it along the road'.

We are now in the spring of 1923. Francis, known by now as 'Chich', was twenty-two and had been in New Zealand for two years. And he wasn't doing too badly on his way to that sought-after fortune. He traded in the motorcycle for an old five-seater open-topped Ford Model T, bought a bicycle and some camping gear and set off to sell the *Farmers Register* to North Island's farmers. He had a polished routine. He would arrive in a new area in the Ford, make camp in the middle of his target farms and then set off on the bike to make the sales. He figured out rightly that the farmers would be more sympathetic to a poor salesman on a bicycle than a middling one in a car.

He gradually worked his way up to Rotorua, the town famous for its boiling mud and geysers. There he stayed in Brent's Hotel, which old photographs in Rotorua Public Library show to be a one-floor rambling clapboard building. It had originally been a 'temperance hotel' but had mended its ways by the time Francis stayed there. As a kind of homage, we stay at the modern and nondescript Millennium Hotel built on the same site. In his autobiography Francis recalls how one evening he was helping a friend build an extension in a shack nearby when suddenly a geyser burst through and blew off the newly laid roof. I go to see one of the famous geysers, which at the time looks annoyingly un-geyserlike. Under a sign saying 'Largest Natural Blow Hole in the Southern Hemisphere' I ask a young lady how likely it is to perform. 'Oh,' she says, '10.30 every morning and 4.30 every afternoon.' 'Ah,' I say, 'so you have an on/off switch?' 'Yes,' she says, 'that's pretty much it these days.'

It was at Brent's Hotel that Francis met a man who indirectly changed his life. 'Harold Goodwin was a queer cuss,' he wrote, 'very quietly spoken; he really ought to have been a Maori chief because he was so adept at grunting. We used to laugh at his

Brent's Hotel, Rotorua; now the site of a nondescript chain hotel

views on women; the girls thought them a great joke. He was like a public schoolboy in the way he regarded women as a nuisance and a useless hindrance to enjoyment of life. He was an excellent companion for me, and we went on many expeditions together. In Wellington he introduced me to his brother Geoffrey in the bar of the Cecil Hotel.' The Cecil Hotel was demolished in the 1950s and is now another mid-rise bank building of no particular distinction and minimal use to mankind.

It's a recurring theme that striving young businessmen meet a kind of mentor or booster who give them that first big break. Geoffrey Goodwin was Francis's booster.

> 'Geoffrey Goodwin was a man about seven years older than me, taller and very strong. He had amazingly strong wrists, covered in ginger hair. He had a freckled face, and looked somewhat like Chairman Khrushchev, with his baldish, roundish cranium and upper eyelids hooding the outer corners of his eyes, which indicated his shrewdness. He said to me, "What are you going to do?" And when I told him I was thinking of heading for Australia he said,

"Why don't you join me in a little business I've started and become a land agent?" "What is a land agent?" "Oh, he sells land and houses and things." "All right," I said. I became a partner of Goodwin & Chichester Land Agents. My savings of the previous years went into a half share of the furniture and assets.'

Throwing his £400 savings in with Geoffrey was the best decision the young Francis made, the cornerstone of his confidence and prosperity, which led directly to fortune and indirectly to flying, Sheila and sailing. They were the perfect twosome, Geoffrey with the experience, shrewdness and local connections that Francis lacked and Francis with the can-do salesmanship and raw vitality that Geoffrey needed. Even their handwriting complemented each other's. In the first year they had gone from being what we would call estate and land agents with a shack office in the nowheresville known as Lower Hutt to property developers with smart offices in Courtenay Place in the capital, Wellington.

A young and assertive Francis, far left, with the land team. Geoffrey Goodwin, far right

They bought fifty acres north of Wellington, divided it up into fifty plots and built houses with gardens on each of them. From the profits they bought 1,100 acres of virgin scrubland above Silverstream, about 20 miles north of Wellington. Francis takes up the story:

We developed this property in two ways. First, we planted it with pine trees. Geoffrey was an enthusiastic tree-grower, and believed in forestry as a profitable investment. I like trees too, so we got cracking. I raised the first 40,000 trees in my backyard from seeds collected from pine cones; it was fun watching the little pine-needle seedlings emerge with the seeds on their backs.

The beds were protected from the sun's heat by scrim stretched across wooden frames. We planted out these experimental seedlings on a hill in rows six feet apart, with nine feet between seedlings. They took well, so we started a nursery of our own, and soon had several planting gangs at work. Overall, we planted a million trees.

We built thirty-five miles of road, and at one time had three teams of surveyors at work. We had to sell off small lots of land as sites for weekend cottages in order to pay for the whole scheme. We bought another property alongside, and cut that up as well. We built up a sales force of thirty salesmen, selling only our own land.

Soon we owned three private companies operating in land which were doing well. By the time I was twenty-six my income was £10,000 a year.

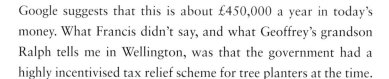

Google suggests that this is about £450,000 a year in today's money. What Francis didn't say, and what Geoffrey's grandson Ralph tells me in Wellington, was that the government had a highly incentivised tax relief scheme for tree planters at the time.

Geoffrey may have been an enthusiastic tree grower but that also meant that Goodwin & Chichester Land Agents paid virtually no tax on the considerable profits.

Like modern developers, they gave their sites romantic, halcyon names such as Pinehaven and Blue Mountain. Nowadays Pinehaven is a rural suburb, while Blue Mountain has more remote, single properties across it. It is while visiting the first of these that I become mightily impressed by one of Francis's achievements for the first time. Pinehaven is actually rather wonderful and he co-created it from nothing. Firstly, the scale is impressive: the eventual 1,900 acres are spread over half a dozen hills. There are still a million pine trees, mostly newly grown as Pinehaven is also a commercial timber venture, run by the current generations of Goodwin & Chichester, Ralph and Giles respectively. And here and there, and by now enormous, stand the original pine trees planted by Francis and Geoffrey ninety years ago.

I am lucky enough to be shown round by Gordon Wilson, who lived at 20 Chichester Drive for many years and now lives nearby, still in Pinehaven. The roads, like Chichester Drive, are named after the Goodwin & Chichester partners and Geoffrey's children and extended family. Most of the original homes have been replaced but the plots and settings remain. Ralph Goodwin shows me the original development scheme, a metre-square layout on heavy paper, with each plot subdivided. Even now it looks remarkably ambitious, especially when considering that each of the fifteen hundred plots had to be carved out of scrubland, landscaped, planted and built upon, roads and water added and communities formed.

Francis's own home is one of the most impressive, at the top of Avro Road, named after the aeroplanes that Geoffrey and Francis used when founding the Goodwin Chichester Aviation Co. On this peak the pine milling is difficult and it is still surrounded by the original – and now venerable – pine trees

Lower Hutt,
February, 1927.

Sir,

How many times have you gone picnic-
ing to find on arrival at your favourite spot that
it was in possession of somebody else ?

Why not a week-end section of your own ?

For £15 down and 10/- per week you can
become the possessor of an ideal section, four
miles from the Upper Hutt, a half-mile off main
Wairarapa Road, situated amidst charming
surroundings.   Prices range from £85 ¾-acre.

Why camp on the roadside when for this
small outlay you can spend your week-ends in
quiet and comfort ?

A number of the sections have Collin's
Stream running through them, and the majority
are timbered with both English and Native trees.

Fourteen of these sections sold in as many days
---don't delay !

RING OR WRITE SOLE AGENT FOR A PLAN :

Goodwin & Chichester

20 Main Street   ::   LOWER HUTT

TELEPHONE : 46-365

*Goodwin &
Chichester flyer*

that Francis planted himself. Ralph points out that some are so old that the local varieties are growing back among them; all are subject to preservation notices.

Nowadays it is easy to view all property developments as a step for the worse, property spivs paving paradise for greed, but what Francis created at Pinehaven is really wonderful, as is the thought that he did all this in his mid-twenties, just a few years after arriving penniless in a new world the other side of the world.

Francis' high mountain hideaway in Blue Mountain, now on Avro Road

If materially Francis was on top of the world, romantically he was in the pit. Every night was a lonely night. Geoffrey had his own family to return to at the end of the day; Francis had rented a bachelor flat at the top of a house behind the Terrace in Wellington. The wonderful night-time views over the bustling harbour were bittersweet, full of the romance of distant shores yet empty with no-one with whom to share them.

Bachelor boy

New Zealand society was layered in ways that Francis struggled to understand. To him people were people; some you liked, others not, and those were layers enough. The chances of a single young man with no local family connections, no church affiliations, not an easy mixer and no natural romantic expression finding a girlfriend were, to all intents and purposes, zero. Public mixing was impossible too: the pubs closed at 6 pm to encourage men to return home. All that happened was that they drank as much as they could before 6 pm and although they then had no option but to return home, most were well past their best by the time they did so. Either way, by 6.30 pm the pavements were rolled up; there may as well have been a curfew.

Francis thus began a series of what he called 'love affairs', although in fact they were merely fantasy flirtations. He met a girl at work and found out where she lived. It was 40 miles away, so he drove out there one night, dimmed his lights and stared into her shack from a distance. He stayed in the car all night, then drove home at dawn. This was one of his 'affairs'.

Another time he met a girl who was sailing to England via Sydney. He bought a ticket for this first leg and hid in his cabin until the boat sailed. His beloved was unimpressed when she discovered him on board. Waiting for the return ship to Wellington, Francis went to the theatre where he heard her distinctive laugh from the circle above.

> It was a distinctive laugh, a ringing melody; it may have been too loud, but it slashed my heart in two that night. What a brutal thing modern love can be; how I wished I had been living in the Stone Age so that I could have grabbed her by the hair and dragged her off, or been killed in the process by a rival.

And so it continued. But Francis did find his cavegirl and married her. Muriel Blakiston was a sweet and totally innocent late teenager, one of eight children living in near-poverty with a widowed mother. She was very pretty and in demand. Francis knew that the only way he was going to bed her was to marry her, so he proposed. I imagine that Muriel's family was delighted: Francis would almost certainly have been the richest suitor and Muriel, knowing nothing of the world at all, would have gone along with them. Even before they were married Francis felt it was a mistake; but he was so in lust that his groin got the better of his brain. 'Sex at last! Whenever I like!' Muriel didn't see it that way and once the double bed became twins, Francis lost interest in her and regained interest in all his other activities. Muriel wanted a domesticated husband and Francis would never be that. Francis wanted a female Francis and she would never be that. She had their baby, George, and within three years had returned to her mother. Francis had lost his virginity, Muriel had lost her innocence, George had lost a father – and the world of aviation had found a favourite son.

It has to be said that Francis had shown no interest in aviation when in September 1928 Geoffrey suggested they start the Goodwin Chichester Aviation Co., just as he had no interest in sailing after Harold Goodwin took him sailing in Auckland. But Geoffrey was an intuitive businessman and rightly spotted that aviation was the next big thing. He arranged to take the New Zealand agency for the English aircraft maker A.V. Roe and bought two of their new model Avro Avian light aircraft. Next he hired four ex-military pilots and advertised joyrides. Over the next three years the four pilots and two aircraft took over six thousand passengers up for quick thrills but, as Francis noted, 'We were lucky that we only lost ten shillings a head'.

The problems were twofold. First, the Avian had a fragile undercarriage and the pilots were more used to landing heavier bombers. Inevitably there were crash landings – partly caused by the second problem: no fixed airfields from which to operate. Farmers' fields had ditches and fences, and the pilots always

seemed to be finding them. When they started the Goodwin Chichester Aviation Co. there was only one aerodrome in New Zealand, at Sockburn (later renamed Wigram) in Christchurch on the South Island and the archives are full of newspaper reports of Geoffrey's attempts to convince the Wellington authorities of the need for at least a landing strip, if not an airfield, in the city. Eventually they agreed to the occasional use at Lyall Bay, now, perhaps inevitably given Geoffrey's nous, the site of Wellington International Airport.

Geoffrey was a keen air passenger and was soon training to be a pilot in his own right. Rub by rub, his enthusiasm infected Francis, so in early 1929 Chich set off for Christchurch to learn how to fly himself. He had a ready-made flying instructor, the Goodwin Chichester Aviation Co. chief pilot, George Bolt.

Geoffrey and Francis's first plane, an Avro Avian.

Luckily for us George later wrote his autobiography, albeit never published, from which we learn that Francis was not a natural flyer:

Towards the end of 1928 I joined Goodwin & Chichester, who obtained the agency for AVRO aeroplanes. I was taken on as Chief Pilot and they had rather grand ideas they were going to sell three or four of these a month. It did not take long to realise this was not going to occur,

so we started joyriding with the Avians all over New Zealand.

Mr Chichester was very keen to learn to fly and the Air Force loaned me a 504K with which I gave him some training. He had no trouble learning to fly the aeroplane but I had difficulty in getting him to land properly as he wore very powerful glasses and had difficulty with his judgment in putting the aeroplane on to the ground. He therefore did not go solo there.

Francis's instructor, George Bolt, and a company plane

Chich, as he was familiarly known, had a very quiet and studious nature. He had a very mathematical mind and would give considerable study to any project he had in his head. He was to make quite a name for himself a year or two after this. I heard that in England he was quite a worry to his instructors because during his solo flights he would disappear for considerable periods, in some cases in very indifferent weather, much to the concern of those who were supposed to be looking after him.

In all fairness the ex-First World War training aircraft, the Avro 504, was more than difficult to fly. It had a rotary engine, which meant the engine and propeller rotated together. Thus there was no throttle as such, rather an engine and propeller that acted like an on/off switch. Coming in to land, the pilot had to judge his glide angle once the engine was turned off and if he undershot the landing field he had to hope that it would restart again. It didn't always comply. Furthermore, the engine ran on castor oil and leaked generously, so goggles always had a good smear on them, and the engine fumes always smelt foul.

But I believe that overwork had something to do with Francis's lack of progress too, as flying training, especially in such unfriendly machines, is not something that can be fitted in around a busy life. Francis remembers:

I struggled away trying to learn, but was a hopelessly bad pupil. By December 1928 I had had eighteen hours fifty minutes of dual instruction, and still could not fly. I think this was partly because of trying to mix flying with an intensely active business life. Geoffrey and I were running five private companies at full blast, besides our partnership, and I was ruthlessly trying to make money for twelve hours a day or more.

At least that part of his life was flying high.

But in spite of his difficulties in learning how to fly – in fact, with knowing Francis a little better now, possibly because of them – the flying bug had taken hold of him. He had found a new way to soar. A plan was forming. He was already planning a visit to the old country. Why not finish his flying training there, where the whole aviation world was far more advanced, and fly a plane back to Wellington? The savings on transport and taxes might just about make the whole adventure cost-effective. And they would have a better plane than the Avian with which to make money. Geoffrey could see that too. A whole new adventure, a whole new life, was just about to take off.

Every flight is moulded into a perfect short story; for you begin – and you are bound to lead up to a climax.

CHAPTER 4

Gipsy Moth

FRANCIS ARRIVED BACK IN ENGLAND on 22 July 1929. He had been away for nine years and four months. He must have felt a sense of 'mission accomplished' as he stepped off the liner *Berengeria* at Southampton docks. He had left with £10 in gold sovereigns all those years go, with only one thing on his mind: to make his fortune – and his fortune he had made. That mountain climbed, he set his sights on a new one: the dream of a record-breaking solo flight to Australia on his way home to New Zealand.

The journey from his new home back to his old home also had aviation at its heart. He had left Auckland for Los Angeles in April 1929 and planned to cross the country test-flying suitable aircraft. But it wouldn't be a Francis journey without struggles to overcome. Almost immediately he became ill and had to spend two months in hospital. He never mentions it and the hospital stay only comes to light through a throwaway line in wife-to-be Sheila's autobiography. I can only assume that he was attacked by some sort of virus, for he was as tough and fit as they come, with will-power and determination to spare. It must have been something extraordinary, a bug caught in California or on the voyage there, to lay him low for so long.

By June he felt strong enough to leave hospital and start the test flights. He wrote:

I had demonstration flights in an American Eagle with a 180 h.p. Hispano engine, a Ryan six-place Brougham, with a Wright 300 h.p., a Whirlwind six-place Kuntzer Aircoach with three 90 h.p. Le Blonds, a Curtis Robin three-place, with a Curtis 180 h.p. Challenger, a Curtis Fledgling two-place trainer, and a Fairchild seven-place plane with a Pratt and Whitney Wasp. Three other types I never tried out because in each case the aeroplane crashed between the time of my making an appointment and reaching the airfield. None of the types I flew in was really suitable, and my visit was aeronautically a flop.

At Southampton docks to meet him was his sister Barbara and together they journeyed to London to stay with Aunt Mary, their mother's sister, at 87 Cadogan Place on the Knightsbridge/Chelsea borders of London. Barbara remembered Francis talked only of flying – so much so that within a week Aunt Mary joked that to keep up with him she too would have to take to the skies.

It didn't take long in England for Francis to have two things on his mind: the record flight home and the fate of his fortune. Between the time he left New Zealand and arrived in London the New York stock market had crashed and the Great Slump had quickly spread to New Zealand. Francis's fortune was made of the wrong sort of paper, mortgage slips from the banks, which he had taken out to buy land and build houses at the time when borrowing to build and sell made good business sense. Now the banks were reclaiming anything and everything they could get their hands on; Francis's fortune had gone from being worth a lot in theory to a little in practice.

It was in these more modest circumstances that Francis went shopping for his aeroplane. The general aviation scene in England was booming, with new manufacturers spinning off existing ones, much like automobile manufacturers were doing. New airfields, new hire and charter companies and new flying schools were opening every month. Later, those of these that had not gone bust would consolidate but in 1930 Francis had a choice of six British light aeroplanes to buy and eight flying schools around London alone from which to complete his licence.

His most obvious choice would have been the Avro Avian biplane. After all, the Goodwin Chichester Aviation Co. in New Zealand had taken out the Avro sales agency and bought two of them to give joyriding thrills. More to the point, the Avian held the existing England to Australia record, flown two years earlier by the Australian ace Bert Hinkler in an amazing fifteen and a half days; it was this record that Francis was determined to break. He knew that he couldn't beat Hinkler on level terms. Whereas he didn't even have a licence, Hinkler had been a First World War ace with a Distinguished Service Medal and after the war was a test pilot for the same Avro company that made the Avian. He'd won two Britannia Cups and a gold medal from the *Fédération Aéronautique Internationale* and even had an international nickname: 'Hustlin' Hinkler'. He'd had a trouble-free journey to Darwin, cutting the previous record in half. No wonder Francis felt a level playing field was not sufficiently sloping in his favour. A faster plane was needed.

Step forward the de Havilland DH.60 Moth. First flown in 1925 by Geoffrey de Havilland at his Stag Lane airfield and factory in north London, by 1929 it had become the Empire's most accepted general-purpose light aircraft. It was still using the same Cirrus engine that Hinkler had used in his Avian. The Cirrus was a fine engine but, being based on First World War Renault engines, supplies were dependent on dwindling stockpiles. With a booming order book, Geoffrey de Havilland decided that his own engine, built in his own factory, was needed. The new engine was designed to be more powerful, lighter and much more reliable – and, of course, available – than the Cirrus. He called the engine 'Gipsy' and so the DH.60 Moth became the DH.60G Gipsy Moth.

Official World's Records Won by the MOTH

Speed

World's record for two seater light airplanes over a closed circuit of 100 kilometers made by Mr. A. S. Butler in a Gipsy Moth, December 7, 1928. Average speed, 119.84 M.P.H.

Climb

World's altitude record of 19,800 feet, for two seater light airplanes made in a Gipsy Moth by Capt. G. de Havilland with Mrs. de Havilland as passenger, July 25, 1928.

Endurance

World's endurance record for light airplanes established by Capt. Hubert Broad in a Gipsy Moth on August 16-17, 1928. Time, 24 hours continuously in the air, beating previous record by 11 hours.

Other MOTH Achievements

Winner of the King's Cup Air Race around England in 1926, 1927, and 1928. In 1929, Moths secured second, third, fourth, and fifth places, the winner being a 400 H.P. military scout. Also won the special trophy for private owners flying their own machines, with MOTHS taking second, third, fourth, fifth, and sixth places.

The first light airplane to fly from London to India, Captain Stack and Mr. Leete, 1926.

The first light airplane to make the flight London-Capetown-London, Lieutenant Bentley, 1927-1928.

Lady Mary Bailey, flying a Moth, on Jan. 18, 1929, completed the longest solo flight on record—from London to Capetown, South Africa, and return, 18,000 miles.

In 1929, the Viscount and Viscountess de Sibour, on a pleasure trip around the world, used their Gipsy Moth for all land transportation, flying 16,000 miles at a cost below $5,000 including hotels, and all expenses.

The Moth is the winner of more contests, trophies and prizes than any other light airplane

MOTH Performance, Weights and Dimensions

Gipsy Moth Landplane
(85-100 H.P. de Havilland Gipsy Engine)

Guaranteed Performance

Performance figures given in Column 1 for total weight of 1,350 lbs. represent machine with pilot and passenger only. Those in Column 2 represent machine loaded up to maximum total weight of 1,650 lbs.

	At total weight 1,350 lbs.	At total loaded weight of 1,650 lbs.
Speed		
Full speed at Ground Level	103-105 m.p.h.	102 m.p.h.
Full speed at 5,000 ft.	100 m.p.h.	97 m.p.h.
Cruising speed at 1,000 ft.	85-90 m.p.h.	80-85 m.p.h.
Stalling speed	40 m.p.h.	44 m.p.h.
Get Off and Landing		
Length of run to take off	80 yards	100-110 yards
Length of run landing	100-120 yards	120-130 yards
Height at 500 yard from a standing start	130 feet	80 feet
Gliding angle	1 in 8	1 in 8
Climb		
Rate of Climb at Ground Level	700 ft./min.	500 ft./min.
Time to 5,000 ft.	9 mins.	13 mins.
Time to 10,000 ft.	21 mins.	35 mins.
Absolute Ceiling	18,000 feet	14,500 feet

Range

At a true speed of 80 m.p.h. the range varies from 4½ hours to 5 hours, according to height—this giving 360 to 400 miles. An additional 13-gallon tank can be supplied—giving a range of 550 miles.

WEIGHTS

Weight, empty (average)	975 lbs.
Crew at 160 lbs. each	320 lbs.
Fuel—23 gallons	140 lbs.
Oil—2.5 gallons	19 lbs.
Weight, fully loaded with pilot and passenger	1,454 lbs.
Permissible baggage	196 lbs.
Maximum total weight	1,650 lbs.

DIMENSIONS

Length—overall	23 ft. 11 ins.
Span—open	30 ft. 0 ins.
Span—folded	9 ft. 10 ins.
Height—overall (tail skid on ground)	8 ft. 9½ ins.

The D.H. GIPSY MOTH

Distinctive Features of the D. H. Gipsy MOTH

Folding Wings

FOLDING WINGS permit storing the Moth in a single-car garage. Commercial users can store three Moths in space occupied by one ordinary plane, resulting in large savings in hangar rent.

Engine Cowling Cuts Wind Resistance

THE NEW automobile-type quick detachable cowling cuts down wind resistance, and ensures perfect cooling under all conditions. The engine is very easy to get at, which reduces the work of maintenance and inspection to a minimum. Cylinder heads are easily removable for valve grinding. The crank-case pan can also be removed easily.

Gipsy Engine. The Gipsy is a four cylinder, vertical-in-line, air-cooled engine, with a normal output of 90 H.P. at 1900 R.P.M., and 100 H.P. at 2100 R.P.M. It is smooth running at all speeds, and has ample reserve power to meet any emergency. Its simple design, like the conventional automobile engine, makes it easy and inexpensive to service. The quick detachable cowling, which reduces wind resistance to a minimum and ensures perfect cooling in all weathers can be folded aside in a few seconds, making the engine readily accessible.

Controls. The well balanced system of controls in the MOTH, which can be operated from either cockpit, makes an instant appeal to both experienced pilots and novices. Controls are very easy to operate, and because of large aileron, elevator, and rudder surfaces, the plane responds immediately to the smallest movement of control stick or rudder bar. The surface areas are designed so that the immediate reaction of the pilot is a feeling of smoothness and harmony. Since the passenger's cockpit and gasoline tank are located on the center of gravity, the plane's perfect balance is not affected by varying loads. The moment a flyer takes off he has a sense of security.

Slotted Wings. The inherent stability of the MOTH is greatly increased by the use of the Handley-Page wing slots, which are furnished as an extra. These small auxiliary vanes, normally lying flush with the leading edges of the upper wings, automatically drop out at stalling speed, deflecting the air stream over the upper wing surfaces in such a way as to restore the wing lift, and prevent danger of falling off into a spin around the low wing. In addition to giving greater stability and safety in the air, the wing slots permit slower speeds and greater safety in landing.

Folding Wings. Moth wings can be folded in a few seconds, easily and without tools. With folded wings, a Moth can be stored in an ordinary one-car garage, or a number of Moths can be stored side by side like automobiles, cutting hangar rent to a third the usual figure. The Moth can also be towed behind a light automobile, even through ordinary city traffic.

Undercarriage. The MOTH super-absorbent undercarriage is of the split axle type, with a wide track to give stability when taking off and landing, and ample clearance to permit landing on rough ground. A combination of resilient rubber units and "Ferodo" lined pistons sliding in the outer casing damps out the shock of the heaviest landing.

Slotted Wings Increase Stability

THE HANDLEY-PAGE automatic slotted wing gear is acknowledged to be the greatest single contribution to safe flying. It prevents involuntary tail spins by insuring complete lateral control at speeds below the stalling point. It can be supplied as an extra.

Undercarriage is Sturdy, Resilient

THE SUPER-ABSORBENT split-axle undercarriage damps out the shocks of the heaviest landings. The split axle permits making landings on rough ground, while the great resilience is invaluable for school flying. Wire bracing is entirely eliminated.

The Gipsy Moth brochure; yours for £650.

When deliveries started in 1929, a Gipsy Moth could be bought for £650, a much better bargain than the alternative Westland Widgeon, Simmonds Spartan, Bristol Bulldog, ABC Robin or, indeed, the Avro Avian. Francis saw the Gipsy-engined Moth as his competitive advantage over Hinkler and the £650 asking price as just about affordable in his newly reduced circumstances.

But first he had to learn to fly – or rather continue from where he left off in New Zealand: he already had eighteen hours of dual instruction in his logbook. He chose Brooklands as his flying base and of the three schools there he chose the Brooklands School of Flying to take him over the line.

It is easy to agree with George Bolt that Francis was not a natural pilot – as, indeed, he was later to find that he was not a natural sailor. What he was, however, was a natural navigator, and then some. In the Brooklands School of Flying brochure the school answers its own question:

> *How Long Will It Take Me to Learn to Fly? The period occupied in taking the course varies with age and temperament. Some obtain their licence after as little as eight hours total flying; others take as long as fifteen hours; but it has been our experience that the average time is from ten to twelve hours.*

Somehow Francis managed to take twenty-four hours of dual instruction before being allowed to fly solo. He had to add five hours at Brooklands to the eighteen already received in New Zealand before the great day, 13 August 1929, when he took off alone for a five-minute circuit of the airfield.

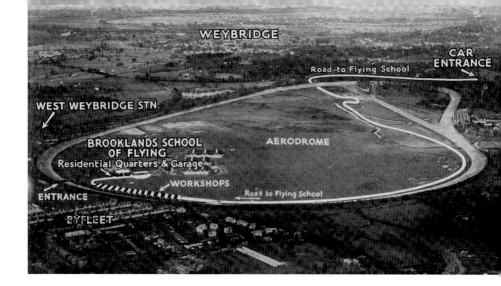

WEYBRIDGE

CAR ENTRANCE

Road to Flying School

WEST WEYBRIDGE STN.

BROOKLANDS SCHOOL OF FLYING
Residential Quarters & Garage

AERODROME

WORKSHOPS

Road to Flying School

ENTRANCE

BYFLEET

Brooklands School of Flying

I am keen to experience what Francis went through during those August days at Brooklands. When I was making sports/racing cars around the turn of the century one of my advisors was Roy Palmer, who ran a very successful marketing consultancy. I remember that he is a keen aviator of the vintage variety and call him for advice for my new venture, viz. writing this book.

Moths at the ready at the Brooklands School of Flying

As good luck would have it, Roy not only knows all about Gipsy Moths but actually owns one and a half of them. More than this, he is generous enough to put the whole one, G-AANL, at my disposal. Brooklands as it was in its Francis-era derring-do heyday is of course no more, the famous banked motor racing circuit mossing away and the infield now mostly the ultra-modern

Mercedes Benz UK headquarters. The very fine Brooklands Museum still stands and thrives, and I'm especially grateful to the archivist there, Philip Clifford, for background and images about the Brooklands School of Flying and Brooklands airfield as it was.

White Waltham airfield near Maidenhead could be said to be the today's Brooklands: its eclectic mix of vintage, aerobatic and home-built aircraft all flying off grass on London's western doorstep – and just under Heathrow's control zone – summons up a refreshingly professional amateur approach to going aloft. White Waltham completes the impression of a modern Brooklands with its wooden bungalow clubhouse, all Biggles and shillings, full of today's The Few, and here I meet my instructor for the day and Roy's own instructor, Bob Gibson.

I suggest to Bob: 'I'm going to imagine you are a Mr C.M. Pickthorn, who had the patience to teach Francis how to fly. Also going to ask if you can imagine I'm the recently arrived from New Zealand Francis Chichester, with eighteen hours under my belt but not yet deemed solo material. And we are both going to take our lives in our hands as you give me-as-Francis a flying lesson.'

'Of course,' Bob replies, 'and not just the flying lesson but the whole Gipsy Moth experience. But there's a flaw in your plan.'

There normally is; I ask him which one this time.

'Francis learned to fly in G-EBPR. That was Brooklands School of Flying's Moth, but it was a Cirrus-engined Moth, not a Gipsy-engined Moth. Francis's – and Roy's – are Gipsy Moths. So we can't be totally like for like – but there or thereabouts. You'll certainly get the Moth experience.'

'Ah. Well can you find me a Cirrus Moth?' I ask.

'No. There aren't any Cirrus Moths left.'

'How come?'

'Well, they were of course pretty fragile, and the school ones would have crashed a lot, but the real reason was that the Gipsy engine was so much better. So if any old Cirrus-engined ones survived the crashes the owners all changed to Gipsies when the time came to renew the engines. But still … the plane's the same and we can give you a good feeling of what it was like.'

We walk around the Moth as Bob explains the pre-flight checks. Close up the old biplane looks amazingly flimsy. We examine each nut and strut and bit of string. There aren't that many of them and the glue you can't see at all. Alarmingly, the wings swing back to ease hangar space – and the hinges are locked in place by a suspiciously simple-looking pin. I mention something about this being a Jesus pin – after the name given by the American flyers in Vietnam to the one bolt that held the rotors onto the Hueys. Bob must have seen me looking wistfully from the grass underneath us to the sky above.

'Don't worry,' he reads my mind, 'she's actually a brand new airplane if you think about it. Just built to a very old design. Back when Chichester was flying, none of the steel was high tensile, now it all is. The glue back then really was glue, now it's adhesive, just like on that Boeing up there.' He looks up at a BA plane on final descent into Heathrow. 'And the fabric's not really fabric, more like some newfangled reinforced ripstop overlay. In layman's terms.'

'Layman sounds good.'

'But apart from having to use all modern materials,' Bob seems a bit wistful now, 'everything else is period, the instruments, seats, screens. The only thing we've changed is the intercom, so we can hear each other a bit more easily. Back at the Brooklands School of Flying they would have had tubes you shouted into and hoped for the best. Instructing involved a lot of yelling, and that was when it was all going smoothly.'

Two other parts of the plane catch my eye. The air speed indicator is a wonderfully simple swing gauge on the port strut between the wings: the faster you fly, the more the needle is pushed back by the wind against the speed markings. Anything below 45 mph is in the red zone, a reminder that when flying the danger is not going quickly enough. Maximum on the gauge is

The Gipsy Moth's air speed indicator on the strut. Buckingham a long way down below, seemingly

120 mph, by which time 'the wings would have gone their own way', as Bob reassuringly puts it.

Secondly – and much in the news that afternoon – is the pitot tube sticking out a few inches from the lower starboard wing. This ingenious bit of tubing feeds information on air speed and air pressure back to the instruments. And why much in the news? The air crash investigation into the Air France 447 Rio-Paris flight had just been published. As Bob says, 'Even the most modern airliners and military jets use the same pitot/static system to provide air pressure information to their instruments. The only difference now is that the information is displayed on glass cockpit displays instead of dials with needles'. In this case the pitot tube malfunctioned, causing the air speed instruments in the Airbus cockpit to read too low. The scandal was that the pilots had been trained to fly computers, not aeroplanes: the aeroplane pilot reacts to slow speed by diving, in the sense that – perhaps counter-intuitively – speed is controlled by climbing and diving, while climbing and diving is controlled by speed, using the throttle. The Air France computer pilots reacted to the false slow speed reading by whacking on more throttle, thereby climbing and losing more speed and subsequently stalling – stalling all the way down into the Atlantic, with the loss of all 228 souls on board. And as even I know, they could always have double-checked the pitot tube air speed reading with the GPS and, realising the instrument error, have gone with the satellite information on the latter – not to mention common sense. And as even I know, too, if the stall warning alarm is shouting at you repeatedly, you do something about it. Shocking, really.

Getting in – and out – of the Gipsy Moth front seat is a real struggle gymnastically. I'm due to sit up there and I'm a big boy and it takes several attempts at contortionist choreography and yogic breathing for me to squeeze in. Francis was medium-built and wiry and a lot younger – and even he remarked about the 'ingress egress bother of the 'plane'. I suggest that baling out in an emergency would be a challenge. Bob agrees, only pointing out that emergencies bring out the lithest in people. He also points out that when the Royal Air Force ordered their Tiger Moth trainers they insisted that, *inter alia*, the existing DH Moths' wings be swept back to solve the problem.

The instruments are all original and pure Francis-era: an altimeter and air speed indicator fed by said pitot tube, a cross-level like a spirit level to keep the plane on an even keel and a compass. Above these are the engine instruments for rpm and oil temperature. There's a chronometer for navigating. Added to the Brooklands spec are a modern radio and transponder for flying in controlled airspace, should the need arise.

'Getting in – and out – of the Gipsy Moth front seat is a real struggle, gymnastically'. Instructor Bob Gibson, left, and your correspondent hanging on tight – and that's still on the ground

Not much to go on, not too much to sit on...a Gipsy Moth cockpit

Time to start her up. Not the work of a moment. Before electric starters this was a two-person operation, one to stand in front of the engine and swing the prop eight times to prime the engine with fuel, the other to catch the engine on 1/4 inch of throttle when it fires up. The engine has two magnetos, basically on/off switches, and in view of the likelihood of disarming or decapitation, the person in charge of the operation is the prop swinger. 'Contact on!' or 'Contact off!' our protagonists shout to each other each time the prop is swung: 'on' means that the magnetos are on and the engine may burst into song once the magnetos have caught a spark. Later, in the Biggles bar, we try to work out how Francis managed to start his engine solo. He would have had to use chocks to stop *Elijah* (as he had named his Gipsy Moth at Brooklands, with a ceremonial bottle of brandy broken on the propeller boss) zooming off, and would have had to set the magnetos and throttle each time. Once it had fired he would have had to rush around, skewer himself into the cockpit and pull up the chocks using pre-arranged ropes. What is less clear is how he did it when *Elijah* became a seaplane. (Actually, once *Elijah* became a seaplane Francis observed naval tradition and renamed her *Madame Elijah*.) He would have had to stand in front of the engine on the port float (as the prop swings clockwise from the front) and somehow get over to the starboard float, all the while with her taxiing across the water, and somehow jump in from that float taking care to keep clear of the rotating prop. We were still trying to work out how he did it at closing time.

So the Gipsy engine starts, Bob runs her up to check that both magnetos are working on full power – 2,200 rpm – and off we taxi. We can't see a thing ahead so we zigzag to the end of the runway, do more final checks and off we go. Bob suggests I hold on to the joystick and rest my feet on the pedals lightly to feel what he is doing. As soon as she starts to roll he moves the stick forward to bring the tail up and at about 45mph, with just a hint of back 'stick, she slowly lifts herself off and climbs away at 300 feet a minute. Progress to the skies is stately rather than startling. Outside it's a lovely September day and soon the thermals are throwing us around a bit.

I actually had a pilot's licence back in the days before inflation, family and yachts, and owned an eighth of a single-engined Piper Comanche, G-AZUL and, later, an eighth of a twin-engined Piper Aztec, rather gaily – as the vernacular evolved – registered G-AYBO. I had also bought a Tiger Moth flight simulator programme the week before today's flight. All this explained, when Bob says the famous words 'You have control', why we don't dive straight into the nearest haystack. Above all, in both senses, it is great to be piloting again.

It would be hard to imagine an easier plane to fly than the Gipsy Moth. Being out in the open must help as you can see and feel directly what happens with every control input. The inputs themselves need only to be tiny for the new/old stringbag to react: an inch or so on the 'stick to port is enough to initiate a turn, half an inch back pressure and the nose pops up over the horizon. This sensitivity is all very well but creates its own problems, very Francis-orientated ones: how to keep her straight and level when you need two hands for doing something else, such as working a sextant or even pouring a coffee or finding a pasty, as he had to do on the long flights. Try leaving her alone to fly herself and within two seconds she is turning or climbing or diving on her own; ditto taking your eyes off the horizon to look at a map. You can trim and balance a modern plane to hold her own for half a minute or so while you navigate; not so a vintage kite, as I must learn to call them.

Then again all this flying happens so slowly and so ensures a strong sense of safety: get something wrong or find yourself lost and you could almost make a cup of tea, rethink and try again and not have gone too far up, down, sideways or forwards. The only quirk is that being relatively underpowered – by today's standards – she stops climbing in the turn; in other words, when the wings are not horizontal, when turning, they lose most of their lift. In fact, unlike the Tiger Moth on the simulator, you can turn and you can climb but you cannot climb and turn at the same time; but you soon get used to that.

Bob takes me through a standard Francis one-hour replica flying lesson. We stall, at what seems strolling speed, and recover, without any drama and with nose down; we emergency land and make a perfect landing at 50 feet above a wheat field; we steep turn with rudder; we set her up for the cruise at 78 mph; we navigate by railway line; we figure-of-eight – and end up more or less where we started. Then we land, without flaps, there being none, being overtaken by a bicyclist pedalling uphill on a country lane on our final approach, or so it seems. Landing is the only remotely tricky part, and even that comes with the option of powering up and having another go. I'm sure that Mr Pickthorn would have told Francis what Bob tells me now: a good landing needs a good final approach, so the landing starts a minute before the wheels first bump off the grass. Half a dozen cracks at it should be enough.

So, it's really hard to see why Francis struggled so much with learning to fly. In his first book, *Solo to Sydney,* he readily admits his lack of flying finesse and recalls some of Pickthorn's fairly frantic comments to him:

Don't jerk your tail so suddenly, or one day in long grass you'll trip and nose over.

Stop swivelling all over the field. Watch a point on the horizon and take off straight.

If you take off before you get up your flying speed, the slightest gust of wind will stall you and you will write off the undercarriage.

Again I say, the regulations state you must not turn until 500 yards beyond the aerodrome perimeter.

You are still turning with too much rudder and not enough bank.

Keep your nose down turning. Your nose is too high, you've too much bank, you've not enough rudder and you are side slipping. You're asking for a spin.

Watch your speed while turning. You'll lose flying speed and hit the deck before you can recover it.

Make all your controlled movements smooth. You're jerking the kite about like a washing- machine.

Then the time comes for Francis to practise an emergency landing.

Pickthorn: 'Cut back your engine. Widen your approach as you are obviously overshooting. Watch your speed on your turns. Try to keep the speed at a steady 60 miles an hour when landing. You have slight rudder on all the time and your left wing is too low. You have flattened much too soon. Put on your engine and go round again.'

Francis tries again. Pickthorn becomes even more anxious: 'Man alive, can't you see you're headed straight for the fence? More engine, quickly.'

At lesson's end Francis has to land. 'Bump!' he reports, 'The wretched machine hits the ground and rebounds fifty feet into the air'.

'For the love of Mike!' (Pickthorn again) 'Put on your engine when you do that or you'll wipe off the undercarriage by dropping back stalled on the deck.'

Francis's day finishes thus:

You then make the world's worst landing in a series of wild rabbit hops. The instructor (what a life!) inspects to see what damage is done. If you are permitted to try another landing, the result will be much the same. At the end of the day, after the humiliating spectacle provided by fellow student, who, with only a third of the instructions you have heard, makes seven perfect landings in succession, you crawl humbly home, the sorriest dog in the world, unable adequately to conceal your tail between your legs.

But – now here's a funny thing. Once Francis had his licence, which he eventually gained on 28 August 1929, his flying came on, as it were, in leaps and bounds. It was if the gods, prescient as ever, had meant him only ever to fly solo. Once aloft alone he was soon singing in the bath:

Next morning I was up with the lark, and make a sorry imitation of him in the bath. I set off for the aerodrome with the nearest resemblance of a rush. Bursting with confidence I board a plane.

At last I make good three-point landings in succession. It is the same as being in love: your heart swells with love for your neighbour, the drone of the Cirrus engine no longer suggests incipient engine-knock with every beat, you forget your creditors, the world is at your feet, flying is child's play. It is incredible that you should ever have imagined it difficult. Your fancy flies ahead, you work out how you consider the control should be moved for a slow roll or half roll off the top of a loop: the intricacies of flying no longer hold any terrors. In short, complete happiness is your portion.

It was enough happiness to make the purchase with de Havilland and on 8 September Francis took the train up to Stag Lane airfield near Enfield to take delivery of his own Gipsy Moth. G-AAKK cost £650, payable on instalments, and the deposit alone used up pretty much all his short-term funds. (Today a Gipsy Moth costs about £100,000 and one with a bit of history well north of that.)

Having got the hang of flying, Francis now had to learn how to navigate. He didn't know it yet but he was about to find his *métier* – and so the words fairly flew off his typewriter:

What about navigation? Suppose I couldn't navigate across country? The first time I ventured away from the aerodrome was most exciting. At first everything was a jumble; then I picked out a railway line, the Thames, the Staines reservoir. With the aid of the map I found Byfleet. Flying at a snail's pace, I recognised other landmarks shown on the map. Thrill, excitement, joy! If I could do that much the first day, competence must be a matter only of practice and experience.

The aeroplane was so new that it had not yet been fitted with a compass. I was 'flying by Bradshaw', following the railway lines across country, and I wondered if I could fly by the sun. The sky was overcast, with ten-tenths at 1,000 feet. I climbed up into the cloud, and proceeded until I had passed through a 9,000 feet layer of it to emerge at 10,000 feet in brilliant sunshine over a snowy white field of cloud. Not only had I no compass, but no blind-flying instruments at all. I reckoned that if I got into trouble I could force the plane into a spin, and that it was bound to spin round the vertical axis, and that therefore I should be sure to emerge vertically from the cloud.

After flying along for half an hour by the sun, I climbed down through the 9,000-foot layer of cloud. I then wanted to find out how accurately I had carried out this manoeuvre, and I used a sound principle of navigation. I fixed my position by the easiest method available – I flew round a railway station low down, and read the name off the platform. By some extraordinary fluke I was right on course. I probably uttered for the first time the navigator's famous cry 'Spot on!'

'Spot on!' It was to become Francis's calling card, muttered *sotto voce* to himself when his sextant confirmed his dead reckoning after an Atlantic storm, quietly to Sheila on seeing their first lighthouse on the Western Approaches, at the top of his voice alone to *Elijah* on landfall over Darwin, and a thousand times besides; always with a hint of pride and surprise, no trumpets to blow – especially in public - but, still, the spot-on sound of Francis in heaven.

Like a child with a new toy, he now set about putting *Elijah* to good use. First he flew up to Liverpool for a rendezvous with an actress. Bafflingly to him, she wasn't impressed with either Francis or *Elijah*. He turned around and followed a different

railway line down to Bristol, then flew west along the north Devon coast to Barnstaple and up his home valley to Shirwell, buzzed the Old Rectory a couple of times and landed at Youlston Park. It was his homecoming after ten years.

That visit home was not a success. Francis had every reason to feel proud of himself. He had left on foot with £10 in his pocket and returned with a fortune – albeit a bit theoretical right now – and flying his own kite. This genteel Devon clergy-squire poverty all seemed so unnecessary. He was disillusioned by the incipient decay of a running-down household after the spick and span of New World homesteads and gardens. Their talk was of who had missed Mass; his thoughts were of record-breaking flights across the world. He now had the confidence to rebel against his father, subtly. Dinners were still held in silence after Grace; he broke that taboo, even if one-sidedly. He laid on the Kiwi accent, which he could tell grated. He boasted of his fortune, knowing that this would annoy them further.

Worst sin of all came when he wanted to buy a wreath for his recently deceased great-aunt, Jinny. The other wreaths already there were small and discreet – and no doubt inexpensive, if not homemade – and fitting in with the scale of a Devon village. Out of devilment Francis bought an enormous, ostentatiously expensive wreath, which eclipsed all the others. He wrote: 'I think that wreath upset my family more than anything else I did; they thought I must be a frightful barbarian to produce such an unusual thing.'

And then the next day he crashed. He had been giving joyrides. After one, with his younger sister Cecily on board, one of the wheels touched down in a rabbit burrow and then went on to meet the steep side of a cart track; the wheels stopped turning but the plane kept moving. The hole in the fuselage looked bad at first but the damage was more to his pride than the airframe or Cecily. He quickly found the family carpenter – and his boyhood sparring partner – George Moore, and together they repaired the airframe's broken ribs and added some fresh ones. The next day Francis and *Elijah* were flying again, this time the passenger being the old family retainer, Wilkie. Clearly terrified by the whole experience, he reminded Francis on alighting that twenty-eight years ago to this very day he had ridden to Barnstaple to fetch a doctor so that Francis could make his very first landing with the midwife. Of all the Old Rectory household, only Wilkie remembered that day was Francis's birthday.

And then he crashed again. After an exhilarating flight back from Devon to Brooklands in a 35 mph wind, he put *Elijah* down at the second attempt and then made a classic novice's mistake: he taxied crosswind and a gust got under the windward wing and lifted her on to the leeward wing-tip. That tip crumpled and another gust levered her up into the air until Francis 'found myself in the undignified position of dangling in the safety-belt and looking down at the ground ten feet below me'.

It took fifty hours in the rigging shop to mend the damage but it was time well spent. Francis still didn't know whether he was still long-term rich or just short-term poor; he did know right now that he couldn't afford to have the chippies and riggers mend it: he had to learn to do it himself under their supervision, much to the chippies' and riggers' amusement – not just at his craftsmanship but the fact that a pilot was actually working on his plane himself.

Francis could not afford any more crashes and by now it was clear that there was more to this flying lark than larking about. He set about a self-imposed, self-instructed intensive training period. He practised landing in crosswinds and even upwinds. He planted a marker ten yards inside a fence and went round and round until his landings got closer and closer and he eventually landed on it. For half an hour a day he practised forced landings. He learned basic aerobatics, lining himself up with a railway line for accuracy of execution. Much as he had learned skiing in New Zealand, by 'falling, falling, falling', he learned to fly in Surrey by landing, landing, landing.

A month later, on 3 October, his compass arrived and he began feeding navigation skills into his daily training routine. By 15 October he was ready for his first night flight, lit only by moonlight. He was in his own kind of paradise:

> I had a feeling of complete isolation and solitariness, and the thousands of lights below intensified the feeling of being completely cut off. I looped, and did a few stall turns for the same reason a dog barks at something which scares him.

When Francis was not flying he was back at Aunt Mary's in Knightsbridge, planning the trip that would break Hinkler's record to Australia. There was a conjunction of time and money to consider. He worked out, for reasons that are not entirely obvious, that the best time to attempt the flight was the shortest day at departure and the longest day at arrival – so ideally to cross the Equator around 21 December, two months away. A last-ditch hope Francis had of funds from the business in New Zealand had fallen flat with a telegram from Geoffrey Goodwin: 'Advise selling plane. Expensive salvage Malay aerodromes. No more money possible. All reserves used up. Expected £2,000 loan unavailable.'

Alongside this conjunction were two further considerations. The attempt to fly solo to Australia was not new – but it was riddled by failure. His licence was only two months old, his solo hours still only in double figures. Much better pilots than Francis had failed – and died failing - in the attempt. The first successful flight was ten years before, in 1919, and took four weeks and two days. Either side of that, one pilot had crashed in Bali in sight of the finish and another at Surbiton in sight of the start. In the five attempts since then, and before Hinkler's record the year before – 1928 – there had been crashes in Corfu, Crete and Turin and two crash-delayed successes, one taking five months and the other seven months. Since Hinkler there had been two more attempts, one crashing in France, the other in Australia. A betting man would have found a willing bookie hard to find.

Conjoining this reality check was a more fantastical notion: he had discovered flying, flying had discovered him, and together they wanted more, more, more. He came up with a wizard wheeze to gain experience and not use up too much of the dwindling cash: he and *Elijah* would spend November burnishing their wings with what Francis called 'a trial spin around Europe'. He was to recall that:

> *That trip was a great experience for me. In twenty-five days I visited eight countries. Of twenty-eight landings, eight were in fields.* [He means here farming fields as opposed to airfields.] *Of these eight landings, three were for fun, two caused by fog, and three caused by fog and darkness combined and made in an urgent hurry. I got away with all except one, yet not without some abominably close shaves.*

And so the trial spin, the 'great sport', came to pass. The insurance company insisted that an experienced pilot should go with him, as the plane was still in hock. They nominated Joe King, recently arrived back from aerial survey work in Bolivia. Joe and Francis very nearly wrote themselves off in the first minute.

'Let's go!' said Joe from the front seat as he pushed the throttle wide open at first, frosty light. Francis assumed that Joe, as the senior pilot, wanted to take her off himself. They both thought they were an unusually long time leaving the ground; eventually they climbed just high enough to clear the Brooklands banking and the trees on St George's Hill.

'What on earth do you think you are doing?' shouted Joe through the speaking tube.

'I'm doing nothing,' Francis shouted back, 'I never even touched the controls.'

'Nor did I!' Joe yelled back.

'Jesus Christ!' they both said to themselves.

Actually this incident has passed into aviation folklore. I remember being told of it when learning to fly, to bring home the importance of the instructor saying 'You have control' and some time later, with relief in his voice, 'I have control.'

Francis had not flown over water before and naturally enough wanted some engine-failure gliding distance over the English Channel. He settled into the cross-Channel cruise over Lydd in Kent at 6,000 feet. I also remember from my flying lessons that you lose 3 degrees Celcius every 1,000 feet you climb. It was still early morning in early November and let's say it was 8 degrees ambient, so at 6,000 feet they were flying in minus 10 degrees Celcius into a 75 mph wind. I can't work out the wind chill factor but you get the p-p-picture.

It wasn't long before Joe was complaining bitterly about being turned into an icicle. He insisted they land and recover and Francis touched down in Abbeville, just off the Boulogne–Paris railway line. They both had a couple of warming Cognac stiffeners and resumed to the Paris refuelling stop. By now Joe had warmed up enough to fall fast asleep in the front cockpit but by Paris he'd had enough, made some excuse about looking up an old female business friend and scarpered – possibly back to the safety of aerial surveying in Bolivia.

On Francis flew, following the railways and the Rhône down to north of Marseilles and then east along the Riviera coast, checking progress on *Tourisme aérien: Carte générale*

The beach at Nice, Francis's refuelling stop

aéronautique internationale aviation maps, cut into strips and concertina-folded by Stanford's on Long Acre, Covent Garden, whose shop still thrives there today. (Stanford's archives can still be seen in the Royal Geographic Society.)

Passengers today at L'Aéroport Nice Côte d'Azur will find it hard to imagine, but on the evening of 3 November 1929, in order to refuel Francis had to land on the Beau Rivage beach, thumb a lift from a passing car into town and return with his tins of petrol in a taxi. He then rounded up two strollers from the Promenade des Anglais to hold the wing-tips while he ran her up and, waving a cheery '*au revoir*', opened up her to take off along beach again.

He flew around the Piedmont to Milan, refuelled and then overnighted in Venice. Leaving Trieste to the east and en route to Ljubljana in what was Yugoslavia, he hit sudden fog. Ahead there were first signs of darkness: 'I had to land in one big and violent hurry.' Below him were cultivated strips of land, each one tiny, in the Napoleonic manner. He had to choose the least worse one – but as soon as *Elijah*'s wheels touched down they sank into the bog and stopped while the rest of *Elijah* carried on for a few more seconds. For the second time in two months Francis found himself suspended 10 feet above the ground looking down on a broken prop. He had to wait ten days in Nova vas pri Rakeku for the new prop to arrive. The villagers were wonderfully hospitable and carried *Elijah* over to a better strip so that the village chief could be taken for a joyride, the least Francis felt he could do to thank them.

It was during that night that Francis had the first of what would become recurring, identical nightmares. He would be flying *Elijah* when suddenly he lost all vision – a white-out – with all certainty gone except the coming crash. The engine noise continued, only sight was lost. He would awake with a start each time, not sleepily, realising that he had just had a nightmare, but violently, upright and in distress. I asked a friend who is a practising psychiatrist and her interpretation was that the nightmare was a mental relief valve against the suppressed fear of crashing from a height, so not an instant death crash, over instantly, but an inevitably fatal descent from height.

The locals were less welcoming on his next forced landing. Having passed through Belgrade and Iasi on the River Prut, he was making for Czernowitz, just inside Ukraine, when again simultaneous darkness and fog got the better of him. Down he came forcefully in Codaesti in Moldavia. He was immediately surrounded by sheepskin-clad, fierce-looking gypsies brandishing firearms of questionable provenance. They had never seen a plane before and were soon poring over it. Francis worried that they were about to 'slice *Elijah* up into small pieces suitable for interior decoration'. Luckily a French-speaking officer rode up and restored order. Less luckily, they then discussed the advisability of shooting Francis on the spot for being a Bolshevik spy from across the border. Francis said he had not eaten all day and could they delay the execution till at least his stomach was full. The gypsies soon knocked up a *goulatsch*; over the meal the ice melted and Francis was spared the bullet, if not the indigestion.

As well as learning to fly and navigate, Francis was learning the system, the endless amounts of paperwork and protocols that any form of travel took in those days – and of which the newfangled sport of flying attracted even more. In his words, 'The only way to cross a country quickly is not to stop in it'. Every landing had the same routine, often liable to delay by officials who were over-curious or officious or lazy – or simply not there. First he had to check in with local police, who would examine his passport and visa, the obtaining of which itself was often the subject of obscuration back in London. Next, Customs wanted to inspect his *carnet-de-passage*, a sort of insurance bond guaranteeing that he would not try to sell the plane in their country, as well as rifle through his bags. Next the military would search the plane for anything suspicious, including camera equipment. Lastly, aerodrome officials would wade through the plane's documents looking for the proof of this and the stamp for that.

Only then, and often after several hours of frustrating delay in foreign tongues, could Francis get on with his trip tasks: checking the *Elijah*'s oil and sparking plugs, refuelling, checking over the airframe and flying surfaces, asking for the latest weather report, telegraphing the next destination and stocking up on food and water.

This extract from the *Bucuresti Dimineata* newspaper of 14 November 1929 is quite amusing, giving a flavour of Francis's adventures, officialdom and newspaper accuracy in the remoter parts of Eastern Europe:

Jassi, 12 November: An English aeroplane landed here yesterday for a short visit, piloted by Mr Chicesterc of New Zealand, Director of Godvin Chicesterc Aviation Co of London.

Mr Chicester is flying one of the company's planes. He left New Zealand last week, Touched at London, then at Paris where he picked up another aviator. On approaching Zagreb his propeller broke at some hundreds of feet and the aviators were in great danger.

The aeroplane, of unusual shape and colour, attracted crowds to the aerodrome of Tecuci. At Vaslui the pilots met fog and were obliged to force land at Codaesti. After satisfactory explanations he flew to Jassi accompanied by Advocate Popovitch. At Jassi Mr Chicesterc was met by a whole of corps of officers headed by Major Argeseanu. After a reception given in this [sic] honour the aviators left for Warsaw and London.

Francis also learned about supplies or the lack thereof, sustenance for himself and petrol and oil for *Elijah*. It was hard enough finding bread and fuel at his stops in Europe and he could only imagine the supply problems across North Africa and Asia. He knew now, if he didn't before, that most of December back in London was going to be taken up dealing with carnets, visas, licences, permits, firmans and authorisations, and with securing fuel dumps along the way.

On he flew to Warsaw, Poznań, Reppen, Leipzig, Dessau, Osnabrück, Jeggen, Abbeville again, and home. I hope you have a flavour of his adventures and so I won't take up more space by recounting every joy and despair of his crash course of continental flying or we'll be here all day.

———— ⚬⚭⚬ ————

I'm also not going to take up much space with the flight to Australia or we'll be here all night too. For readers interested in the blow-by-blow, I can recommend *Solo to Sydney*, his first and in many ways brightest book, written the following summer in the von Zedlitzes' garden in New Zealand. Suffice to say here, he failed to break Hinkler's record for reasons I shall go

*The Von
Zedlitz
garden,
where
Francis
wrote Solo
to Sydney*
into over the next few pages, but he succeeded in making the
journey in good time and in one piece. Considering his amateur
status compared with Hinkler's, Francis's achievement was very
remarkable and could stand proudly on its own.

I should still like to mention some highlights – and lowlights
– of his flight to Sydney. Just as by now he knew that a good
landing starts with a good approach, so a good flight to Sydney
starts with good approach in London. December was indeed
a whirr of preparation as Francis hurried from Stanford's
map emporium to the Air Ministry, from Shell's offices to
the Meteorological Office, from ordering a rubber dingy to
requesting permits to fly over fifteen countries – one permit at
a time – then on to square the insurance and then off to de
Havilland to pick-up the auxiliary fuel tanks, back to the Air
Ministry to research this landing strip against that landing strip,
which meant a trip back to Stanford's, and the round repeating
itself daily. In the meantime he was buying all the bits and pieces
needed for the flight, plus all his sheepskin and tropical clothes,
navigation tools, survival food and water, sixty-three spare parts,
the dingy with mast, sail and oars, and so on and so forth.

His refuelling calculations were based on beating Hinkler's record. Hinkler had averaged 640 miles a day. Francis reckoned:

It was not much use trying to beat his time by a few hours, so I divided the distance as nearly as possible into five hundred-mile stages. I would try to make two of these stages each day. To do this would necessitate daily average of 12½ hours in the air and the only way to manage that would be to leave every morning in the dark, at about 2 o'clock.

So for the ten days before departure Francis took on his record attempt routine. He would get up at 2 am to familiarise himself with the monastic timetable. He worked on his maps, mostly. From London to Rangoon/Yangon the scale was perfect at a millionth, or 16 miles to the inch. After that they became less useful, and over what was the Dutch East Indies, now Indonesia, more or less useless. He marked every possible landing site on his route, every forty-mile/half-hour 'peg', every change in magnetic variation and time zone heading east, then cut the maps up into nine-inch strips, joined all 71 feet of them together and made five scrolls. Later, still before dawn, he would work on *Elijah*'s final fettles. Now a new sense of urgency drew in: the de Havilland finance company wanted a guarantor for the £275 still owing, in case he crashed and burned. Clearly the manufacturer's bankers did not share their customer's belief in himself. Francis calculated correctly that the best way of finding a guarantor was to escape without one.

Finally, finally, the great day came. At Croydon airport – the Heathrow of its day – at 1.30 am on 19 December 1929 Francis 'stowed away some bacon and eggs'. At 2.30 am he had the weather reports and went through the starting procedure. In the hangar was a familiar face he couldn't quite place, which said: 'Aren't you Chichester?' Francis confirmed. 'I've just arrived here in my own kite. I shall never forget you turning up in Liverpool in a new machine without a compass and that ridiculous map of yours. Have you had any flights since?'

'Yes,' replied Francis modestly, 'I've flown all around Europe.'

'Great heavens! But you've only just got your licence. Perhaps you are planning to fly back to New Zealand!' he joked.

'Well, as a matter of fact I am.'

'Not possible! When?'

'Just now,' Francis replied, heading towards *Elijah*. 'Oh by the way...'

'Yes?' the man replied.

'I've just realised, I've forgotten to stow something important.'

'Can I help?'

'You couldn't spare me a corkscrew could you?'

He could; and did; and so Francis fired up *Elijah*, fully equipped for the great adventure.

Outside it was pitch black as the airfield lights were down, so Francis found a couple who agreed to walk ahead of him in the dark so that he didn't taxi into the hangar. It was bitterly cold and he was so wrapped up that it's hard to imagine how he could feel any of the controls. They waved him goodbye. 'The girl was particularly nice in the way she said "Goodbye!" to me. I sang out "Cheerio!" and with a wave, off we went.'

He got lost in the freezing fog over the Channel and eventually arrived an hour late at his first stop, Lyons, where he refuelled *Elijah* with fuel and himself 'with an enormous omelette washed down with a bottle of red wine', while he enquired about the day's best route over the Alps. The recommended minimum height was 10,000 feet and Francis knew *Elijah* could not manage that so fully laden. He had, however, by now learned to fly her by rudder alone, having learnt the knack of trimming her for level flight by changing the trim lever gears and using the rudder to yaw her, lifting a wing to keep her straight as well as level – and so freeing up both hands – thus solving one of our White Waltham how-did-he-do it mysteries.

He crossed the Aiguilles d'Arves pass at 6,000 feet and minus 20 degrees Celcius, ice and snow everywhere and no immediate prospect of finding an emergency landing field. Ahead, 'the Alps presented an impenetrable snow-capped wall, backed by innumerable humps and mounds covered in snow and stretching for a seemingly endless distance. The sun shone in flawless weather.' So high, so alone, he was close to heaven literally and metaphorically: Francis swathed from head to toe in layers of wool and sheepskin, *Elijah* and he at one with each other, the instruments for company, the intense whiteness all around, broken only by the four blue flames from the Gipsy's exhaust, the profound silence outside contrasted with the Gipsy's urgent throb, Mont Blanc towering over on the wing-tip, the wing-tip towering over the valleys deep below, the compass offset for Pisa four hours away, somewhere beyond the jagged, lonely, snowy range. With some fuel burned off, he climbed to 9,000 feet to cross the Cenis Col, descend over the Piedmont, which he had crossed a month before, and on through some stormy weather into Pisa for a night landing and a bout of chaotic Italian officialdom: 'My wants were simple enough, merely petrol, oil, engine work, sleep, food and a 2.00 am start. It took me four and a half hours solid talk and argument to arrange everything bar the sleep.' After twenty hours of intense wakefulness, including flying 780 miles in a tiny biplane

Cold, very cold

over freezing fog at sea and freezing air on high, being bashed about by a storm, sometimes lost and always on his wit's edge, he was so tired he couldn't sleep.

—⊶⊷—

Francis failed to beat Hinkler's record because the next night he crashed in Tripoli, now in Libya, then an Italian colony. The new prop took ten days to arrive and fit, and that time taken meant the end of the record attempt.

After leaving Pisa he had a fast run down the Apennines, past Vesuvius, across to the Straits of Messina to Sicily, to refuel in Catania. He was running late due to Sicilian paperwork chaos but was assured that there was night landing at Homs airfield (now Khoms, next to Leptis Magna) on the north African coast. When he arrived at what he thought was Homs, he only saw a reddish light. He dived to look 'and was disgusted to find it appeared to be a bonfire lit by some Arab peasants (or whatever they are)'. Later he was to learn that this was in fact Homs: in the absence of electricity, the Italians had helpfully lit a bonfire to show him the landing spot. Chagrined, he reluctantly flew west, away from Sydney to the certainty of the main Italian Air Force base at Tripoli.

The weather was worsening, the altimeter was malfunctioning and Tripoli was not where it should be. Francis became frightened and disorientated. The right side of his brain was telling him that as long as he was flying west along the coast he must eventually see the town; the left side was imagining that Homs wasn't Homs and he was miles to the east – or west – of anywhere. Lost. In the dark. With lowering weather. And the Italian Air Force's Mellaha airfield near Tripoli not expecting him. Maybe unlit. Both sides of his brain had been flying solo for the last twenty-six hours out of forty, with less than an hour's snatched sleep, all the while on the limit of alertness, constantly anxious, frequently occupied by raw fear, exposed to unnaturally loud noise levels, reacting to his cold and cramped body, fixated on breaking someone else's record.

Ahead, through the gloom, he saw a flashing light. The airfield! He dived. It was the sea- and not the airport lighthouse; but it was Tripoli. Then a minute later, another flashing light. The airfield! But this time it was a car playing silly buggers with its headlights. Then ahead, a searchlight moving. The airfield! It was. Francis dived past to let them know he was arriving and the searchlight followed him briefly in acknowledgement.

And then – after all the hostages to fortune – he had some simple bad luck. Maybe a fully functioning Francis would have sensed that something wasn't quite right. He knew that the British Empire's air forces used searchlights to light up the runways. He didn't know that the Italian Air Force, then still called the Regia Aeronautica, used them to light up the dangers. The searchlight settled on a hangar and collateral light showed space to land but not enough to go round again should the landing not be right first time 'and it was very unlikely that I would make a good landing first shot after so long in the air and in the dark on a strange 'drome'. Francis circled slowly and low and 'noticed a splendid square of ground enclosed by trees and the hangars. There was plenty of water about but I didn't worry too much about it as water makes sand hard'. He did two practice runs 'to get my eye in'. The third time he touched down sweetly. Joy, relief, at last! Then, a second later, 'Wonk!, which is the noise an aeroplane makes when it goes over on its nose'. For the third time in four months Francis was suspended 10 feet above the ground, held only by his seat belts and his feet braced against the pedals.

He clambered out. Splash! 'Bless my soul', he thought, 'I'm in the sea; how on earth did I get here?' The water was only up to his ankles. He tried to light his pipe, couldn't, and set off towards the searchlight. The searchlight found him first, then shone on *Elijah*. 'Write off', he thought, distraught, and looked the other way, only to see dozens of figures silhouetted running straight towards him.

He was soon the Italians' guest of honour, being cheered and suited in the officer's mess, then congratulated by the commandant, Colonel Ranza, and 'his extraordinary attractive wife. I must have been a queer object for society, unshaven, dirty, sheep-skinned and wet to the knees. I told him my bus was a complete write-off and fell asleep as I talked'. That night, the vision loss nightmare returned; but deep, restful sleep returned too.

The next morning all was clearer – and better. The Italians had righted *Elijah* and brought her back to the hangar for inspection. Francis had landed in a salt flat next to the airfield and – unbelievably – *Elijah* had only broken her prop and the interstrut, which had damaged but not snapped the wing spar. The fuselage damage was easily fixed by the crew there; the prop and interstrut would need shipping from England. Telegrams flew back and forth from Tripoli to de Havilland. There would be a delay of ten days. Francis was bitter-sweet: the record attempt had failed, but *Elijah* was still a flyer; when they weren't bombing Arabs, the Italian Air Force were lauding him; and if Hinkler's record was out of reach, Francis now sought a new record to beat – his own against himself, as yet undetermined, but still a target at which to aim.

It's not known if old copies of the British newspapers ever reached the officers' mess at Tripoli, but if they had this headline from the 21 December 1929 edition of *Daily Mail* would have made Francis laugh and his creditors cry:

RICH MAN'S AMAZING FLIGHT
12,000 MILES DASH ALONE TO AUSTRALIA
3 AM START, ACROSS FRANCE IN A DAY

One of the most audacious flights ever attempted is now in progress. At 3 o'clock yesterday morning, as exclusively announced in later editions of the Daily Mail, *Mr. Francis Chichester, a rich young New Zealander, set out from Croydon Aerodrome to fly alone to Australia…*

❤

After leaving Tripoli Francis stayed the first night with the British consul in Benghazi. Bad news from New Zealand awaited him: Muriel had died during an operation. They had been separated for two years and the pathos of the mismatch and the tragedy of her young death put Francis in touch with a different set of realities than his mere survival – looking after young George, for one – and how he must not repeat the mistakes of his own father with his own son. That night, the same nightmare.

On he flew, leaving Italian-controlled Libya, flying along the Barbary coast to British-controlled Egypt; in fact he was to be flying in British skies all the way to Singapore – and from Cairo to Delhi, following the Imperial Airways route and stopping at Imperial Airways aerodromes.

Their Empire Route had been established nine months earlier, with passages from London to Karachi. The service took seven days and cost £130 and was deemed to be of more benefit to the mail – and all that quick mail meant – than to the passengers.

Even for the Imperial Airways passengers it was not an easy ride. The first day took them to Paris for refuelling, then on to Basle for the overnight *wagon lits* train through the Alps to Genoa. Awaiting the train at the port station was a Short S.8 Calcutta flying boat. If the passengers had not seen one before, they might have wondered how on earth this three-engined barge ever left the water. But somehow it must have done, for that day they would be refuelling in Ostia, Naples and Corfu before arriving twelve hours and a thousand miles later, shattered, shaken and practically deafened in Piraeus for the next overnight stop. The third day was slightly less far but possibly more fraught, flying over the expanse of the southern Mediterranean. They stopped at Souda Bay in northern Crete, now a large NATO base where our own yacht *Vasco da Gama* spent a happy week's refuge from storms, and Tobruk for refuelling; then again along the North African coast, stopping at Alexandria for the third night stop at the Grand Royal Hotel, as was; then on to Cairo by slow train to meet the next plane.

By Francis's time, nine months later, the air service started at
Alexandria, part of a gradual improvement to make the route
more continuous. Likewise, at the other end the route now
stretched from Karachi to Delhi; thus with the de Havilland
DH.66 Hercules – to all appearances a scaled-up Gipsy Moth
– Imperial Airways was spreading its wings at the end of the
1920s. The middle part of the route stayed the same: from
Cairo to Gaza, Rutbah Wells (now Ar-Rutbah), Baghdad, Basra,
Bushire (now Bushehr), Lingeh, Jask, Gwadar and Karachi. Due
to the difficulties navigating across the featureless desert, British
engineers build an enormous furrow from stop to stop, still the
longest furrow ever built, even if now reclaimed by the shifting
sands. We're going to pick Francis's passage up at Rutbah Wells,
an oasis on the old caravan route from Damascus to Baghdad.

Francis had noticed the low compression on the Gipsy's no. 2
cylinder becoming dangerously lower during a routine check at
Gaza and knew he had to work on the valves as soon as he
could. Luckily, at Gaza he met Major Herbert Brackley, the head
of Imperial Airways, who was flying back from the inaugural
flight to Delhi. Brackley suggested to Francis that if *Elijah* could
hang on just a few hours longer, the Imperial Airways base at
Rutbah Wells would be better equipped to help.

Francis would later write that he was

*extraordinarily intrigued by the whole outfit at Rutbah
Wells, a romantic spot in the middle of the desert, a large
square fort with building backed up inside its high walls.
There were camel caravans inside, and a squad of Iraqi
infantry. It is a stopping place also for the motor caravans
which run from Baghdad to Damascus. These are owned
by Nairn Brothers, who are New Zealanders.*

I enjoyed reading that, as in our kitchen in Hampshire is a most atmospheric Nairn Brothers poster we bought in Ramallah, Palestine. Under the banner 'Overland Desert Mail to Iraq, India, etc.' it shows two of the desert trucks, one for mail and the other passengers, leaving a large, square fort with palm trees and camels scattered about. The lower banner says 'Direct Cross-Desert Service; Haifa – Beirut – Damascus – Baghdad'. Looking at Francis's route and the available options, it's not too fanciful to hope that the large square fort was the oasis of Rutbah Wells.

Rutbah Wells airfield a few years later

Back to Francis. He soon found the Imperial Airways mechanic promised by Brackley. At first the mechanic wasn't too keen to help, as it would mean working into the night. Then he declared that he was only trained to service the Imperial Airways DH.66s' Bristol Jupiter radial engines – massively large and complicated units compared to *Elijah*'s five-litre four-cylinder engine. But somehow he melted and between them they folded *Elijah*'s wings and pushed her through the barbed wire surrounding the fort, across the parade ground and up besides the mechanic's bedroom window. They found an extension cord, clipped a spotlight onto one of the prop blades and Francis told the mechanic how to strip off the manifold and cylinder head while he tried to snatch a quick respite in the arms of Morpheus.

Francis was shown his quarters in the officers' block and what seemed the pleasing prospect of some sleep soon soured when the Iraqi officer in charge entered and 'ruined it by snorting and sniffing, sniffing and snorting and asking silly questions in French. Of course time means nothing to people living out there; they cannot understand anybody finding such an absurdly small unit of time such as an hour being of any value'. But bit by bit Francis drifted off to sleep, accompanied by the imaginary soothing sound of tinkling bells and flowing flutes and 'outlandish instruments' he had not heard before. But still, that night, the nightmare.

After a 5 am breakfast of desert grouse, they tried starting the restored Gipsy engine. Nothing doing; it was 'exceedingly cold and had frozen during the night'. By 7.30 am the sun solved the problem. Francis took off and headed off across the desert towards Baghdad. Navigation was no longer by furrow but by a trunk road, the old caravan route to Damascus, so crowded that Francis saw two motorcars in the first 100 miles, as well as several black-tented Arab caravanserai.

If the thought of flying for up to ten hours a day in an open biplane, cramped and noisy, windswept by hot and dusty air, always living on the edge and on wits over *terra incognita*, if the very thought of all this seems tiring enough for the rest of us, for Francis the really trying part of the enterprise was after landing, the dealing with officials and well-meaning well-wishers. He complained of 'the continual conversation and negotiation with your host for the night, with acquaintances and officials, together with the considerable amount of work that has to be done on the engine every day'. This was not a quick routine of checking the dipstick and heading off for the bar, but rather involved 'changing or cleaning the eight sparking plugs, removing and cleaning the petrol filter, drain and replace the oil and filter, check and adjust the tappets, grease all moving parts and fill up all tanks with petrol'. And that was if petrol was ready and waiting; quite often he would have to arrange supplies or even go and find petrol himself – which meant even more time dealing with inquisitive strangers. When all that was done, he had to make sure *Elijah* was safe for the night, in itself not the work of a moment in far flung aerodromes.

Then of course he had to refuel himself. He was usually too tired after landing to service the engine, preferring to take a short nap first, when he could, officialdom permitting, then returning to work on the engine later. Most nights he had no more than four hours sleep, often interrupted by that nightmare. As he preferred to leave before dawn, he had to arrange for the next day's food and drink before turning in. Even this required care and attention, as the last thing he needed was diarrhoea aloft. And even turning in was subject to the vagaries of officialdom, availability and transport from and to the aerodrome.

It's no wonder that Francis felt relief every dawn as he opened up *Elijah*'s revived and rested engine, gathered speed along the runway and left all the troubles of the world on the ground behind him.

We pick up his flight again in Bima on what is now the Indonesian island of Sumbawa, at that time still part of the Dutch East Indies. Why there rather than anywhere else en route across the Indonesian archipelago? Only because we are short of space, his experience there was not untypical – and because it rang a large and sonorous bell: I was shipwrecked off the southern coast of Sumbawa and taken without clothes, passport or money by horse relay to Bima and spent a happy month staying in the very house in which Francis had stayed while the authorities worked out what to do with me.

After Baghdad, Francis had continued imperially east: to Delhi following the Imperial Airways route and then stopping at Raj military airfields on to Calcutta. It must have been a wonderful flight across the Indian Plains, navigating by the Ganges and the Grand Trunk Road, in the perfect climate of the north Indian winter. After Calcutta, things became somewhat leery, organisationally and meteorologically, but on *Elijah* flew, through monsoons like waterfalls, across what seemed unlimited jungle with no emergency landing options and confused officialdom at recognised landing options.

Sometimes the monsoon rain was so dense that Francis was forced down to sea level, which of course brought its own dangers when the rain and sea became an amorphous, horizonless mass of grey pain and gloom. He would slow down as much as he dared to ease the pain of the 'flying needles of hail' and came as close to crashing as ever when he stalled *Elijah* at 80 feet above sea level, lost flow over the wings and felt the joystick to be like 'shaking a dead man's hand'. He only just recovered flight as the wheels skimmed over the sea. 'Hades!' as he put it, 'there is nothing funny about stalling at 80 feet over the sea'.

The scenes following our respective crash landings on exotic beaches were unchanged by the forty years between 1930 and 1970. Francis's was caused by trying to avoid a wall of water from the sky, mine by trying to avoid a fury of water from the sea. Inexperience on both our parts, really: the golden rule of flying is 'If in trouble, head high'; of sailing 'If in trouble, head out'; but we were both young and foolish. On landing there is exhaustion, gratitude, a jumble of conflicting priorities, resignation and a sense of 'now what?'. Soon 'at the other end of the aerodrome a curious sight: a stream of humanity like a swarm of ants issuing from the woods flowed in my direction. I sat tight and was presently the centre of a hundred or so Malays. Both Francis and I had a few words of Bahasa Malay, the world's simplest language, spoken in Malaysia and Indonesia. Francis's were from a guidebook, mine from having lived there for a few months. Eventually a head man arrives, takes charge, throws open the doors of hospitality in a wooden-floored, leaf-roofed, open-plan shack on stilts – and, with chickens and women clacking around in the compound, all is well.

And thus to Bima, the capital of Sumbawa. For those not shipwrecked or force-landed thereabouts, the Indonesian archipelago heading south goes Sumatra, Java, Bali, Lombok, Sumbawa – and then on east, island to island, to Timor, the jumping-off point for Darwin. Francis landed in Bima by plane in short order; I, shipwrecked off the southern coast, arrived a week later by pony relay though a Garden of Eden that lay across the island.

In the Dutch-ruled days each island capital had the equivalent of a British Raj Resident, a European whose job was not so much to rule but to advise, but whose advice it would be unwise for the sultans to ignore. Francis somehow managed to pick a fight with the island vizier. Seeing one of the natives making a self-important nuisance of himself, Francis gave him a screwdriver and told him to open a can of oil. Not a good idea. The vizier took great exception and demanded that Francis pay for twenty of his tribesmen to guard *Elijah* overnight. Francis noted: 'Fortunately wealth for him was represented by a quarter of a guilder per man. No doubt he collared the lot.'

And like the Raj, the Dutch regime built government guest houses, or 'rest houses', to accommodate their own officials and visiting dignitaries. It was in the one in Bima that Francis and I stayed. In his Dutch days and my Indonesian days they were called *Pasangraham*. I remember there was one suite with a balcony on the first floor and smaller bedrooms with patios on the ground floor. I imagine that Francis, like me, was given the VIP suite overlooking the mayhem of the main street. This had not changed either:

You pay so much for a bed, and the man in charge buys food, which he cooks for you at a very reasonable charge. There is some sporting uncertainty as to what you will get, considering that he understands you no better than you understand him. Sleeping is quite simple: you have a bed netted off against mosquitoes, a hard mattress covered over with a sheet, a pillow for your head and a long bolster, the use of which I am not quite certain about. Apart from pyjamas you do not have any covering. As I had no pyjamas, it was simpler for me.

Again that night, the nightmare: 'The lizards must have woken with a start'.

The stories end well. The Resident drove Francis to the airfield the next morning. 'He had been extremely polite and pleasant to me, so when he asked me to fly over his house for the edification of his wife I gladly agreed'. I flew out too, in an Indonesian Air Force helicopter to Bali, then on to the British embassy in Djakarta for a new passport, some money and some clothes – and the first meeting with a life long wife.

Francis would later say that the question most people wanted to ask about his flight to Sydney concerned the 320-mile, so just over four-hour, crossing of the Timor Sea, from the island of Timor to Bathurst Island on the way to Darwin. It would certainly be the question I would have liked to ask, having crossed the Timor sea in a yacht, on my way to the shipwreck, just three men in a boat and frights of hammerhead sharks looking up at us, licking for what passed as their lips.

Francis was typically sangfroid about the whole affair, pointing out correctly that neither the plane nor its single engine knows that it is over the sea – therefore you should be as unconcerned about an engine failure as you would be if it was flying over four hours' worth of perfect landing strips. In theory, of course, he was quite right; in practice, of course, he was quite wrong.

I remember flying single-engined over the sea. We used to fly quite regularly over the English Channel on a duty-free run to Le Touquet, throw in a pissy lunch at L'Escale restaurant on the airfield, and fly back to Lydd, as people did in those drink-and-fly, duty-free days. It's only 25 miles, less than 15 minutes, over the sea and yet the thought of a forced landing was always to mind, at least on the way over. Then we used to fly to Le Mans for the *Vingt-Quatre Heures* every year, leaving England from the Isle of Wight to cross the French coast at Cherbourg. Again, only 60 miles or 30 minutes, not enough danger, you would have thought, to raise a Franciscan eyebrow. One year, mid-Channel, the four of us on board all heard the engine miss a beat – just the one – but one was enough. From then on we took the long route via Dover and Calais, just in case the one missed beat turned contagious.

Yet for all his insouciance, Francis knew that a sea landing in a single-engined aeroplane with a fixed undercarriage is a sinking waiting to happen:

The question of coming down in the sea with the landplane is an interesting one, and I have discussed it with several experienced pilots, without being able to come to a definite conclusion about it. The general consensus of opinion seems to be that every landplane, falling into the pond, puts its nose right into it and goes straight to the bottom. Theoretically, the wings are supposed to keep the bus afloat for a short time, but I understand that in practice they never do. It is wonderful what you are ready to do in emergencies. That is to say, theoretically, before the event. What happens in practice, it is generally fortunate nobody is there to see.

And he took precautions seriously:

I trotted out the rubber boat, blew it up to see that it had no leaks, took off the front cockpit streamlining, and arranged it in position so that I only had to pull a rope fastened around its middle and yank it out of its place in order to float it on the water. I fastened the sail, mast and oars up together with an inner tube, so that they too would float, provided I could reach them, before Elijah and I sank. The drink and iron rations I put in a sack and placed in the cockpit. I'm afraid they would not stand much chance of getting out in the event of landing in the water, but still one never knows one's luck.

It was in the spirit of taking enough precautions to meet luck half-way that Francis set off single-engined for four hours across the Timor Sea:

You certainly get a kick out of crossing a good stretch of sea with the single-engined land machine. I felt moderately excited, and slightly elated. The fact is, if you are confident you have done everything possible to have your engine and plane in good order; if you have taken every precaution in the event of you falling into the pond, in that case it does you no good to worry, and it becomes a great gamble which you can sit back and enjoy.

The great gamble paid off and this navigation was once again 'Spot on!', hitting Rocky Point, Bathurst Island, as planned and then on to Darwin. On his way in he saw a stream of cars racing to the aerodrome to meet him after he had buzzed the town to let them know he was arriving. It didn't occur to him that he might be becoming famous, that all the time he was cut off in the Dutch East Indies the Empire newspaper wires were taking up where the *Daily Mail* had left off three weeks ago.

———∞———

The prospect of fame, or 'fuss' as Francis always called it, must have dawned on him on arriving at Charleville, Queensland, about 600 miles north-west of Sydney. He wrote:

> *I never saw such an enthusiastic place as Charleville. The whole town had turned out, which made me nervous as the deuce in landing. Then the mayor and town council held a reception in the town hall, complete with beer and lemonade.*
>
> *I have often been asked what was the worst moment of my flight, and I think it was this moment, when I was called upon to try to make a speech.*

After lunch he flew onto Bourke, now in New South Wales, to another civic reception and dinner: 'Life was getting strenuous.' Just as well he did not know what Sydney had in store for him. But while flying into that other sort of storm, the media sort of storm, he had time to reflect on what he had achieved:

> *1) I had not beaten Hinkler's record. 2) I had not done what I had really wanted even more, namely, to fly solo half-way round the world. To do this is exceedingly difficult without crossing the Atlantic or Pacific. I think flying from Spain to New Zealand is the only way a true flight half-way round the world can be made without crossing the great oceans. 3) Even my attempt to cross Australia in three days had failed. The best I could claim*

*was the 12,655 miles between Tripoli and Sydney which
took me 22 days, an average of 575 miles per day, against
Hinkler's 760 miles a day'*

His mood grew even darker as the end came into view:

*I was a human 22-day clock beginning to wind down.
After being wound up at Tripoli I began ticking away
every day from before dawn to after sunset. It had become
a habit. And now the clock was just about to stop, to leave
a desolation, an emptiness, a solitariness in place of its
steady tick. Lor! I should soon again be a slave to petty
circumstances and petty officials. In the air ... well, one
was a slave there as much as anywhere else, if not more
so. Yet how much greater the masters: Father Time, as
usual; Aurora, the goddess of dawn; Vesper, the goddess
of night; Jupiter the god of weather; and lastly, of course,
Minerva, goddess of wisdom.*

His worst fears came true in Sydney. It seemed that every light
aeroplane that could fly took to the sky to escort him in, flying
around like 'like a flock of deranged seagulls'. One by one
they landed; then it was his turn. With the world watching
he botched the landing, of course, but that was the easy part:
'Ensued for me a turmoil', he wrote, before going on to describe
the demands of celebrity by someone who sincerely did not seek
it, yet found it inconceivable not to answer every request for
information or to thank every well-wisher personally. If we are
all famous for fifteen minutes now, back then fame could last
fifteen days: Francis's flight had caught the moment, the angle
being that a novice pilot with no money had accomplished what
had previously needed experience and a weighty budget.

Francis did not wear this adulation well. Instead of being
proud of seeing his photograph on every front page, he withdrew

into himself, noting that he had been at work for over 350 hours in three weeks. However, his exhaustion came not from the flying but from the agoraphobia from which he had begun to suffer. He dreaded interviews and ran shy of any spotlight. He grew a beard, solely to hide behind it. And then the nightmares were becoming worse, now visiting him 'every night almost without fail for nine weeks between three and four o'clock. Usually I woke to find myself clawing at a window or wall, trying to escape'. But the high of flying overrode the low of the nightmares:

> Flying is the most fascinating sport in the world. That feeling of cutting out big distances in an apparatus controlled only by you; the attempt by you, a solitary should from among two thousand million to do something that none of the other 1,999,999,999 has done, it tickles your vanity, your sense of power, your sense of romance, your love of excitement, as nothing else in the world can do.

He was already planning the next one, the big one, crossing the Tasman Sea westabout. There was a lot of thinking time during those 350 hours aloft: 'I found myself planning how within a month of finishing one flight ... I can make and save enough money to do the next'.

But first he had family business to which to attend, a welcome break from the maelstrom of attention in Sydney in the quiet of the von Zedlitzes' garden in Lower Hutt, Wellington.

———— ∞ ————

Elijah and Francis shipped back to New Zealand. His own house on top of Blue Mountain was rented out, so he took a cottage in the von Zedlitzes' grounds, rescued George and set about making enough money with Geoffrey to go flying again.

Rescued George? Hardly. Since Muriel had died two months previously, the 4-year-old George had been brought up by his aunt and grandmother in their family home. He was a quiet and timid little chap and was as happy as he could be hanging off the skirts of his elderly relations. Then out of the blue this strange action man, his father, apparently – although they had never really met – arrives to take him away from his cosy certainties to a new life with new people. Muriel's family, the von Zedlitzes, the Goodwins, everyone warned against it. But Francis was stubborn and determined that George should have the father-centric childhood he never had. He took George swimming but George was frightened of the water. George had good eyesight, unlike Francis, so his father determined he must play catch; but George hated ball games. Friends were throwing a house party up-country; Francis was never allowed to go to anything as frivolous as a party, so George must come with him and join

George, second from left and Francis, second from right.

in the charades. But shy George didn't enjoy charades. Instead in reaction he developed asthma, which made him even more withdrawn. At last, having made enough of a stab at fatherhood to have convinced himself that he had done his best, Francis handed poor George back to the comfortable bosoms he had craved all along.

Francis's other ventures were more successful. He rushed out *Solo to Sydney*, his first and best book, while he and his flight were still hot news. The book had good reviews and sold well. The slump was still on, so property sales were slow, but he and Geoffrey made enough from forestry interests to keep some money coming in. He joined the Territorial Air Force, so someone else paid for his flying.

Thus passed the rest of 1930, with Francis working and earning, fathering a little and flying when he could. But it was never going to be enough; those nightmares of crashing in a void had been replaced by daydreams of solo flights and world records. *Elijah* was down at the 'drome and Francis was up in the hills. It's a big, wide world out there. At some stage Francis, *Elijah* and the big, wide world were going to meet again – and in the New Year, New Zealand summer of 1931 they made plans to do just that.

There is no such thing as an impossibility.

CHAPTER 5

Spot On!

T HE CRAZIEST IDEA OF ALL CRAZY IDEAS came to Francis when he was shaving. It was as 1930 was turning into 1931. For six months, since his return to New Zealand, he had been brooding about long distances and world records, about completing a circumnavigation by flying *Elijah* around the world back to London, working on the permutations, the scenarios and the routes. Every dawn of a bright idea was soon followed by the dark dusk of seemingly intractable problems. The more he brooded the more he felt trapped in the small, comfortable world of minor prosperity in New Zealand.

To fly anywhere he first had to cross the Tasman Sea. Only Charles Lindbergh had managed to cross a serious ocean, the Atlantic, and he had financed that by public subscription to convert a Ryan monoplane, the famous *Spirit of St Louis*, for the task. Could Francis do the same? No: Francis was not a Lindbergh extrovert, quite the opposite, and backwoods New Zealand was not the continental USA, also quite the opposite. To raise money for any sort of attempt he took passengers joyriding, hundreds of them, but by then professional barnstormers in properly powerful Curtiss biplanes – and even flying circuses – had made poor old *Elijah* seem rather tame and the enterprise did what is known locally as a 'fizzo': it fizzled out. Without a similarly adapted purpose-built plane to carry enough fuel to make the crossing, *Elijah* would have to carry her own weight in fuel, which in turn meant she would be too heavy to fly. No matter which way round he held the chart, it simply couldn't be done.

And then came his eureka shaving moment. A globe was next to the handbasin and between shaving strokes he noticed two small dots in the middle of the Tasman Sea. Why hadn't he thought of them before? They would break the journey neatly into three equal parts, distances he knew he could fly in a day. Splashing the soap off, he looked more closely: Norfolk Island, off the north-east tip of New Zealand, and Lord Howe Island, a smaller hop off the coast of New South Wales. Then he looked at the scale: New Zealand to Norfolk, 480 miles; Norfolk to Lord Howe, 560 miles; Lord Howe to Sydney 480 miles. Doable! Yes, by Jove, very doable! And once Sydney had been breached, then he knew that the land route back to London via Asia and America was doable too.

He rushed to the Wellington Public Library to find out more. Norfolk Island was a glorified rock five miles square, about the size of a Kiwi sheep farm, with no landing strip of even the most imaginative kind. Lord Howe Island, on the other hand, looked like a crescent around a large lagoon, which would be perfect if it were made of concrete, but it wasn't: the lagoon, annoyingly, was made of water. But then again the notations on the chart were so romantic: Sugarloaf Passage, Smooth Water Lagoon, Coral Reef Awash Here, Heavy Surf Here and Boat Passage at High Water. Francis knew he must fly there.

Looking at the chart in the library, Francis had his second eureka moment of the day. Of course! Convert *Elijah* into a seaplane. 'The idea of blowing in and settling on the lagoon of an untamed island caught my fancy. I decided to learn seaplane flying at once.' He looked again at Norfolk Island. There was no sheltered anchorage, only Pacific rollers pounding in to the 300-foot cliffs. That, Francis agreed with himself, would be a challenge; but he liked one of those.

Francis knew exactly the call he had to make: to the New Zealand Air Force's Director of Aviation, Wing Commander Grant Dalton, the air chief who had enlisted Francis as a Territorial Pilot Officer. The NZAF had a seaplane – even better, a Moth-based seaplane – which had just returned from Samoa, where it had been hassling rebels as they uprose. TPO Chichester to WC Dalton: 'Could I do seaplane training instead, sir?' WC Dalton to TPO Chichester: 'Of course, old boy, she's all yours!'

Francis soon found the seaplane rekindled his joy of flying:

I found seaplane flying much more thrilling; there was something wild and free about it, and it called for more flying skill. You must rely on your own judgement for choosing the best water to alight on, estimate wind and tide, and survey the surface for rocks or even small pieces of wood which might pierce the thin floats. A seaplane needs more skill in handling because, with its big floats, it loses flying speed and stalls more easily. If too steep a turn is made, the floats catch the air and tip the plane over, possibly on to its back.

Francis now knew that flying a seaplane was the solution to flying around the world. He also knew that island-hopping from New Zealand to Norfolk Island to Lord Howe Island to Australia was the solution to flying across the Tasman Sea. And he knew that he had a related problem: actually finding the islands. He was totally confident in his ability to navigate overland by dead reckoning, that is, the calculations that interrelate speed, time and distance, which had taken him around Europe and from London to Sydney. Navigation over the sea posed a whole set of new problems. Radio navigation had yet to be invented. Compasses on small planes were notoriously distracted. Undetectable wind shifts out at sea would cause havoc with any dead reckoning calculations. On the one hand, using dead

Francis and lady friend floating on water

reckoning from Timor it would have been literally impossible to miss the massive island of Australia 320 miles to the south. On the other hand, using dead reckoning from New Zealand it would be equally impossible to find the tiny speck of Norfolk Island 480 miles to the north-east.

Thus began the quest for what would become Francis's greatest skill, one that even the likes of Bob Gibson find impossible to reconstruct today. 'The only possible way of finding the islands', he decided, 'was by using the sun. I should have to take shots at the sun with a sextant to measure the height of the sun above the horizon, and work out my position from that.'

Bob Gibson had given me the experts' view: 'In a word, impossible', he had said. 'How could a man flying a plane solo use a sextant to take astro sights? For a start, a plane is going so fast that the sights will be instantly redundant. And the pilot would not be at sea level, so all reference points in the astro tables will be u/s [unserviceable or more popularly, useless]. And what happens in clouds? And who is going to fly the plane straight and level while the pilot takes the sights? And even if he could take a useful sight, where is he going to find the space in the cockpit to make all the calculations? And how is he then going to transpose them onto his charts? No,' Bob shakes his head, 'I just can't see how it can be done. It simply cannot be done.'

Francis would have disagreed, of course. If I could put words in his mouth: 'If a sea navigator can navigate a steamer by the sun, I can navigate an aeroplane by the sun.' And he did.

———— ∞∞∞ ————

I ask one of our Unicorn authors, Rear Admiral Kit Layman, author of *The Wager Disaster*, to explain how astronavigation works in practice. Kit says:

'A sextant will measure the angle of the sun or moon or a star above the horizon. In the case of a star, the only time you can see both star and horizon clearly enough is at sunrise and sunset. You must note the time, accurate to the nearest second, at the exact moment that you take your sextant reading. These observations must be absolutely accurate: an error of only one degree in measuring the sextant altitude will place your position 60 nautical miles out. And an error of one second in time will place you a quarter of a mile out at the equator and much more at higher latitudes.

'Given the time and the angle, you make some adjustments to both and then dive into a fairly complex book of tables. You can now calculate, not a position, but a position line, and this you draw on your chart. Your position is somewhere on that line, but you do not know where yet.

'You must therefore take another observation preferably at right angles to the first one, which gives you another position line, and where the two position lines cross you have at last a fix. In practice one always takes three observations if possible, and if they all go through the same point, or nearly so, you can feel confident as to where you are.

'On a stable platform it is quite easy with practice and good eyesight to take an observation of the sun above the horizon. Aboard a ship it is a bit more difficult as you have to contend with the movement of the ship. On a yacht it is much more difficult unless the sea state is very steady.

'For air navigation, where you are most unlikely to see the horizon clearly enough, you have to use a bubble sextant. This recreates the horizon on the instrument itself in much the same way as the spirit level does around the house. As anyone who has tried to put up a shelf will know, balancing the bubble brings its own problems, and I would have thought taking a sight while trying to balance the bubble and while bumping around in a small aircraft would be at least as difficult as using a regular sextant on a yacht in a rough sea.

'If all this sounds physically demanding, what comes next is equally mentally demanding. You have to perform a number of careful calculations from the tables.

'You can do some of this work in advance on the ground for the sun, moon or stars you expect to see at certain times, and Chichester would certainly have done as much as possible. But remember, every observation gives you not a position but a position line, which must be related to the chart; and between observations of different objects the aircraft is moving its position, so that positional movement has to be taken into account before you can get your two, preferably three, position lines to cross on your chart. And there you have your actual position.

'The more I think about how he did all this in his tiny plane the more extraordinary it becomes. To take a good sight in these circumstances would be close to miraculous. Taking the exact angle and the precise time, and then making the calculations – all this needs total concentration, whereas he had a plane to fly at the same time. And all the while in the background he had to contend with the certainty that failure to get it right first time meant missing the target and flying on to an ignominious doom.

'To a simple sailor the word superhuman seems not an overstatement.'

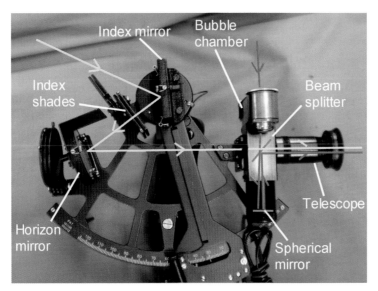

The bubble sextant, mastering it aloft while flying a biplane seaplane not the work of a moment

Labels on image: Index mirror · Bubble chamber · Index shades · Beam splitter · Horizon mirror · Telescope · Spherical mirror

Back on land Frances threw himself into mastering the sextant and logarithmic tables as only he could. He practised in the car at 50 mph and on foot. He practised in a dinghy and capsized for his troubles. When the sun went down he practised his mental arithmetic. He practised them both together in the air too: the first time his error was 108 miles and the second time 740 miles. If he didn't know already, he was discovering quite how much of a challenge he had made for himself.

While all this micro-navigating practice was honing his skills, a macro-navigation question loomed. Given the inherent degree of inaccuracy of his astro, due to inexperience and the very nature of the challenge, how could he realistically hope to find the Norfolk Island needle in the Pacific haystack? The answer was that he couldn't, so he arrived at the very solution that sea captains had been practising for years: the navigational tactic known as Aiming Off. Let's say you want to navigate to Norfolk Island five hours away. In spite of your best endeavours, by the time you think you should be there, it is nowhere in sight. Now comes the dilemma: with limited fuel and daylight, do you gamble to turn left or right? It's a form of 'double or quits' as you move away from or closer to the target.

The solution is to miss the target on purpose by Aiming Off, aiming deliberately off the island to an imaginary waypoint. When the time says you should be there you then turn at right angles on to a much shorter heading, knowing that your target is at least somewhere in that direction. So if Francis knew that after exactly, say, five hours and 40 minutes' flying he would be south-west of Norfolk Island, all he would have to do would be to turn north-east and he would surely come across it. Surely? What could possibly go wrong?

<hr>

By March 1931 Francis felt he had to go, if only because the Tasman weather was about to turn seasonally against him. On 25 March he plucked the date of 28 March out of thin air as the day to go – and was then delighted when the Met Office predicted perfect conditions. Grant Dalton was worried enough to write to him officially, urging the flight be called off for the sake of aviation's image in the event of its certain failure. Luckily the letter did not work its way down the chain and Francis blagged a new pair of floats from the NZAF and then asked the Wellington Base Commandant, Squadron Leader Len Issit, to help him fit them. Len, who was an experienced seaplane and flying-boat pilot, said, 'I don't like this flight of yours. I doubt if you can find your way alone by sextant; even if you can, suppose there is no sun? If you reach Norfolk Island there is nowhere to put down a seaplane; if you succeed in getting down, you won't be able to take off again because of the swell. If there should chance to be no swell, it would be impossible to take off a Moth loaded up like yours without a stiff wind.

'Don't forget that you have ideal conditions at the moment. Strong breeze against you, tide with you, and choppy sea to break the suction of the water of the floats. I'd like to see you carry out a forty-eight hours' mooring test to make sure the floats don't leak; and also some long flights, to test your navigation farther.' Francis noted: 'It would certainly have been wise to do all this, but probably I would have had no flight if I had.'

But Issit was at heart a flyer and a sportsman and he knew that Francis had to do what Francis had to do. That night he joined in the team fitting the floats to *Elijah*, which in seafaring tradition went from a he to a she and now became *Madame Elijah*. At 5 am the next day Mrs Issit was cooking them both bacon and eggs. At 6 am they broke a bottle of brandy over the prop and fired her up. Len cast her off to the sea and Francis cast his fate to the winds.

⌾

It was 6.45 am when Francis turned out of the Wellington harbour entrance and headed north. It would be sunset at Norfolk Island at 6.45 pm, so he had twelve hours of daylight with ten hours' flying to do. First he had a three-hour flight to the northern tip of New Zealand, where he would fill up with petrol for the sea crossing.

Almost immediately Francis noticed the first of the day's problems: although the heavily laden *Madame Elijah* had taken off sprightly enough, with the new floats she was harder to trim than she had been. Previously he only had to tilt his head backwards to start her climbing, but now he could not leave her for more than a few seconds without her going into a steep dive or climb. He put it down to the unusual weight distribution as well as the floats and lack of practice flying her so fully laden. It wasn't as if he hadn't been warned.

After three hours of dead reckoning he splashed down on Parengarenga Harbour, the refuelling spot. Spot on! Maddeningly, the Maoris there were not only not expecting him but had no fuel anyway. Then *Madame Elijah*'s anchor began to drag and Francis couldn't persuade the Maoris to help him with theirs. The miscommunications between the time-crazed Tasman solo flyer and time plenished natives only made time stretch further. As Francis said, 'My request for them to get the petrol in a hurry was strongly worded. The Maori is a devilish fine fellow, friendly, good-natured, sporting and with perfect manners.' It's just any sense of urgency isn't immediately forthcoming.

Launches crossed the harbour this way and that. Every time Francis was sure it was bringing his precious petrol, but none of them did. By now it was 11 am; he should have left at 10 am. He was tearing his hair out. At 11.23 am the petrol arrived but by then Francis had already decided that he'd better wait until tomorrow. Then a launch appeared 'with a white man waving a telegram'. 'Forecast from Dr Kidson', he read out. 'Weather expected fine; fresh to strong south-easterly breeze; seas moderate, becoming rough.' Francis's reason told him to delay until the morrow; his instinct said ride the wave now. Francis was an instinctive person.

But now more problems. Whereas *Madame Elijah* had taken off enthusiastically at dawn, by now at noon she was decidedly sluggish. Francis was baffled; what he didn't not know yet was that one of the floats was leaking, a problem that was to dog the Tasman adventure and later to dog him all the way to Japan. After three attempts she caught a wave just right, the wings bit the air and they were off. Francis was back in heaven:

All my miserable anxieties and worries dropped away, and I was thrilled through and through. Over my left shoulder, the last of New Zealand receded rapidly. Ahead stretched the ocean, sparkling under the eye of the sun: no sport could touch this, it was worth almost any price. I seemed to expand with vitality and power and zest.

Now here was his plan:

I estimated the time when I should arrive and I computed the distance of the island from the sun position an hour before that time. Then I marked a spot on the chart 90 miles to the left of the island, which would be the same distance from the sun position at that time. This was my first target. By the height of the sun a sextant shot at the time would then tell me if I had reached the spot or not. As soon as I reached the spot I would turn and keep the sun abeam, which would bring me to the island. I had to aim well to one side of the island in case an error in the dead reckoning caused by a faulty compass reading or undetected wind effect should put me on the wrong side of the island. Above all, the island being out of sight, I must be certain that when I turned to the right I was turning towards it and not away from it.

He flew his tightest dead reckoning to give his astro the best shot. It was easy to see how at 80 mph an unexpected 30 mph wind from the north-east would cause him to drift 24 miles to the side of its route in an hour, and every hour. Over time he had developed what other pilots said was impossible: a method of determining the angle of drift over the sea. He explains it in *Tasman Alone*; I can't understand it, so won't try to explain it. What can be understood is this:

The work required extraordinary concentration. It had been easy enough in a car driven at 50 mph by someone else; in the seaplane it was at first difficult to concentrate enough while attending to the five instrument readings, maintaining a compass course, reducing the sun sight, and solving the spherical triangle involved. The 90 to 100 mph wind of the propeller slipstream, which struck the top of my head just above the windshield, made concentrating difficult; so did the pulsating roar from the open exhausts.

In the cockpit the passage was being marked off on a chart in a device he had invented himself to save space. It looked like a scroll roller with a knob to turn the chart at one end and a roll holder at the other. He did not use log tables for working out a sight, as trying to transfer the six figures accurately while glancing across the instruments and flying the plane was impossible. Instead he used a Bygrave triple circle slide rule, just small enough to squeeze into the cockpit.

On he pressed, into the blue above and the blue below.

The refuelling flap before starting had now disappeared, and my brain was ticking over coolly and steadily. I knew that everything depended solely on accurate work. Conditions were perfect; the sun shone in the cloudless light blue sky, the wind astern and brisk. The exhaust gave off a steady rolling note. The needle of the revolution indicator might have been cast in metal, it was so steady.

All the time he was working his dead reckoning and taking sights. At half distance he noticed the wind had shifted to the south-east 15 degrees; he compensated by heading north-west but found that this projected him 200 miles to the west of Norfolk Island. Half of him wanted to believe it could not be right, the wiser half that he had to trust his instruments and calculations. He visualised *Madame Elijah* crabbing her way across the ocean and held his new course. To take a sight he would descend to near sea level, undo his seat belt, put his thickest manual, *Rayners Harbour Guides*, under his bum, sit on that for extra height – and added wind blast – and try to trim her steady to take a sight of the sun and horizon in one sitting. But with her new trimming quirks he found this not only impossible, but terrifying:

I trimmed the tail as delicately as I could to balance the plane, but she would not stabilise, and I had to use the control-stick the whole time while adjusting the sextant. To be quite sure that I was using a piece of horizon vertically below the sun, I had to wipe out the plane's balance from my mind, and concentrate only on the sextant. I had just got the sun and horizon together in the sextant, when terrific acceleration pressing my back made me drop the sextant. I grabbed the stick and eased the seaplane from its vertical nosedive into a normal dive, and then flattened it out. I reset the tail trimmer till the seaplane was bound to climb as soon as I left the control-stick alone. I tried again, and this time managed well enough, easing the control-stick forward with my left elbow whenever the seaplane climbed so steeply that the wing cut off the sun from view.

More miraculous flying/navigating was to come. Again, best let Francis tell the tale:

A few minutes before the end of the half hour I realised that there would be no sun available for a shot. The clouds ahead were darker, and I could see no opening. Could I rely on the previous sight? No, I must have another. The whole enterprise depended on turning at the right moment. The clouds looked whiter away to the left. Close to the half hour I turned left, away from the island instead of towards it, and opened up the throttle. After 3 or 4 miles I spotted a round patch of sunlight on the sea ahead, and slightly to the right. I opened the throttle wider still. I was so impatient that time seemed to stop while I raced for that sun-patch, yet it could not have been more than 5 miles away. The area of sunlight was small, and I set the seaplane circling in a steep bank. I used my feet on the rudder to fly it while I worked the sextant with both hands. After each shot I straightened

out the seaplane, and flew out of the patch while reading
the instrument. I got four shots in this way, while the
seaplane was chasing its tail in a tight circle. I corrected
them for the lapse of time since 4.30, and compared them
with the figure already computed. They agreed. I was
on the line! I had expected to be, and yet it was a great
surprise, and immense relief. I turned round and headed
for where the island should lie 85 miles away.

And so for the run in to Norfolk Island. Of course there were
dramas, such as the engine changing note and the building seas
below on which to land – payback for that lusty tailwind. The
exhausting effects of four and a half hours of non-stop mental
calculations, difficulties with handling the seaplane, worry
about the engine and the sea – all concentrated by the near-
certainty of death if the calculations should be out or the plane
deficient – were offset by the excitement of landfall. But landfall
was there none. His right brain was telling him it must be there,
his left brain now full of doubt and dread imagination. At 5.08
pm it should have been in view; it wasn't. At 5.12 pm, still no
land. Each cloud looked like a hill. He relaxed, telling himself
there was nothing he could do; and there was nothing he could
do. The island was either there or in one hour the fuel would
be gone and he'd die in short order. Then the clouds parted
and he saw an island. It was the only one for 500 miles in all
directions. It had to be the one. Norfolk Island. He had made
it, albeit less elated at being alive than with the fact that 'my
navigational system had proved right. I doubt if Captain Cook
was as delighted to find Norfolk Island by sea as I was by air'.
As it turned out I was more worried about him not finding it
eighty-five years later than he was at the time.

He swept low over Cascade Bay and saw some men on the
jetty. His luck was holding: they did not know he was coming
and just happened to be on the pier. Now, as then, the pier is used

for offloading all the supplies for the island. A freighter anchors off and a team of longboats ferries the goods onto the jetty, to be hauled off with a pulley crane. If they need to import something large and heavy, like a bulldozer, they tie two longboats together to make a catamaran. The only concessions to doing it today's way are the engines in the longboats and the crane; in Francis's time they rowed in an out through the swell and hauled on the pulley crane's chain.

The Norfolk Islanders who had never left the island may not have seen a plane before; *Madame Elijah* was the first to fly there and the island was served just once a month by steamer from Sydney. Quite what they made of Francis's spindly biplane landing on the water we can only imagine. But soon they were rowing a longboat over to meet him. A giant of a man was steering with a rudder oar.

Cascade Bay, Norfolk Island today. The jetty and crane are still the only way to bring goods to the island

'Stand off, you're going to ram me!', Francis shouted.

'All right, skipper, all right,' sang out the helmsman, 'don't get excited, we won't hurt you.'

Francis considered that 'they were very patient, considering that they must be some of the best boatmen in the world'. They still are, diesel engines in the longboats notwithstanding.

Francis intended a quick in-and-out overnight stay in Norfolk Island. In the event he spent three nights there. Various degrees of disaster followed one after the other.

As he had arrived unannounced and literally out of the blue, the islanders were not prepared to receive him. Nevertheless, they soon arranged for him to stay at Government House, in a converted cell from the days when Norfolk Island had been a British prison colony for the most recalcitrant of prisoners, a kind of Alcatraz lost in the Pacific Ocean. Today the island is a more or less self-governing territory under the auspices of Australia in general and New South Wales in particular. Government House is occupied by the Chief Administrator, elected by nine independent councillors, themselves elected by the 2,000-strong

Government House, Norfolk Island

adult population. The cell where Francis stayed is still used for the occasional guest, although in greater comfort.

Francis was soon being looked after by Gussie Martin, whose family owned Martin's Agency, a general stores trading company until 1970. Gussie organised *Madame Elijah*'s aeronautical and Francis's personal top-ups and was his host for the next two nights. That first morning, after the usual island breakfast of bacon and eggs and whisky and soda, they re-launched *Madame Elijah* and stood back to watch her take off across Cascade Bay for Lord Howe Island. Francis immediately noticed that she was mysteriously sluggish. The same reluctance to take off that he had noticed leaving Parengarenga Harbour was now even worse. He tried three runs, including one across the waves, which broke every rule in the seaplane pilots' handbook.

Gussie and the boys soon had *Madame Elijah* hauled up onto the jetty and inspected the floats. Sure enough, one compartment on the starboard float was full of sea water. It must have filled overnight as she lay to anchor. Francis found a tube in the cockpit and began sucking to syphon it out. It was horrid work; after half an hour he had syphon-sucked and spat out four gallons of sea water, yet still some remained. Francis felt sick, his jaw was

Madame Elijah being hauled out, Cascade Bay, Norfolk Island. Most islanders had never seen a plane before.

Brent on the case, Francis on left looks on

cramped and his mouth rotten with sea water and metal filings. Not ideal so soon after bacon and eggs and whisky and soda, presumably. It was also way past the take-off time to make Lord Howe Island; even Francis had to call it a day.

While *Madame Elijah* was on the jetty one of the islanders, Brent, whisked off her cylinder head. He soon pronounced Francis lucky to be alive: one of the valves was about to disappear into the works and blow it all up – and no engine, no Francis. Even he acknowledged that after all, his survival had less to do with his navigation than with his fate.

The next morning was groundhog: more bacon and eggs and whisky and soda, more aborted take-off runs, more head-scratching about the problems. They had replaced every screw in the floats and assumed that they had fixed the problem. They hadn't. Meanwhile, Francis was becoming more and more foolhardy in trying to make *Madame Elijah* lift off, the propeller frequently splashing the waves and covering her and him with salt water. Lastly, in one last desperate attack on the waves, he heard a loud twang and saw an inter-float wire snap.

Limping back to Cascade Bay, he was dive-bombed by an irate flock of seabirds as he taxied past Bird Island. Desperate to keep them out of the propeller, he speeded up, which made the prop even less visible; then he slowed down, which made him even more of a sitting target. Eventually they bored of him and squawked off back to the cliffs. I can report that their ancestors are still very much in evidence, squawking and dive-bombing off the cliffs as they see fit. Twitchers are among Norfolk Island's most enthusiastic tourists and apart from them I spot white terns, sooty terns, red-tailed tropicbirds, masked boobies, white-capped noddies, black-winged petrels, wedge-tailed shearwaters (known locally as 'muttonbirds'), as well as unidentified flying feathered friends wheeling and dealing and flying around just for the hell of it.

Another night of hospitality with the Martin family, another morning of bacon and eggs and whisky and soda. The islanders liked Francis and Francis liked the islanders. He liked the romance and revolt of their *Mutiny on the Bounty*, Pitcairn Island back-story. They threw all their hospitality and assistance onto him then as they do onto me now. Gussie's daughter Odette was too young to remember anything about Francis's visit then, and anyway too old to remember anything about much now, bless her. Her daughter and Gussie's granddaughter, Jackie Pye, still lives here. Francis's flying visit is fondly recalled with displays at the Norfolk Island Museum, the Bounty Folk Museum and at Norfolk Island Airport; he remains very much part of the island's history and up until a generation ago everyone knew someone who remembered Francis's flying visit.

Brent repaired the wires, emptied the float and wiped off the salt. They then lightened

FIRST AIRCRAFT TO VISIT - 28 MARCH, 1931.

SIR FRANCIS CHICHESTER 1901-1972

14¢ NORFOLK ISLAND

Norfolk Island
Commemorative Stamp

Madame Elijah of everything except enough petrol to fly her round to what seemed a smoother bay, Emily Bay, which runs along the old prison colony ruins. Here, lighter and in calmer waters *Madame Elijah* was happier, but still not her usual self. They drained the floats again and reloaded her up with the minimum weight needed to make the almost 600-mile crossing to Lord Howe Island. Everything not essential was sacrificed, even, amazingly, the rubber dinghy, its oar and sails, and Francis's survival rations.

Francis would leave at first light; this time his life really would be on the line.

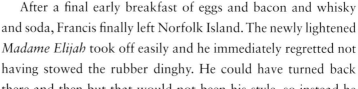

After a final early breakfast of eggs and bacon and whisky and soda, Francis finally left Norfolk Island. The newly lightened *Madame Elijah* took off easily and he immediately regretted not having stowed the rubber dinghy. He could have turned back there and then but that would not been his style, so instead he dived back to Emily Bay and saluted the well-wishers with his wings and, with a last cheery wave to them from the cockpit,

Emily Bay, Norfolk Island, Francis's taxi- and runway

headed west 600 miles out to sea, 500 miles to Lord Howe Island plus the 100 extra miles to the turn-off waypoint.

Almost from the start something didn't feel right. Although the sea water was dripping out of the float, it was also sloshing about within it and upsetting the balance. Not only was it hard work constantly having to fight the controls, the effort also told him that something was wrong with the set-up. Something, but what? Nagging doubts ensued and consumed him.

Worse than poor balance was to come: an hour later *Madame Elijah* started vibrating, slightly at first but within another hour more violently. Francis suspected that it was damage done by crashing into the waves repeatedly as he was trying to take off. Soon there was evidence of problems in the cockpit: the vibration had caused the compass housing screws to loosen and now the altimeter and air speed indicator needles started swinging freely. If these were the loosenings he could see, what about all the hidden fastenings vibrating free? Francis noted that a few months earlier he would not have flown over the safest land in the world in such an unsafe plane, never mind miles out at sea without a dinghy. Yet the curious thing is he was only two hours

out, with easily enough fuel to turn back, repair the seaplane and start again. The thought never seemed to have occurred to him. Once more, the fear gene seemed to have bypassed him.

Soon, even vital navigating was proving difficult:

Holding my log-book in my left hand with the little finger crooked round the control-stick, and my other elbow touching the side of the fuselage, I found it impossible to write. This drove home to me that the vibration was not only severe, but dangerous. The whole fuselage was shaking, with a quick short period, and the rigging wires, which should be taut, were vibrating heavily. Why? It was not the motor, because the exhausts were firing with a steady, even bark. I decided that it must be the propeller. I thanked heaven for a following wind and perfect weather; if the seaplane struck bumpy air in this condition God help us.

Half an hour later it was clear that his latest fix was wrong. 'I knew that there was a mistake, either because of the blast of wind on top of my head, the roar of the motor, the salt air, or my weariness', and then as an afterthought, 'or perhaps anxiety about the seaplane's breaking up'. He consoled himself with a light lunch in the shaking cockpit:

I pulled a tin of pineapple through the hole cut in the seat of the front cockpit, and my mouth watered as I cut open the tin. The juice was like nectar. I cut the slices across with my sheath knife, and ate the chunks with a pair of dividers.

The pleasure did not last long: 'The vibration was breaking things. I felt despair. The dashboard airspeed indicator, the compass seating, and now both altimeters broken. How long could the aircraft stand the strain?'

So there he was, 250 miles away from anywhere, his life dependent on a plane that had already lived a hard life, had flown him more than half way round the world, and was now shaking itself, and him, to bits. Worse, *Madame Elijah* was now her own life-raft, the real one jettisoned on Norfolk Island, and this particular life-raft didn't float. Now more problems, bad problems: on the horizon clouds were forming and then becoming darker. They looked less than an hour away; they darkened and spread and shaped up for a squall. He had no option but to fly straight into it because the turn-off waypoint lay directly beyond it. How he must have dreaded the punishment he and *Madame Elijah* were soon to endure. Then the even worse thought: being unable to tell how deep the squall lay and if his vital sun sights lay behind it.

Luckily the squall was short and sharp. That was the good news. The bad news: behind the squall lay drooping clouds and an obscured sky. Next followed more extraordinary flying and skating on the thin ice dividing courage from foolishness:

I spotted a patch of wintry sunlight on the sea lying away to the north. I swung off course and set off through spits of rain to chase the sun-patch. The seaplane was now plugging dead into wind, yet the sun-patch which had appeared close enough at the start seemed to keep its distance. Afraid of the gap's closing before I reached it, I opened the throttle, and sat tense waiting for an explosion from the propeller flying to bits, followed by a runaway roar from the motor.

I pushed the throttle wide open. Several times I had a glimpse of the sun at the edge of the cloud, and at last I thought I was in position, and turned sharply to take the sight broadside on. But as I lifted the sextant, the shadows raced over the plane, and on again. Angry, I turned sharply, and set off again at full speed. Nothing else seemed to matter. I adjusted the sextant to what I estimated would be the right angle, and held it ready. I put the nose down, the speed rising until there was a shrill note in the rigging wires. I turned with a vertical bank, and got a single shot while still in the turn, pulling the seaplane out of its sideways dive just above the sea.

As any pilot will confirm, all of the above should be impossible, even in ideal conditions. Out at sea, solo, exhausted from fighting a failing plane, anxious, with no life-raft; it defies all limitations.

He was now in dull rain, flying westwards, working the slide rule in the cockpit. He transposed the result onto his home-made rolling chart, all the while looking up to keep *Madame Elijah* straight and level. He put his position 21 miles short of the turn-off point. What trust could he put in that last, miserable, sketchy sun-shot? But there was no more sun. 'Fifteen minutes after the observation, I reckoned that I had reached the turn-off point. I turned, and headed SSW, changing course by nearly 70 degrees to Lord Howe Island'. Or Davy Jones's locker.

Now he was flying on blind trust. Either his workings were correct or he would die. He noted the squall had given up a large wind shift and he was now flying into a 40 mph wind. His speed across the angry-looking sea was only 40 mph too. More calculations, adding forty minutes to the flight. No need to worry about drift now, the island and the wind were on the nose. There was enough fuel but would she hold up? Only now did Francis recall: 'I bitterly regretted not taking my rubber boat'.

He resigned himself to triumph or death, reached forward for something to eat, when

a distinct, clean-cut land showed ahead and a few degrees to the south, a dagger of grey rock thrust through the surface. A hot flood of triumph and excitement swept through me. I could have smashed things with excitement.

Then, good God! There was an enormous black bulk of land right alongside me. I stared astounded. It was little Lord Howe Island emerging from a dense squall cloud. It looked as big as Australia it was so close. What I had spotted was a rock off the south end of it.

He soon found the lagoon landing spot but even here the waves had build to a white horse swell. Now throttling back to land, the vibration grew even worse. He was being so badly shaken that his sight lost its focus on the waves, when suddenly a downdraught pushed *Madame Elijah* onto them. He landed without even knowing it.

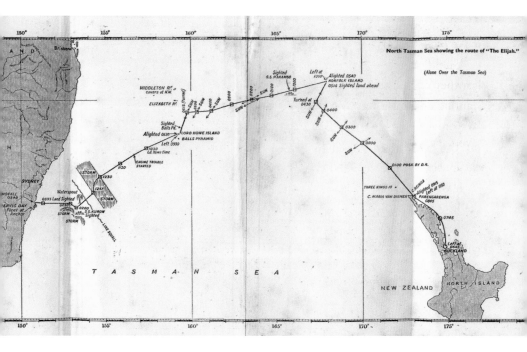

North Tasman Sea showing the route of "The Elijah."

(Alone Over the Tasman Sea)

Francis' route map across the Tasman Sea, as seen at the Lord Howe Island Museum

These islanders had been expecting him and soon two launches were circling the seaplane. Their helpfulness and generosity was equal to that on Norfolk Island and Francis soon found himself, mightily relieved, being looked after in one of the islanders' houses, while *Madame Elijah* found herself, equally relieved I would have thought, comfortably beached on the shore.

The squall returned during the night and at dawn Francis awoke with a start, not from the usual nightmare, but from the terrific noise of the gale blowing through the iron roof. After the usual island breakfast of bacon and eggs and whisky and soda, spent looking at the swaying palm trees in the first morning light, he and his host, Phil Dignam, went down to work on *Madame Elijah*.

'Isn't that where we moored the plane?' Francis asked him.

'Yes!'

'I don't see her', Francis said.

They walked on. 'Ah, there she is!' said Francis uncertainly. A little closer, he added: 'She looks queer to me.'

'She looks queer to me too', said Dignam. They could not make out why through the dawn mist.

'Sunk!' Francis said, though not yet believing it himself. At last they could see only too clearly: the tail of the seaplane was slanting above the surface, like a big fish diving into the water. 'We dragged out a boat and rowed across. She had been carried off the beach and flipped in the squall. The entire seaplane, except the tail and the float ends, was under water.'

It was clearly a disaster. As daylight broke they waded out to see how badly she was damaged. Badly. Both wings were torn, the engine and front half of the fuselage was upside down and lying in sea water, the cables were all snapped and the rudder flapping about listlessly. Waves were washing past her, bouncing her on the bed with every ebb and flow.

Francis was full of conflicting feelings: clearly distressed at seeing his partner wrecked, almost humiliated; yet also relief at not having to make the next leg the following day. He had already determined that overnight, knowing that he had been very lucky she didn't fall apart on the crossing from Norfolk

Madame Elijah turning turtle in the night

Island. Then depressed again at the thought that having starting off across the Tasman by aeroplane with such a flourish, the very thought of creeping in to Sydney in a miserable steamer was humiliating. 'I felt that I would rather sail the rest of the way in a dinghy; it would not matter how long it took, or how I finished the passage, if only I could finish it as I had started – solo'.

'Solo' always had the last word with Francis.

Nine weeks later, when he finally did take off, he reflected that these had been the happiest nine weeks of his life. And having relived most of the weeks of his life, I can confirm that they certainly were; well, if not the happiest (he had yet to meet Sheila) then the most fantastical and limitless. These weeks had also demonstrated his great motto for life: 'There is no such thing as an impossibility.'

To repair *Madame Elijah*; how impossible it must have seemed. He had already written her off, along with the whole enterprise. The island's population comprised barely forty adults and only two of them were mechanics. There were no cars, only the two diesel-engined launches that had come out to meet him. The only tools the mechanics had were related to these diesel engines. There were no electricians and no electricity. There was not much knowledge of outside life either, just the monthly visits from the Sydney steamer.

But that very self-sufficiency, another of Francis's favourite graces, was to prove to be a more valuable skill than all the specialist skills put together. Day by day, he and the islanders convinced themselves that the impossible might, after all, be possible:

> *I had expected men who had never seen an aeroplane before to be bamboozled when asked to unscrew rigging-wire turn-buckles, or wing-root bolts, or to slack off control-cables, or airspeed indicator tubes. But it was the quickest*

and slickest salvage job I have ever known. One stream of people carried pieces to the shore, while another came back for more. The seaplane was dismantled in twenty minutes, and I was the only person who lost anything – some shackle pins that I pocketed before realising that there was a hole in my borrowed pair of shorts.

In two hours they had built a beach workshop from local materials and laid out in careful piles inside it all the parts salvaged from the wreck. Amazingly, the skeleton of the workshop so hastily built still stands, albeit with re-clad panels and roof – and on it is a brass plaque commemorating *Madame Elijah*'s rebuild. Francis reflected on this strange new paradise in which he found himself: looking out from the workshop, a paradisiacal view onto an aquamarine lagoon edged by swaying palm trees standing on shimmering white sand; inside the workshop, strangers, now friends, working as a team in ingenuity to repair the opposite of paradise, the ruin of his beloved *Madame Elijah*.

In the workshop two men named Kirby and Keith helped me to dismantle the motor. We managed everything until we reached the crank-case. The propeller boss had to be drawn off the shaft before the crank-case case could come away, and this required a special tool, which we lacked. Kirby walked off, and came back with a gadget he had made himself, of two iron strips and some long bolts. With this he drew off the propeller boss, and freed the crank-case.

The engine rebuild was the easiest part of the restoration. They stripped down every single part, cleaned and oiled each one and put them all back together. If any nut, screw or washer was left on the bench, they knew that they must have missed a part and would have to strip it back till the omission was found. They didn't omit anything and in three weeks the engine was rebuilt, fired up and passed off as fit for duty.

The fuselage was going to be more problematic:

I went over it carefully. The plywood covering the fuselage was tacked and glued to the framework. If salt water had destroyed the glue, the plane might as well be made of cardboard. As far as I could tell, by pricking it with the point of my knife, the glue was unweakened. I decided that the fuselage could be used again, if every bolt, wire, fitting and tube were removed, cleaned of rust and salt and repainted.

That night Francis sat down with Phil Dignam and made a list of parts they would need to order from Sydney. Everything not made of wood or easily bendable metal had to be shipped in: all the instruments, magnetos, wires, paint, dope, glue, everything – plus, of course, blueprints from de Havilland's rep in Sydney. On the

Francis and Eileen Wilson repairing Madame Elijah's wings

list were four new wings and ailerons. The list was over twenty pages long. Dignam asked Francis's least favourite question: 'What about the money?'

The list was crumpled up and rethought. The wing spars were undamaged. The island's carpenters were willing – but building a workshop in two hours was not the same skill as building a wing containing four hundred pieces and tolerances of down to fifteen hundredths of an inch. Francis was optimistically dubious. Dignam's way was island style: 'She'll be right, mate.' Francis had no option but to go with the island flow. The list was reduced to fourteen pages. (Phil's great-granddaughter, Kate, still lives on the island. I had hoped that she might by some miracle still have the snagging list in an old drawer somewhere, but she doesn't.)

They set to work on the different sections, doing as much as they could before the steamer arrived. Francis became Chicko. He was loving the madness, the impossibility, the ingenuity of it all. Lord Howe Island became a heaven:

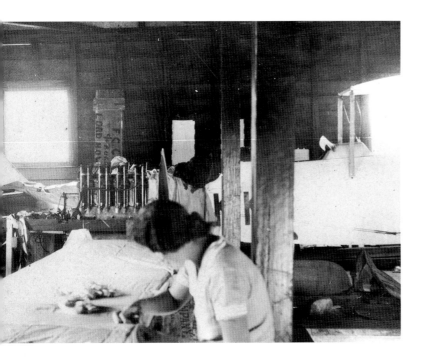

Then began a strange, but strangely happy period of my life. I began to find the island the most attractive spot imaginable. I settled into life on the island, fishing and enjoying being a member of one of the friendliest communities I have ever met. As far as I could see the island was communistic in the Biblical rather than any political sense.

The islanders were happy, lovable people, the men interesting and the girls charming; the island itself a paradise. The beach of white coral sand was a romantic spot in the white light of the full moon with the lagoon at hand. Sometimes at night, the beauty would swell one's heart. The still air was pure, and strangely clear…

Talking of romance, Lea Petherwick tells me that her grandmother, Joyce, had it that 'while the husbands helped Francis with his plane, Francis helped himself to the wives', including a reputed fling with her great-aunt, Jenny.

Thornleigh, Francis's Lord Howe Island home for nine weeks

Amazingly enough, in view of time and tempests, Thornleigh, Phil Dignam's house where Francis stayed, still stands. No longer owned by Kate's family but by a holidaymaker from

Sydney, it is looked after by Brendon Cong, who is kind enough to allow a neighbour to show me around. It's threadbare now but would have been substantial enough when Francis stayed there. Then it was part of a small farm, as the island had to be largely self-sufficient; now it is a smallholding with free-range chickens clucking around. The outbuildings have turned to corrugated rust. The new owner plans to restore the farm as a tourist attraction; meanwhile, nearly all the food is flown in daily from Sydney.

Some other of Francis-era descendants are still on the island. Larry Wilson is the son of Roley Wilson, who was effectively Francis's foreman. Roley's niece, Eileen, who was in charge of sewing up *Madame Elijah*'s skins, has a granddaughter, Tas, on the island. Bill Retmock is the son of Charlie Retmock, who was in charge of painting and doping the skins. The communistic aspect of island life ceased when the New South Wales government stopped subsidising the kentia palm crop. Now the island's population has grown tenfold to 400, all servicing tourism. *Madame Elijah* might have been the first plane to land here but now three forty-seater prop planes arrive every day from Sydney or Brisbane. What remains of Francis's version of paradise is a modern version of paradise – providing you can live without mobile telephones, meaningful internet access or any semblance of a budget.

The steamer arrived with the new parts and Francis was the only one who knew what went where. 'I had to think day and night. It was not a question of making as few mistakes as possible; I mustn't make any mistakes.' With the work now in full flow came another realisation: the season was changing. His love of island life cooled with the certainty of the coming winter westerlies. Now his mind was turning back to Sydney and completing the flight. But that brought fresh worries, largely self-inflicted.

For reasons not clear even to himself, he had decided to fly directly to Sydney, 480 miles over water, rather than to the nearest landfall, Macquarie, only 365 miles over water. Maybe he felt like applying some fresh self-flagellation after the nine weeks in paradise:

> *My stay on the island was nearing its end. It had been the happiest nine weeks of my life, perhaps because I knew it was a crazy, dangerous flight which I had to face, the most foolhardy I had ever attempted; to fly across 483 miles of ocean, with a seaplane and engine which had spent a night bumping on the bottom of the sea. I dreaded the idea of the flight.*

But apparently not enough to make it as problematic as possible…

Slowly *Madame Elijah* was starting to look her old self again. They had rebuilt four wings and two ailerons, painted them first with oil and then with dope-resisting paint, taped and covered them, applied serrated tape along the line of the ribs, applied seven coats of dope to the surfaces, fitted the automatic slots and replaced the fixtures and fittings, struts, rigging wires and aileron controls. It was an amazing achievement from a team that had never even seen an aeroplane before, or even read a technical drawing.

The overhauled motor was back in place, the fuselage carefully enamelled inside and out, the floats painted, ninety-six new screw threads drilled through the manhole rims, the wings loosely assembled in pairs ready to fit to the fuselage, the bent float boom repaired, and the bruised longerons strengthened with steel plates.

Now came the most critical a part of all: setting the wings at just the right angle. Back at de Havilland a whole floor area would have a permanent jig set at the perfect right angle to do the job. Francis himself had often 'watched in awed silence a rigger performing this semi-mystic ritual'. Now he studied the de Havilland manual:

> *The wings must be dihedrally rigged, 3½ degrees upwards, and this angle must be correct to one sixth of a degree, measured with a variable inclinometer. The leading edge of each wing had to be higher than the trailing edge, so that the wing made an angle of 3½ degrees with the horizontal fore and aft. After that we had to rig for 'stagger' – the upper wings had to be 3½ inches ahead of the lower wings.*

All very well, but the island had no solid floor and no inclinometer. I doubt if they had ever heard the word before. There was no library, let alone access to the Internet on which to look up instructions. All they had to go on were Francis's recollection of seeing riggers go about their 'semi-mystic ritual'.

Three days later he had his solid floor and inclinometer.

The following day all four wings were in place and the rebuild completed. But would she fly? The necessary bottle of brandy was broken over the prop.

> *I went aboard at once for a trial flight, thinking that if I waited I should get nerves, imagining all the things that could be wrong with the seaplane. I taxied well out, faced into wind and opened the throttle. The seaplane left the water as easily as a fairy dancing off. Now I began hurdling. I put her through her paces, increasing the strain steadily. She had never been more fit, I thought. Then I jumped her up 200 feet, and trimmed the elevators for hands-off flying. I left the stick alone – she flew dead level. The rigging by our island plane factory was perfect first shot.*

The team relaunching Madame Elijah

His enthusiasm was infectious and within a few hours half the island's adults had been up for a joyride. But Francis was noticing that each time she took off, she did so a little more reluctantly and when landing would yaw to starboard. Of course he suspected the leaking float, but on checking he found them dry. It was becoming more and more mysterious.

The next day Francis loaded her up for a trial flight with the weight for the third and final part of the Tasman crossing. She was flying more sluggishly with each kilo added. Having already sacrificed the dinghy in Norfolk Island, he was now reduced to syphoning off petrol, so that he only just had enough to make Sydney. Still he refused the shorter crossing to Macquarie Island. It was as though he was upping the odds against himself all the time. The islanders were now worried too: they gave him two homing pigeons to release in case of a sea landing. If the pigeons did not return home, they would know he had made it.

Still she did not like taking off. Francis wrote: 'It is hard to understand why I did not realise that the starboard float was nearly full of water, and that a few more gallons would have sunk it'.

(The mystery would only be solved later: earlier in its life the starboard float had been dropped on the deck of a warship. The keel had to be repaired and the only material to hand was stainless steel, which reacted electrolytically with the duralumin rivets and skin of the rest of the float. This reaction caused the top part of the float to be pressed away from the keel, and the water flowed in. As soon as they came out of the water, the water inside pushed the sides of the float against the keel and stopped the leak.)

Looking around for other weight to leave off, Francis chose his spare parts kit – after all, he could always replace them in Sydney and he would hardly be using them before he reached there. The same was true of all unnecessary clothing, in fact anything and everything not entirely essential to completing the next leg of the flight.

He was becoming desperate with *Madame Elijah*'s reluctance to fly, yet the cause still eluded him. What to do?

I changed my tactics, keeping the seaplane down until she had long outrun the distance usually sufficient. Off? Yes! No, touched again. I held her down for another cable's length. Now, back with the stick. Would she hold off? Yes-no-yes. She was off. It had been a horrible take-off, but I determined to stay up.

The seaplane had no flying speed, and I had little control over it; it was quite unresponsive. Slowly it righted, and lurched heavily. I pushed the stick hard over, and it righted to an even keel. Suddenly the port wing was struck down by an air bump, and the seaplane seemed to collapse on its side. I struck the control-stick hard over. It had no bite, and the ailerons flopped. The seaplane continued its slither to the sea. 'That's the finish of it!' I thought.

My anxiety ceased and I felt resigned. Then the wings seemed to cushion on a layer of air a few inches from the water, and the seaplane slowly righted. Only the slots hanging out like tongues of dead-beat dogs gave me the least control. The wall of palms ahead blocked my path, and it was impossible to turn right or left. The only chance was to keep down in the thicker surface air to gain enough speed to jump the palms. They rushed at me. Every nerve rebelled, urging me to rise now. But too soon meant certain destruction.

At the last moment I jumped the seaplane as high as possible. I knew that the jump would lose me all the flying speed gained; and I knew that the seaplane must drop after the jump. Could it get flying speed before striking the trees? The foliage came up at me, but suddenly a strong gust of wind reached the plane. I could see its blast spread on the tree-tops; it gave the wings lift, and the controls grip. It saved us.

Finally, nine weeks later, riding their luck and a following wind Francis and a sorry version of *Madame Elijah* were bound for Sydney – and glory.

But it had been, and was still to be, a damn close run thing.

———— ✕✕✕ ————

Francis's first two trans-Tasman solo flights had started off cheerily enough but both soon descended into fear and desperation and ended with a close shave. The third leg was no different; it wouldn't be a Francis flight if it were all plain flying.

After the first hour he had covered over 100 miles under a blue sky in perfect visibility, with a stronger than expected tailwind. I'm sure a strong wind from any direction would have caused him concern, as they can only back or veer. This one backed. Half an hour later it had blown him miles too far south. He altered course 15 degrees to the north, certain that the backing was a trend.

Then, calmly settling down to his new course, he had a tremendous shock: out of nowhere the engine gave a loud backfire. It had never done this before in flight. He knew there could only be two causes, electrical or fuel flow. He sat utterly upright, waiting for the engine's final splutter and death – and his death too. He flicked to the port magneto and back; the revs dropped and the running was rough. A defective magneto – but he had two. Thank God it wasn't the carburettor; he only had one of those.

Still on edge, he took another sight. The wind was backing even more and he was steering her even further north. Looking at the chart he noticed – as if for the first time – that the 'Australian coastline had a receding chin, and that every degree I flew south of the course rapidly increased the distance to land which might soon become greater than my range, whereas every degree north of the course would have shortened the flight over the sea'. Still, he pressed on for Sydney rather than head due west for the nearest piece of coast.

Now he was becoming fraught, with the engine uncertain and the ever-backing wind, a new problem arose. Clouds. He could see that soon he would be unable to take a sun sight. At first he was not too worried; after all, he had a 2,000-mile target of the Australian coast to aim for. But still the wind backed and *Madame Elijah* was flying like a crab into the wind to keep across the course. If it backed more it would become a headwind – and there wasn't enough fuel to survive that. He could only turn her further north to keep a south-easterly heading – and hope the wind would veer or die down.

Instead it backed further and now brought rain, heavy rain. The drift was becoming alarming and now he had drastically reduced visibility. The rain was now a downpour, just like a Dutch East Indies monsoon. Water was everywhere: pouring down his neck, filling the cockpit floor and spraying off the windscreen. The rebuild had not been 100 per cent true after all: the old *Madame Elijah* had draining for the cockpit and a slightly higher screen or lower seat. Francis recalled:

I was flying blind, as if in a dense cloud of smoke. I throttled back, and began a slanting dive for the water. Panic clutched me: if I got out of control, I would be too low to recover. But panic meant dying like a paralysed rabbit. I remember saying out loud, 'Keep cool! Keep cool! K-e-e-p c-o-o-l!' The seaplane passed through small sudden squall bumps, which shook it violently.

He was now flying blind by instinct and engine note; if the revs increased, the dive was steepening. He dared not try to climb blind, for if he stalled and spun he would not know where the sea was to give him a levelling-off point. He sat still and tense, looking for glimpses of the sea and the compass. If the revs increased he would ease back the joystick.

But intense concentration can only be kept up for so long. Just in time, out of the wall of water he saw the spume off the waves below the port wing-tip. He opened the throttle but the engine only misfired. He opened it wide, nothing to loose. Certain death. This time it shook and backfired but gave him just enough power to lift the nose clear off the spume. Heaven knows what his course was; all his energy was given to keep her flying in any direction.

I dared not take my eyes off the water to look at the compass or the rev indicator. One thing helped me – the violence of the gale itself. Although the seaplane headed in one direction, it was being blown sideways, so that it crabbed along. I could see the next wave between the wings instead of its being hidden by the fuselage. I steered by the drift, keeping the angle of it constant. Otherwise I should have wandered aimlessly about the sea. There was a furious cross sea. Waves shot upward, to lick at the machine, but were slashed away bodily southwards by the sheer force of the gale.

After 10 minutes of hanging on, hanging in there, Francis thought he must navigate again. The compass showed that he was 55 degrees off course, heading too far south towards Tasmania. The wind must have backed another 45 degrees; he was in the eye of the storm.

I had to think hard. I picked up the chart case on which my chart was rolled, but the soaked chart was useless. Before the storm I had drifted so far south that I was right on the edge of the chart; during the storm I was blown farther south at the rate of a mile a minute, and was now far off it. I had been only four hours thirty-five minutes in the air: it seemed a lifetime.

But the eye of a storm is good news too: once through it, all that went before is reversed. The gale was now helping him along and behind the front he found enough of a break to take two sun sights. Soaked to his skin, with water up to the rudder pedals, distracted by a backfiring and spluttering engine, it took him half an hour to work out where he was and how much fuel remained.

The wind now veered. Helpful. Yet only now did he give up the idea of reaching Sydney; any piece of Australia would do. He flew due west, as he should have done hours ago.

I felt intensely lonely, and the feeling of solitude intensified at every fresh sight of 'land', which turned out to be yet one more illusion or delusion by cloud. After six hours and five minutes in the air I saw land again, and it was still there ten minutes later. I still did not quite believe it, but three minutes later I was almost on top of a river winding towards me through dark country.

It was Australia – but he had no idea which bit of it, only that he must be north of Sydney. Actually he wasn't even sure if he was in New South Wales. To the south, in the fading light, he saw a bay. Wherever it was, he would land there and find directions. Closer in he saw three grey ships: the Royal Australian Navy. At random, he chose to land, exhausted, next to HMAS *Albatross*.

Incredibly, Francis's first thought was to replenish himself and *Madame Elijah* and fly down the coast south to Sydney. A naval launch came out to meet him and told him he was at Jervis Bay, 80 miles south of Sydney, not north. Such was his disorientated. He asked them to hold *Madame Elijah* while he started her, so that he could complete the flight that evening. Standing on the float, he noticed the engine cowling streaked in soot from the backfires. Still he insisted to himself he must fly to Sydney; only when she failed to reach anything approaching take off speed did he ask for sanctuary.

HMAS Albatross

On board he was fêted by the officers and a few whiskies later he resigned himself to a good meal and dry berth on board the *Albatross*. Yet even now Francis felt the self-inflicted pain of failure just as all the officers were acknowledging his achievement and celebrating his success.

Yet I felt isolated, horribly cut off from other people by some queer gulf of loneliness. I had achieved my great ambition, to fly across the Tasman Sea alone, I had found the islands by my own system of navigation which depended on accurate sun-sights worked out while flying alone, something which no one had ever done before and perhaps no one ever would do in similar circumstances.

And then his famous, telling remark: 'I had not then learned that I would feel an intense depression every time I achieved a great ambition; I had not then discovered that the joy of living comes from action, from making the attempt, from the effort, not from success.'

But that day had one more nasty trick up its sleeve. The duty officer wanted to hoist *Madame Elijah* on board for the night so that they could steam for Sydney. Francis felt he had to supervise. Mentally and physically exhausted, and several whiskies for the better, he caught his fingers in the winch loop as the crane took up the slack. Francis cried out in agony but by the time the loop was slack his fingers were crushed. Next thing he knew: 'When I came to I was in the ship's hospital. My right hand was crushed, but I lost only the top of one finger. The surgeon cut off the crushed bone and sewed up the flesh'. But the evening was not over yet. 'I then became the guest of the wardroom officers as well as of Captain Feakes, and it is hard to recount such marvellous hospitality. It was like staying in the best club with the mysterious fascination of naval life added.' They knew, and he knew they knew, what an extraordinary act of navigation, daring and skill he had just pulled off.

Six mornings later the Albatross steamed into Sydney harbour. Francis and *Madame Elijah* had made it, even if not quite as planned.

———❧———

In the same way as we didn't have space here for a blow-by-blow account of Francis's London to Sydney flight, we don't have space for a blow-by-blow of his attempt to land-hop his circumnavigation back to London via Asia. He wrote a comprehensive book about those four months, from July to October 1931, *Ride on the Wind*, from which these are some of the more startling endeavours. Rarely can anyone have packed so many adventures, met so many aspects of humanity, had so many near scrapes and moments of ecstatic relief as Francis had in that short period.

By the time she limped onto the Australia seashore *Madame Elijah* was in urgent need of some mechanical TLC. Luckily the Australian agent for de Havilland was a flying-works family man, Major Hereward de Havilland, known to everybody in Sydney as 'D.H.'. D.H. was just Francis's cup of tea and Francis, with his Moth exploits, was D.H.'s *cause célèbre*.

Under D.H.'s supervision *Madame Elijah* had the ultimate makeover and emerged a new girl: engine rebuilt, new prop, rigging tested and tightened – and even that starboard float mended – or so Francis thought. He had his own hand mended and filled his days journeying from consulate to consulate seeking landing and flyover permissions for the first stage to Japan. He needed to find places with empty landing waters every 500 miles, where a seaplane could anchor safely overnight, with access to food for airman and fuel for seaplane and where some sort of pidgin English could be used. Frustrated by officialdom, Francis's great *bête noire*, and delays to *Madame Elijah*'s rebuild, D.H. asked him why on earth he didn't just built a yacht and do it the easy, sunbathing way. Francis recorded: 'Thirty years on,

Afloat on Elijah

now that I am a sailing man, this idea seems a great joke; I get far more sunbathing in the middle of London in a month than I ever have on a yacht!'

With an eye on the weather in Northern Canada and Greenland, Francis grew increasingly impatient to leave. None of the consuls was much moved to help, the petrol situation en route was undiscoverable and, to cap it all, the money promised from New Zealand failed to arrive. D.H. rode to the rescue, lending Francis £44, enough to buy petrol and food to reach Japan, by which time the New Zealand money should have arrived.

Eventually, on 3 July, all was ready. Francis said his good-byes and thank-yous to everyone who had helped him that last month in Sydney. They were all apprehensive about what he was setting out to do; it must have seemed as crazy as it was. Captain Feakes from HMAS *Albatross* took Francis to one side and said what they all felt: 'If you find it's impossible, give it up, won't you?' As if! A few moments later Francis was flying again, free as a bird, and wrote in his log what Feakes and the stay-at-homes could never understand: 'This is the supreme ecstasy of life'.

The flight up the coast was uneventful enough, stopping at Brisbane, Rockhampton and Cairns, mile after mile of pristine emptiness. It wasn't until passing Cape Lee in Princess Charlotte Bay that the boredom of wonder was relieved. Sharks! A whole fright of them. Francis had always had a fascination with the marauders of the deep and was disappointed not to have flown over any across the Timor Sea seven months earlier. Now, when most of us would have given a shiver and flown on gratefully, he went down to have a look. He landed on the exact spot where they had been, turned off the engine, jumped out of the seaplane, took off his flying suit and lolled about on a float hoping for a good close up. He smoked a pipe and ate some sandwiches. It never occurred to him that his floats must have looked like two juicy seals to his new friends down below. At least I presume it never occurred to him. He waited a few minutes but his natural impatience got the better of his natural curiosity, he fired her up and took off again for Thursday Island.

Ah, Thursday Island. The last stop of Australia heading north and west. A place of some notoriety among sailors for being the home of women of easy virtue, as they used to say. I remember sailing around there in the early '70s and, being the junior crew and a relatively fit teenager, rowing a stream of pissed-up Sheilas back and forth from bar to yacht. Luckily a doctor's surgery was next to the bar, or perhaps intentionally, for the next morning four rather sheepish crew members lined up for their penicillin shots.

Visiting airmen seemed not to enjoy similar visiting rights, as Francis's welcoming party consisted of a man called Vidgen, a local pearl merchant. Luckily Vidgen was throwing a dinner party for a visiting Dutch captain that evening and invited Francis to spend the night and join in the party. Francis was impressed: 'The manners of the party were gentle and punctilious, after the Dutch style. We had a huge, excellently cooked dinner, the sort of feast that one had fifty years ago in an English country house in the middle of winter.'

Talk soon turned to the cannibals thereabouts. After making sure that there was no missionary in the soup, one of the Dutch crew asked Francis what weapons he had if he came down in cannibal country.

'I have a .410 double-barrelled pistol', Francis declared proudly, 'and I've made the shot solid with candle grease'.

'What range would it kill at?' asked the Dutchman.

'Ten yards', Francis replied, 'for sure'.

All around the table there was laughter, shaking heads and knowing looks.

'What's the joke?' Francis asked.

'My friend,' Vidgen replied, 'you will never see any Papuans. They keep behind the trees. They then shoot poisoned arrows at you from 200 yards. The arrows are barbed so can't be pushed through or pulled out. They won't approach you until they are

Contemporaneous cannibal, Merauke

sure you are dead. And then they eat you.'

'So this idea of boiling you alive is nonsense?' asked Francis.

'Yes, nonsense, they prefer you dead, if that's any comfort.'

'Cold comfort', said Francis.

He took off over cannibal country early the next morning.

—⟨∞⟩—

Actually the nearest Francis came to cannibalism was twenty-four hours later, when he was preparing to leave Merauke. The town is now just inside the Indonesian half of Guinea but was then part of the Dutch East Indies. Once more, the Dutch had proved hospitable hosts, putting him up in a guest house overnight. On his way back to *Madame Elijah*'s mooring they passed a column of prisoners being marched off in a chain gang. One of the Dutchmen pointed out two particular prisoners, who were chatting away busily and happily to each other. Turns out they were from hill country and had got into the habit of coming into town, selecting a local fatty, conning him into eating some drugged sago, lighting up a spit and chowing down. They had been caught and tried. The judge thought it unfair to hang them for doing what they had been taught was right. Instead, he put them to work building roads. Apparently they thought the bargain fair as, although having to work hard, they were given food without having to hunt for it.

This was food for thought for Francis, whose route that morning took him across the middle of Frederik Hendrik Island. 'No white man had ever seen the interior of this island. All that was known was that natives attacked any ship becalmed near the coast.'

At Dobo, a completely remote, tiny island en route to the Philippines, Francis landed to spend the night and refuel. It is likely that the islanders had never seen a plane before, even a seaplane. As he taxied up to the jetty, 'a tremendous press of natives, thousands of them, suddenly burst into a shout, a thrilling sound that would have raised the sky'.

On the jetty a Dutch official pushed through the crowd. He proudly showed Francis the island's fuel supply from which he could fill up *Madame Elijah*. There was quite an array of oil drums, all full … of diesel. Soon the Dutchman found Francis his petrol; in the search for this Francis found three Australian bachelor pearlers, with whom he spent a most amusing night – he doesn't reveal what they were doing, but knowing bachelor

Dobo

pearlers... They lived in a typical Lord Jim compound house on stilts, with wide verandas and rattan curtains for doors.

Before leaving this tiny paradise, Francis was introduced to the local prince. It made his morning: 'The Rajah was small, quiet, delicate and aristocratic, and he wore white flannels with a Savile Row cut. His wife was perfectly charming, with tiny feet and hands, a perfect little figure'.

Feeling that all was perfect in the world, Francis took of for the Philippines. Half an hour later he was writing up his log when, suddenly: silence. The nightmare comes to life. He turned 'instantly from a tolerant philosopher into a primitive animal'. He turned into wind to land, switching the magnetos on and off, when equally suddenly the engine cut back in.

Two hours later he had a Spot on! landfall at Cape St Augustine in the Philippines. Feeling again that all was well in the world, he switched off the engine and circled the lighthouse in a steep, spiralling glide. When level with the lighthouse, he switched on the engine again. Nothing happened. And this time he had little height with which to bargain. Primitive animal again, he flicked the mag switches frantically. Just before the forced landing the engine cut back in again. He flew on without further playfulness, determined not to risk his luck a third time.

<hr>

The first overnight spot in the Philippines was at Mati, on the island of Mindanao. As he climbed up on to the jetty there was an even bigger crowd of curious natives than there had been at Dobo. In front of them stood a handsome young Filipino.

'I am the Chief Postmaster. When do you leave? Doctor Mendez wants you to take our mail bag.'

Francis replied: 'Very well but I must get some petrol first.'

'Petrol?' he said as they swayed to and fro, jostled by the surging crowd. 'There is no petrol here.'

Francis grew uneasy; he knew Mati was cut off from the rest of the island except by steamer, but here was the steamer in the harbour. It seemed incredible that there was no petrol. He asked again, 'Have you no petrol at all?'

'No, no petrol here on the island.'

'But your radio station', Francis replied. 'How do you work that without petrol?'

'Press a key, just the same as for telegram.'

Just then three more Filipinos forced a passage through the crowd and strutted up. The Postmaster said quickly, 'I introduce you to Chief of Public Works, to the President-elect, and to the Chief of Police.'

Francis thought: 'Public Works – petrol'. He asked the Chief about it; the Chief shook his head: 'No, no petrol here.'

Francis thought of trying the steamer in the harbour, but it was impossible to force a passage though the throng, so he asked the Chief of Public Works to make an inquiry on board. A messenger was dispatched to the steamer.

The messenger returned; the captain regretted that he had no petrol; could Francis not use gasoline instead? But the question was theoretical rather than hopeful; whatever you called it, it was not actually to hand. Francis took the Chief Postmaster by the arm and asked him if he could find his favourite stalwart, a nice cup of tea.

Now a new uniform arrived and announced, 'I am Commandant of Military here. The Governor-General has wired me about you. You will stay at my house. Do you carry passengers?' Francis replied he only had room for one. 'Do you know that the President likes flying? It is possible that the President might find you some gasoline.'

As they walked towards the Commandant's house, it became apparent that not just the President but the Governor-General, the Chief of Public Works, the President-elect, the Chief Postmaster, not to mention the Head of the Police and his cowalker the Commandant of Military all thought that they would like flying too. Francis was beginning to fear that they would be offended when at last the Army chief said, 'What would happen if Governor-General Davis,[12] Governor-General of all the Philippine Islands wanted a ride in your plane?'

Francis felt he was being made into an early version of the Philippines Airlines. 'He couldn't have one', he said promptly and firmly, hoping that if he refused the Governor-General the rest of the bigwiggery would not feel insulted.

On the Commandant's veranda the guest's party was served tea, cigars and brandy.

'About the gasoline?' Francis asked after a polite interval.

'No problem, no problem', said the Chief of Public Works. 'But first you must see the President.'

'Oh, I'm really very tired', Francis replied, 'it's getting dark. I'd really like to sleep first. If you don't mind'.

But they would have none of it, hinting that the matter of the gasoline would be helped enormously by seeing the President.

Soon Francis was a passenger crammed into the back of a car coming down a country road. Every now and then they forced aside a bullock and cart driven by a Filipino boy in a large, floppy, strawplaited hat smoking a fat cigar. Every time Francis asked about the coconut grove or banana plantation they were passing through he was told, 'This belongs to President Lopez'.

They drove up to Lopez's palace with terrific horn-blowing and carved a way through the throng of supplicants. President Lopez himself greeted Francis and took him upstairs to a wide veranda. Lopez wore expensive golf trousers of pepper-and-salt flannel, black silk stockings and white kid shoes. A handsome .32 calibre automatic with a mother-of pearl handle made his cartridge belt sag at one hip. He gave Francis a superb cigar, the best he had ever smoked. Fireflies spangled the darkness, like twitching stars. The tropical night was cool and scented. Endless formalities took ages. Francis was now hungry as well as dog tired.

Next Lopez took Francis to see his crocodile. He shone his torch on a tough, leathery brute about nine foot long lying beside a concrete pool against some wire netting twelve inches high. It had a merciless, unwinking stare. Then the President shone his torch round the wall of the snake house.

'Where are the snakes?' Francis asked. The president flashed his torch round again, but all Francis could see was a thick brown beam under the rafters on top of the wall.

'Can you not see it?' asked the president. 'It dined on a cat the other day and is sleeping it off. Surely you see the cat in its stomach?' Then Francis noticed that the thick bar all round the hut on top of the wall was mottled, and he saw a bulge in it like a football.

They went back to the veranda and sat there forever. Nine o'clock came and went; ten o'clock too. Finally dinner arrived. Francis sat next to the President, the various henchmen and chief of this and head of that around them at a circular table. They spun this round and stabbed at whatever morsel they fancied. No one said a word; the only noise was the clatter of knives and forks and the creak of the revolving table. It was quick work while it lasted. One after another the guests finished abruptly and moved away, to let the women have an innings. Francis was by now desperately tired and every few seconds his eyes closed.

'Is there any chance of sleeping here tonight?' he asked the President. 'I'm really all in'.

'Sleep?' Lopez replied, surprised at such an early request. 'Oh, no, no, no. The Chief Postmaster has arranged a dance at the Commandant of Military's house, and we must return to Mati. And party.'

So off they went again, but not only after the President had presented Francis, in full show in front of his lined-up household, with three tins of gasoline, some of those splendid cigars and a freshly salted wild cat skin. He had, he boasted, shot it himself the day before.

*The
Presidential
Palace at
Mindanao*

They returned to the Commandant of Military's house to
find the vast central room clear of furniture. Francis woke up
a little at the prospect of a lively evening among the maidens
of Mati. But although some coy maidens did drift in from the
darkness, they were tightly cased in Spanish-looking dresses of
stiff brocade and each was guarded by a chaperone with the eye
of a bird of prey. He was led round and introduced to everyone,
one by one, with a long speech in each case.

By these early hours Francis could take it no longer, literally
falling asleep where he stood. After great protestations from his
hosts he was led to his bed next to the big drum of the dance
band. In spite of the booming banging, he fell asleep as soon as
he lay down.

Francis's sticky end came in Japan. After the ramshackle
informality and gentle chaos of the Dutch East Indies and
Philippine islands, the deep formality and spick-and-span
suspicion of imperial Japan brought a cultural clash of no mutual
comprehension. No wonder the islands to the south came to a
sticky Japanese end too.

Japan was by 1931 in military hands and Francis was permitted to arrive from Shanghai at one place and time only: Kagoshima at 3 pm on 13 August 1931. Awaiting him were three launches with ten officers in each one. The launches and officers were immaculate: the former of varnished mahogany and shiny steel, adorned with a plethora of Japanese flags, the latter in blue uniforms with white caps and gloves. Awaiting them was an unkempt young Englishman, alone, unshaven, ununiformed, unwashed, windblown from a solo flight half-way round the world, standing on a float of a tiny civilian seaplane, throwing an anchor into their sea, waving an informal salute. He thought they were a comic opera. They thought he was a spy. You can see their point. How else to explain such blatant eccentricity as a civilian flying for private pleasure other than by a typical *gaijin* double bluff?

After an excessive display of politeness, when each officer had bowed his respects and Francis grunted a hello in reply, the party disembarked at the jetty. They found a civilian interpreter, Hayashi-san, and once out of sight of the public the questioning began. On one side of the table sat Francis, alone. Facing him was the interpreter flanked by a dozen officers, now slightly less polite.

'Where did you cross into Japan?' Each officer asked it several times. At first Francis thought it was just each one having to ask it to save face, but then they each asked the same question again and again.

'What was your course to Kagoshima? Show us on your chart.' Again, the question did a couple of laps of the table, each officer having a turn by seniority.

'What is your trade?' Francis told Hayashi-san that he was a company director. That really got them excited. Impossible! You are far too young. Again and again, they fired back the question, then came the turns that Francis was by now expecting.

'You are really an army officer, aren't you? You must be a military pilot.' Francis tried to explain the concept of private aviation, flying for fun, flying solo for fun being even more fun.

Kagoshima in 1930

They had absolutely no comprehension of how it was possible governmentally, and why it should be enjoyable materially. The line of questioning was going round in increasingly aggressive, insistent, tight circles. Francis recalled he 'got bored with this line of questioning after a while and, to liven the party up, said I was in the Territorial Air Force. The party was electrified'.

Of course he really *was* in the New Zealand TAF but it was impossible for him to explain – or for them to understand – the concept of a territorial force. Francis upped the stakes, mischievously, when he said he was 'Reserve, I am in the Reserve'. 'Then you are officer in Army, yes?' they shot back. Francis was by now tired and exasperated: 'Yes, no, yes, damn it!'

All this while other officers were searching *Madame Elijah* and going through his bags and equipment. Great enthusiasm was shown for every aspect of his and *Madame Elijah*'s paperwork. Then the Mayor, the Chief of Police and Customs Superintendent arrived, to a whole new round of bowed introductions and fresh questions. Poor Hayashi-san was as tired as Francis. Sandwiches arrived and to Francis's great relief he heard the sound of a popping cork, 'for a glass is as good as a bottle to a tired aviator'.

Now the Chief of Police pulled rank and insisted that Francis be handed over to him for the night. Francis found him 'affable, easy-going, smooth-mannered and pleasant and it was just incredible that any human being could be so polite'. With Hayashi they motored along interminably long, narrow ways through a densely settled area towards the hotel. Each time Francis dozed off he would be jerked awake by another polite question.

You can sense Francis's relief when the day was nearly over:

We arrived at a hotel as per a state visit. As we entered, a row of smiling girls knelt on the raised floor before us, bowed till their foreheads and palms touched the floor, then settled back on their heels repeating it all time after time. Hayashi and the policeman bowed profoundly in response; I did an Englishman's best. My shoes were removed by dainty fingers. They tried to fit me with a pair of slippers from a row of them on the ground, but the largest only just admitted the tip of my toes. I heartily agreed with Hayashi's suggestion of a bath.

As usual, Francis was too discreet to continue.

The next morning the questions turned to the future. Francis, by now in the hotel's kimono, asked for his chart. He showed them his route to Kochi.

'But it is not permitting to go to Kochi', said the Chief.

'Oh, but it is; I have permission', Francis replied, producing a letter from the British Consul-General saying that the Japanese permitted him to alight at Kochi.

'No', insisted the Chief, 'if you please I have new instructions. Between here and Tokyo there is only one permitted stop and that is here.' He pointed to Katsuura on Francis's chart. Thus began Francis's fateful final flight.

You can quite see why the Japanese rerouted Francis to Katsuura: if Kagoshima is on the south-western tip of Japan, Katsuura is on its south-eastern tip, about 50 miles south of Tokyo. To fly from Kagoshima to Katsuura means flying the 600 miles over the sea, by and large. It suited both Francis and them: the Japanese military to keep the spy over the sea and Francis to keep the comic operaticians on the land. Moreover, it was a perfect flying day:

> To be flying round the world on such a day was the perfect adventure. The sunlight was balmy; the water sparkled. The Pacific Ocean was friendly, and I skimmed the surface to be close to it. It seemed to give me strength. Life was grand; flying had become an art, and that morning I felt that I was master of it.

Sure enough, at Katsuura a welcoming party of launches was there to supervise him. Among all the officials was a middle-aged, dapper little fellow waving an umbrella. He turned out to be Suzuki-san; he had lived in the United States for twenty years; he spoke a form of English Francis could understand; he had been nominated to look after Francis; he was 'unusually efficient'; he invited Francis to stay with him overnight. After the unpleasantness of the military company in Kagoshima it was good to be back in pleasant civilian company. Mrs Suzuki cooked them a good meal and opened up the *sake*. Mr Suzuki put Francis in Japanese clothes so he could show him around the town less conspicuously. This was, Francis felt, in every way more like it. Ahead lay the ice floes of north-eastern Russian and Alaska; for now he was enjoying the warm hospitality and friendship of a westernised oriental gentleman.

It was in this spirit of cooperation and friendship that the next morning Francis agreed to do something he had hitherto always refused to do: a barnstorm. But Suzuki had made a special request: 'Will you make circles round the town? The peoples would like to see your aeroplane.' It would have been churlish to refuse, even if it meant reversing normal policy.

Katsuura is a natural, hilly harbour with a narrow entrance out to the Western Pacific. *Madame Elijah* was soon skimming along the waves and airborne. Francis headed out towards the entrance to gain speed for manoeuvring. At the entrance he turned back to make a low pass over the town, then thought he needed more height. He was already higher than the harbour rim, yet still lower than the high peaks beyond that. There was no cause for even the slightest alarm as he had more than enough speed and height to deal with anything. Except, of course, an unmarked obstacle, such as seven telephone cables strung across the harbour between the peaks, ready to be turned into a catapult should an unsuspecting seaplane fly straight into them. What happened next is best left to Francis:

I pulled back the control-stick, and the seaplane began to climb sharply. I was looking at the township below me on my left, thinking what a pretty sight it was with the cluster of roofs at the base of the hill and the sunshine strong on the green harbour water beneath me, when there was a dreadful shock, and I felt a terrific impact. My sight was a blank. Slowly, a small aperture cleared, a hole for sight, and through it, far away, I saw a patch of bright green scrub on a hillside. But it was a long way off, like a tiny glimpse seen through a red telescope. Now it was a round sight, half of sparkling water and half of rooftops, straight before me. I was diving at it vertically, already doing 90 mph. I remember thinking, 'Well, this is the end,' and feeling intense loneliness, a vague sense of loss – of life, of friends. Then, 'I'd better try for the water,' I was vaguely aware of lifeless controls, but suddenly all fear was gone. The next thing I knew was a brightness above me and in front of me.

The wreck of Madame Elijah

Francis regained consciousness, remembering the brightness and taking it as a spiritual experience, that he was in heaven. Then the pain kicked in and brought him back again. He knew that, incredibly, he was alive. Flitting in and out of consciousness, he saw dozens of hands clutching at him and felt stitches being sewn into his arm. Then he was lost again, coming to in a hospital. More intense pain, then the relief of morphine and sleep, then the coming to and the dreadful thought: was he a eunuch?

When he next saw daylight he still seemed to be alive. Daylight was only a sheet of light, nothing defined. He asked the room about his sight. Suzuki-san answered. He had been with Francis all night. 'The sights can be saved', he said, now by the bed. Then Francis asked 'the only question that mattered to me at that moment; was I a eunuch?' Suzuki stole a look; all was well with the undercarriage. For Francis, 'That was one of the greatest moments of my life, and I put everything I could into the effort to get well again quickly'.

As he recovered, Suzuki-san told him what had happened: 'You have wonderful good luck. The wires cut up your plane. Nobody understands. They rush to pull you out before the fire catches. You must be dead. Great is their wonder to find you still alive. It was terrible a sight. I am nearly sick. Everybodies is so sorry for you. Everybodies prays to God for you. The doctor thinks you do not live for ten, twenty minutes.

'We decided to send you to Dr Hama's hospital at Shingu 10 miles away. All young men carry you to train, very careful. They carry you all way one hour train journey.'

As he recovered, Francis took stock. Overwhelmed, he remembered the nightmare he had had so many dozens of times, of flying blind, waiting for the inevitable crash. He counted thirteen bone breaks or fractures. Not surprisingly, the damage to his back was the most long-lasting; it would eventually take ten years to make a complete recovery.

Francis's crash, survival and repair were enormous news in Japan and he was now something of a local attraction. Group after group came to visit him, all with the usual deluge of politeness and kindness, so much so that Francis feared that

the Japanese kindness would make me mad. They were immensely sorry about the accident, and sympathetic with the foreign birdman who had come to grief. Thousands came from near and far to visit me. All day they passed through my room at the end of my bed. If Suzuki were there he would introduce them to me: 'This is directors of the ice factory at Katsuura; they pray to God for you, and send you ice every day.'

If putting on a show of being alive was tiresome, there were moments of relief and genuine kindness, such as the letter from Hayashi-san, his interpreter at Kagoshima:

Sir,

Receiving the report of the mishap I have profound regret which never could be forgotten.

I expected you will success as I said you, I hope you will success, when bid farewell on the beach.

I hope you will buy fresh eggs with money that I present to you (I enclose a money order, ten yen, which you must ask for post office) and take them to make you healthy.

Your truly,

Hayashi.

The *Nichi Nichi Shimbun*, a major circulation Japanese daily newspaper, wrote about the crash. They printed a letter from a lieutenant of the Naval Air Force that said:

Aviators Amy Johnson and Jack Humphries visiting Francis in hospital

We had been hoping that he would not encounter an accident when taking off at Katsuura. Kitsugura Bay is about 2,000 metres in diameter, flanked by rocks 100 metres high. The outlet of the bay is narrow, and just in front of it is an island. It is an ideal port of refuge, but a very dangerous place for seaplanes to come and go.

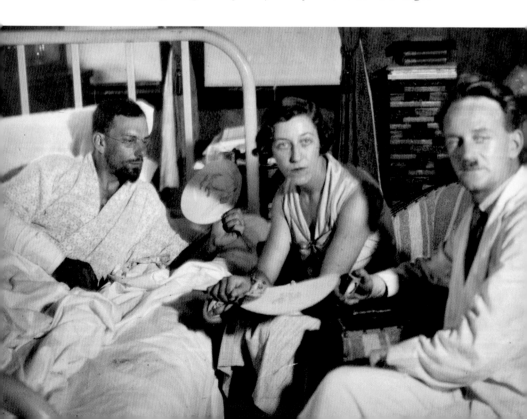

Being Francis, his thoughts soon turned to completing the journey, even as his broken bones rendered him helpless. He thought about writing a book from his bed and with the money buying a Katsuura fishing boat to enable him to keep going, a seaplane being beyond all hope of a budget.

A month later, still bed-bound but now in Suzuki-san's house and being nursed by Mrs Suzuki, he wrote left-handed, the only way he could write: 'Every flight is moulded into a perfect short story; for you begin – and you are bound to lead up to a climax.'

It was to be five years before the broken Francis would fly again, to start another short story. It was the quietest five years of his life; the only quiet five years of his life.

Francis chose to recuperate in Devon and set off for the family home in Shirwell. This visit was no more successful than the last one; less so, in many ways. Whereas before he had been the brash and cocky prodigal son with his rough colonial outlook, now he was broken, physically and mentally, and not too well financially either – and Shirwell did not do nurture and repair.

Luckily help was at hand, both to his broken body and broken spirit. The body was rescued by his cousins in nearby Instow, who found him lodgings on the estate. There he spent nine months in repair, a physically imposed exile that gave him time to write *Seaplane Solo*, his book about the flight from Sydney to the telephone wires in Katsuura.

His spirits were restored by being awarded the Johnston Memorial Trophy by the Guild of Air Pilots and Air Navigators. Now that navigation can be done by mobile phones, GAPAN has become The Honourable Company of Air Pilots, the largest livery company in the City – and very helpful in the writing of this book. Francis was presented with the trophy by the Prince of Wales, later King Edward VIII, for his navigation across the Tasman Sea. The award was a tremendous honour and big news in Devon, but even this failed to move the stony hearts at the Old Rectory, Shirwell.

After writing his book and receiving the award, a mended Francis made his way back to New Zealand. In his autobiography he passes over the next four years in two sentences: 'For four years I led an easy life. In the fishing season, I used to go off every evening after work to fish dry-fly for brown trout.' There's nothing much to add to that, except that he and Geoffrey Goodwin tried their best to make the land pay again, which it did to a reasonable extent, if not like the gold rush days before the Crash.

It is likely that Francis would have stayed happily enough in New Zealand for the rest of his life had he not met a sheep farmer, Frank Herrick. Frank was bored of counting sheep and falling asleep, was looking for adventure and floated the idea of himself and Francis flying a Puss Moth to England – and maybe back again. Francis would be the pilot and navigator, Frank the passenger and paymaster. Francis agreed, the Puss Moth was shipped to Sydney and two months later they set off.

What the flight showed above all else was how much aviation had evolved in the seven years since *Madame Elijah* and Francis had left London on his first great adventure. The Puss Moth itself was an advanced Gipsy Moth, now a monoplane capable of cruising at 100 mph, offering the comfort of a proper cabin. On the ground, too, aviation had evolved: Francis could put away his sextant and rely on the simplicity of radio beacons. The arrival of a light aircraft no longer caused the sensation – and frequent aggravation – that it once had. The Imperial Airways route now stretched all the way from London to Sydney. Pioneering was a forgotten art, a redundant science.

Theirs was strictly a tourist excursion. The original plan was to fly back across Siberia, but after reaching Peking via Singapore and Hong Kong they found the Russian overflight permission refused and decided to go back the old Empire way

across southern Asia. In Peking Francis had one of the few *De Havilland Puss Moth* diversions on the trip. He met 'an enchanting young lady ... so small that my two hands could meet round her waist. I visited her in the old walled city, although I was told that I was taking a big risk travelling through it at night by myself in a rickshaw'.

Other diversions were not so diverting. In Persia they were surrounded by guards with fixed bayonets, assuming that he was Lawrence of Arabia disguised with a beard, and proposing to proceed up-country to start a revolt. In Baghdad Frank managed to walk into the rotating prop in the dark, breaking an arm – and he was lucky at that. By Cairo they had had enough and flew back to Brooklands, old-Francis-style, in under thirty hours.

Thus back at his home base at Brooklands, Francis's seven-year flying career came to a satisfactory conclusion. Apart from towards the end of the coming war he would never fly himself again – but he would navigate, which to him was largely the point of flying. He repaired to Devon for one last attempt with his family. There he met Sheila. And Hitler invaded Poland.

NOTES:

12. After whom tennis's Davis Cup is named.

It's clear to me that God is an Englishman.
Don't mention that to Sheila. There'd be a
frightful rumpus.

CHAPTER 6

Sheila and the War

IN HIS AUTOBIOGRAPHY Francis has a chapter titled 'Sheila and the War'. No doubt he meant it chronologically as they were married just before the Second World War, but to me it reads more generically, for Sheila was – shall we say – combative. You would want her on *your* side, undoubtedly. Today we are used to feminine assertiveness and it ruffles few feathers unless demonstrably strident but in the 1940s, '50s and '60s women were supposed to be demur – and if they had any opinions to keep them to themselves, not, as the leading man in the black and white movie would say, to worry their pretty little heads about things.

Brusque would have been Sheila's reaction to such patrimony, for she had little time for purposeless chit-chat, idle chirping or reactionary opinions. In disregarding the expected feminine role, she was decades ahead of her time and her assertiveness found a willing correspondent in Francis, who didn't care much for frivolity either. Francis was a tough and wiry bird, a man's man with no feminine side to him at all; Sheila didn't have much of a feminine side to her either; thus the two chums had a long, happy and humour-filled marriage and friendship.

There's no doubt that even now Sheila is remembered for being abrupt and terse. That she was large – in the sense of being big-boned, not overweight – and certainly bigger-boned than Francis, reinforced the impression of a powerful woman best left undisturbed. Researching this biography, I came across the same joke many times, all versions of 'The only reason Francis sailed around the world was to get away from Sheila'. Like many quick quips it is not just unkind, but untrue. They were both unusual people, very unusual people, whose individual quirks suited each other perfectly. Francis sailed around the world to be with himself, 'to intensify life', as he put it, not to escape from Sheila. Sheila let him go, often when unwell, because she understood perfectly that free birds must fly – and that caged birds were no good to anyone, especially to her.

Sheila's autobiography starts with: 'My father committed suicide when I was three days old'; as we would expect, this tragedy changed her life before it had really begun. This was in 1905, making her four years younger than Francis. The family on her father's side was extremely rich: her grandfather, Thomas Craven, had made his fortune in industry and now resided in the stately Kirklington Hall in Nottinghamshire and, when not there, in 'Millionaire's Row', next to the Russian Embassy in Kensington. Both residences bristled with butlers and their

Kirklington Hall, Sheila's family home – but not her home

Sheila,
aged 4

underlings and the extended panoply of Cravens, major and minor. Sheila was born a major, her first few days spent in Belle Eau Park, one of the grace-and-favour mansions in the parks around Kirklington. Then, for reasons not completely clear, old Thomas Craven blamed Sheila's mother for his son's suicide and ceased supporting her, so casting Sheila and her mother into polite penury in a small estate cottage, yet still surrounded by their enormously rich relations.

Sheila's mother was one of eight sisters and the only one to have married, thus giving Sheila an early attempt at the world record of having seven maiden aunts. One such unsullied aunt was in religious orders and arranged for Sheila, by then eleven, to attend a convent school, St Mary's, Wantage, dedicated to preserving the cult of the Virgin Mary. Like Francis a few hundred miles away, Sheila had a terrible time at the hands of perverted

clergy, in this case the nuns in general and one sadistically and
sexually confused nun in particular. At a reunion many years
later the then current Mother Superior apologised: 'Yes, I'm
very sorry', she told Sheila, 'that woman was not suitable for
children'. At least Francis only had to doff his cap when the
headmaster walked by at Marlborough; at St Mary's the girls
had to get down on their knees and pray out loud when the
Mother Superior sailed past.

Yet it was at the convent that Sheila discovered her great
gift for art, particularly drawing. She won the Royal Drawing
Society's prize and was hailed in the national press as a 'child
genius'. There was talk of an art scholarship to Oxford but
Sheila's mother, as keen as Francis's father to discourage any
enthusiasm or individuality, could not imagine such a thing and
refused on the grounds that men did not marry women who
were too clever.

Instead Sheila was shuffled off to a more 'ladylike' finishing
school in Paris and soon found another talent in dress design. She
modelled dresses too and was offered a place at a Paris fashion
house, drawing, designing and modelling. Again her mother held

her back and instead, noting Sheila's fondness for fashion, found her a job as a shop assistant in a dress shop in Bond Street, which of course Sheila loathed. I think of Sheila now mostly as an unrequited artist, a naturally creative spirit held back by an inadequate rather than a manipulative mother.

By now aged twenty one – and not unattractive, in a rather gawky way – she had her first affair, with 'a glamorous young man I had met at a ball in the south of France. He had brown and white shoes and a car and a chauffeur, which seems to be the last word elegance.' In those days an affair meant that an offer of marriage was expected fairly promptly, as we shall see with Francis's courtship of her. She was jilted by the handsome lothario with the car and chauffeur and rebounded into a long affair with a married man in the Canary Islands, as she herself said, 'old enough to be my father' and which left her mother 'frightfully upset', written as if that was a satisfying part of the affair.

In her mid-twenties she experienced a life-changing – more a life-affirming – event borne of initial misfortune. By now working in the dress shop in Bond Street again, she contracted chickenpox from her mother while visiting home and, although cleared locally of the disease, came back to work in London with a tell-tale spot or two. Promptly sacked from her job, evicted from her Cromwell Road lodgings and thrown out of her mother's home, she eventually found a shabby room to rent in her mother's village belonging to the doom-laden widow of a policeman. The chickenpox now took good hold and Sheila couldn't shake it off, became depressed then deeply depressed in her surroundings and with her circumstances. She had a nervous breakdown. In her own words, she...

...was finally restored to health by meeting a wonderful healer. She did not use drugs and she herself had had a miraculous recovery from Bright's Disease. She used to

talk to me and give me absent healing and it was entirely
through her that I was able to lead a completely normal
life again. I learnt a great deal from her about prayer and
meditation and constructive thoughts.

Thus was born Sheila's unquestioning belief in natural healing
and prayer, not to mention her vegetarianism and, being Sheila,
an equally strong distrust of doctors and drugs, a philosophy she
applied throughout the rest of her life and one that she later used
to save Francis's life.

Her healer was Mary Winnithorpe, a West Country follower
of Mary Baker Eddy, the founder of the Christian Science
movement in New England. The absent healing to which Sheila
referred enabled Mary to heal Sheila through prayer even
when they were apart. These prayers recognise that ultimately
the spiritual realm is all that really exists and that all worldly
appearances, including illness, are illusions. It followed that,
for example, the best way for Mary to treat Sheila's nervous
breakdown was not by medication but by correcting the
mistaken belief that reality is what appears to exist rather than
that which is aware of its existence.

That which the Eastern mystical tradition holds as the
transpersonal Absolute or *Brahmin* the two Marys held as the
personalised God: 'The great I AM; the all-knowing, all-seeing,
all-acting, all-wise, all-loving, and eternal; Principle; Mind;
Soul; Spirit; Life; Truth; Love; all substance; intelligence'.[13] This
metaphysical Love is beyond the mind-induced limitations of time
and space and so can be anywhere, at any time; all that is needed
is union between the person praying and God. The similarities
with Eastern mystical traditions are remarkable and I must admit
that it was at this stage of research I became rather fond of Sheila.

Soon after recovering her equilibrium, Sheila had a piece of
bad and then good fortune. Her mother had been ill for some
time and died from what the now-Naturalist Sheila saw as 'death

by doctors and injections'. However, her mother's death meant that a minor inheritance had somehow slipped through Sheila's mean grandfather's net and with it she embarked on a Grand Tour of Empire.

The Cravens had never been short of connections, it was just Sheila's branch of the family that could never afford to use them. Now in quick time she sailed first class to Raj India on the steamer *Strathaird*, was hosted by the governors of Madras and Bombay, visited the Maharaja of Bundi, stayed with and danced with the Viceroy in Delhi, visited the North-West Frontier, rode elephants, was danced off her feet in the officers' messes of the Plains and was courted opportunely wherever she went. Giddy with the glamour of Empire, she set sail for Abyssinia, staying with the Resident in Aden and from there sailing for Djibouti to stay with the British Minister at Addis Ababa, where she met the Emperor Haile Selassie. On the passage from Aden the Somali captain, worried that a 30-year-old woman was unmarried, gave her a set of charms to help her find a husband. Francis arrived in short order and she always made sure that, when sailing alone, he sailed with one of the Somali captain's charms.

And so to Francis. Piecing together tales of the courtship from their autobiographies, we can imagine how it all happened.

On 30 December 1936 Francis and Sheila both happened to be house guests at the house in Westward Ho! in Devon of Francis's cousin Douglas Blew Jones. Douglas was famous for having size 24 feet and would become even more famous as the father of Bindy, Lucien Freud's favourite model. Francis was a very bachelory thirty-five and Sheila a proto-spinstery thirty-one. Nearly all their contemporaries were married, and with issue. Before Sheila arrived, Francis was told that she was coming from a dance in Wiltshire and instead of driving down was putting her car on the train. Francis noted 'this unusual move intrigued me' but thought not much more of it and went out shooting with the other house guests.

Sheila arrived around teatime and was chatting by the fire when in walked Francis holding a dead goose in one hand and a broken 12-bore shotgun in the other. Sheila was less than impressed: 'I was repelled by this because I didn't like killing. However, he laughed and I thought he seemed quite nice'.

Over dinner Sheila explained how she preferred to put her car on trains so that she always arrived fresh. Francis approved of the freshness: 'she liked comfort, and appeared rather languid. I felt that she should have a black boy following her with cushions, a rug and a parasol over her head'. The conversation turned to travel. Francis noted that 'Time seem to have a little importance to her. She was always interesting to listen to, and often had original views. I was surprised when I discovered that this languid personality had just returned from a voyage alone to India and Abyssinia.' She then explained how she had always wanted to go exploring and planned to do some more. Francis thought 'that this was just a bit of airy verbal thistledown; if it had been revealed to me that she would one day sail across the Atlantic with me, I would have laughed at the joke'. Francis doesn't seem to have mentioned his adventures even though he was by then one of the most famous aviators in the world. (Sheila claimed the significance of his fame had not dawned on her until told of it by Amy Johnson after they were married – but I find that rather hard to swallow.)

The next day the Westward Ho! house party repaired to a New Year's Eve party in Cornwall. The acquaintanceship continued. Francis had lived most of the last eighteen years in New Zealand and Sheila couldn't help being rather sniffy about it. 'I thought he had well-cut clothes for a man who had come here from the Dominions. Later I discovered that his evening clothes had been made by the Duke of Windsor's tailor. In those days one tended to look on people from New Zealand as being a bit uncivilised.' Francis must have been quite attentive as Sheila noticed that 'he made quite a set of me and I felt his personality'.

Sheila's next party was in Winchester on 2 January. She again decided to put her car on the train and on New Year's Day drove to Bideford with Francis as her passenger to make all the arrangements. He then stayed on with other cousins at Instow. He spent most of the night thinking about Sheila and about marrying her. The following day she duly boarded her train at Bideford, a train which then stopped at Instow. To her amazement, onto the train jumped Francis and onto the point he jumped straight.

'I've got on the train to ask you to marry me', he announced. Before she could reply, he added: 'I've got an overdraft of £14,000, a million trees and a thousand acres, a hundred pounds in the bank and that's all.'

Sheila didn't know what to say, but said, 'Well, you know, I spend £50 a year on my hair.'

'I'd like you to do that', Francis replied.

Sheila thought to herself: 'Men are so impractical, but this an interesting one'; she said to Francis: 'We are both fairly mature, and we've lived alone. We might be able to make a go of it.'

Francis then sang the praises of life in New Zealand, where he intended to take her. Sheila remembered that her mother had been out there when first married and had always spoken well of it. An hour later the train stopped at Exeter and Francis alighted.

'I'll think about it', Sheila promised, and they went their separate ways.

She took soundings from her friends. Most of the men were dismissive: 'You can't do that, he hasn't got any money.' Then she asked her mother's old maid Hester, whom she had inherited along with the small change. Hester gave her a cheerier, if rather frank, reply: 'Well, I think he sounds rather good, quite different from all the others you've had. I always worried about you taking up with these married men.'

When Francis telephoned to ask how she felt about it, she replied, 'I think we might make a success of our lives together'.

They arranged to meet again in her London flat, where Sheila had prepared a supper before they went to the theatre. The evening didn't get off to a good start.

'You know, I've been thinking it over', Francis announced. 'I don't think I can get married. I'm so used to being alone, and I don't think I'd like to be married.'

'I absolutely understand how you feel', Sheila replied, 'but let's go to the theatre all the same. Don't feel tied at all, because it's a dreadful feeling and it would be stupid', and off they trooped to her box at the theatre.

The next morning Francis reappeared on her doorstep. He had changed his mind; he did want to get married after all. So did Sheila and they became engaged on that very doorstop.

They had met on 30 December 1936, became engaged on 7 January and were married on 25 February 1937. The British Minister from Addis Ababa, Sir Sidney Barton, gave her away in Chelsea Old Church; very apt, as since staying with the family Sheila had adopted him and Lady Barton as her proxy parents. They tried to keep the wedding small but once Sheila discovered that Francis had thirty-five first cousins alone, the Craven contingent grew to match and it was quite the hullabaloo.

Their time together in New Zealand was not a success. The outdoor, gun-blasting, fish-hooking New Zealand life that Francis remembered so fondly didn't export to Sheila, especially the gun-blasting, fish-hooking part of it. For some reason he rented a villa, 77 Duthie Street, in the hillside suburb of Karoni, miles up twisty roads from what little life there was in Wellington. Even when there, there was a further steep walk up six flights of stairs to the house. To get to the villa they had to pass Francis's snazzy old penthouse apartment on The Terrace, which would have been much more up her street. Sheila, who didn't even suffer wise men gladly, felt she was in a hilltop prison. Constrained in their suburban villa in Wellington, her bohemian life in Europe was now unimaginable, with restaurants closing when they should be opening, the wit of sophisticated banter replaced by talk of sheep and trees – and as if they mattered. She soon longed for the cut and thrust of cosmopolitan London.

For Sheila the best part of their time in New Zealand was getting to know Francis's son, George. He'd had a hard time of it, his father leaving when he was less than a year old and his mother dying when he was three. He had also developed very bad asthma. By the time Francis returned he was eleven and Sheila set about giving him the happy home life he'd never had. In doing so she limited her own life even further, as his asthma meant that George wasn't able to go out easily and couldn't be left alone at home.

Before a year was up she drew stumps. Francis wasn't sad to pull them too, partly because he had to agree with her about dominion life in suburban New Zealand and partly because she wanted to take George with her, but also because the drums of war were rolling in Europe. And surely an aviator of his renown would make an essential fighter pilot in helping defeat the Hun?

Actually, no. The first time he applied to join the Royal Air Force, in 1938, Francis was turned down flat: at thirty-seven he was much too old and he had poor eyesight to boot. He was much chagrined and set about trying to find a job. It took six months but eventually his contacts in the world of navigation came good: Arthur Hughes of Henry Hughes & Son created a job for him developing bubble sextants at Hainault in Essex, about a dozen miles east of London. Francis found himself content at work: 'the job involved many hours in the air taking sights, and on the ground checking achievements'. But he was discontent at home, hemmed into Sheila's tiny flat in Chelsea, with the daily grind of the commute to Essex on the District and Central Underground lines, his off-work life restricted after the outdoor freedoms and space of New Zealand.

Six months later war broke out. Again Francis applied to join the Royal Air Force; again he was rejected. He was by then even older and his eyesight certainly hadn't improved but that

didn't stop him being equally chagrined a second time. He then had a brainwave, which even the dunderheads at the Royal Air Force couldn't turn down: together with his 'too old to fly' chum from the Royal Aero Club, the distinguished aviator Wing Commander Lord Douglas Hamilton, he decided to form a sort of suicide squadron, formed solely of known flying aces who lacked a limb or 20/20 vision or were 'too old'. The idea was that, by dint of their superior navigation and flying skills, members would be able to fly low and deep behind enemy lines, pinpointing bombing or photographing strategic targets that the novice pilots had no hope of reaching. It was implicit in this scheme that the members were expendable, the sorties being dangerous in themselves and the pilots being of no use to the regular RAF anyway. The idea was considerably ahead of its time and, as Francis wrote, 'I believe that this would have shown the value of the Pathfinder Force and brought it forward by a year or two. I was disgusted with being turned down a third time by the RAF and said "if they want me after this they can damn well come and get me".'

Henry Hughes & Son site in Hainault

Getting him would now be a little harder: the lease on Sheila's Chelsea mansion flat had expired and she leased a new house, Pages in Chigwell Row, then a small village in Epping Forest, much nearer to the Henry Hughes & Son offices at Hainault. With bombs now falling, young George was sent to stay with Francis's mother, Emily, in the West Country; the danger was no idle threat, as by the end of the war Pages had been damaged by bombing eight times.

Sheila found her war role, working for the YMCA in the blitzed East End, meaningful and personally rewarding. Francis though was soon bored at Hughes, no doubt made worse by his constant awareness of fighter pilots in derring-do action above the Essex skies. He broke the boredom by writing a series of short stories and articles on navigation for *Flight* magazine, which in turn led to a commission to write two books for Allen and Unwin, *The Spotter's Handbook* and *Night and Fire Spotting*, both published in 1940 and both aimed at telling bomb-threatened Londoners what planes were overhead and, Francis hoped, stop them running for shelter every time an aeroplane engine was heard overhead.

Although he was dismissive of these books, describing them as containing a lot of nonsense, by early 1941 they had attracted the attention of the Air Ministry. Word was sent to Hughes & Sons that the country needed Francis, an instruction with which the company was obliged to comply. An interview with Air Commodore the Hon. Ralph Cochrane, head of navigation training at the Air Ministry in Queen Anne Street, followed quickly. Cochrane listed Francis's civilian occupation as 'Air Navigation Specialist'.

The wheels of war moved quickly and on 14 March Francis received his commission as a Pilot Officer in the Royal Air Force Volunteer Reserve, the lowest rank that could be commissioned. As he soon found out, the word 'pilot' in Pilot Officer was a cruel misnomer. He was assigned to the Training Navigation section

*Air Vice
Marshal
Cochrane,
Francis's
recruiter*

of the Air Ministry Directorate of Air Member Training (AMT). Flying a desk from a fourth-floor office in Adastral House in Kingsway he might well be, helping write navigation manuals for instructors and students he certainly was, but he was at least in a uniform and contributing to a war that so far had seemed to hold a grudge against him. For the first time since returning from New Zealand his spirits were lifted; they were lifted further on the one or two nights a week when he stayed at his club, the Royal Aero Club at 119 Piccadilly, rather than suffer the Central Line commute to and from Essex.

At Adastral House Cochrane had thrown Francis into a small team with two very distinguished Air Force navigation experts, Group Captain L. 'Kelly' Barnes and Group Captain F.C. 'Dickie' Richardson. Nicknames were clearly the order of

Adastral House, Kingsway, Air Minsitry HQ from where Francis flew his desk in the early war years

Francis's respite, the Royal Aero Club building in Piccadilly

the day: Francis, who had been 'Chich' in New Zealand and 'Chicko' on Lord Howe Island, became 'Frank' during his part in Hitler's downfall. With Kelly he never got on at all; with Dickie he formed a lasting bond of respect and friendship. His problem with Kelly had begun before Francis ever met him.

When Francis was in New Zealand he had heard a story about a Royal Air Force seaplane navigator who had got so fed up with an interfering VIP that he socked him on the chin. The good news was that the plane landed safely; the bad news that said navigator was court-marshalled. Like many a good pub story, the facts had been improved in the telling and by the time Francis had turned it into a short story, *Curly the Navigator*, it really was a work of fiction. Unfortunately for Francis, the officer delivering the real-life punch was none other than Kelly; double unfortunately for Francis, Kelly had read *Curly the Navigator*.

'Frank' was duly summoned

to meet my boss, Group Captain Kelly Barnes, a big red-faced character who looked and acted exactly like the traditional John Bull. He had been the flying-boat navigator whose story I had dished up. I was decidedly uneasy as to what sort of reception I should get. He called me into his office and, as I did my best to stand smartly at attention, he said, 'You know, you got the end of that story wrong; what actually happened was that I was court-martialled in the morning, and called up before the Air Council in the afternoon to be awarded the MBE'.

To make Frank feel even smaller, the MBE was for 'his outstanding contribution to the advancement of air navigation' – by writing no less than the voluminous *Air Publication 1456*, the second part of the Air Ministry *Manual of Air Navigation* (1938).

With Dickie things were easier. They bonded personally and professionally, Dickie fully aware of Francis's solo flights to Sydney and across the Tasman Sea and the navigation skills and sheer bravery required. Dickie recalled that 'we were joined by Flt Lt (*sic*) Frank Chichester, then nursing a duodenal ulcer by constantly sipping milk and munching digestive biscuits. Frank and I had our way in reshaping the *Air Almanac*, which became the foundation in the revolution of astro navigation'. Francis wrote:

Dickie was one of those sterling, stalwart citizens who make a country great if there are enough of them. He left the Air Ministry to become Chief Navigation Officer of Coastal Command, where he introduced a navigation drill which raised the standards of navigation and with it the standard of safety. Dickie's navigation drill was almost precisely the same as the system I had worked out for navigating to Lord Howe Island and Norfolk Island.

Dickie was working on the new navigation guide, *Air Publication 1234*, which was to replace Kelly's earlier one – perhaps another reason for Kelly's hostility. In early 1943 it was translated into all Allied pilots' languages and inevitably a captured one fell into German hands. Dickie had been rather stumped for chapter headings, so he had borrowed some from Lewis Carroll: six from *Alice's Adventures in Wonderland* and six from *The Hunting of the Snark*. After the war he met the former Luftwaffe Focke-Wulf Fw 200 Condor navigator Dr Karl Karwarth, who in 1943 had been asked to translate the captured *Air Publication 1234*. All was easy enough, reported his former enemy, except the chapter headings: 'Tell me now we are at peace: what on earth was their code?'

Apart from his ease with Dickie, the free-spirited Francis found it hard to fit in with his superiors and the hierarchy of military ranking when outside the confines of Adastral House. And being Francis, he didn't take it upon himself to hide his feelings. No doubt the Whitehall regulars resented a civilian navigator being drafted in to advise them, and no doubt he resented being told what to do by a bunch of blackboard-wallahs, who had probably never navigated further than Dover, and that by train. He amused himself making navigation games for Allen and Unwin, firstly '*Pinpoint the Bomber*' and then a '*Planisphere of Navigations Stars*'.

In early 1943 Francis's boredom was lifted somewhat. Dickie found himself operational, being sent from Adastral House to put his skills to better use as Coastal Command's Chief Navigation Officer, based at their headquarters in Northwood, West London, now the site of the UK Permanent Joint Headquarters. Under his wing, as it were, were Nos. 15, 16, 17, 18 and 19 Groups responsible for patrolling the channels, seas and oceans all around the British Isles. By 1943 most attention was centred on

No. 15 Group, based at Derby House in Liverpool, responsible for fighting the Battle of the Atlantic, protecting convoys and sinking U-boats. (By early 1943 the U-boat fleet had grown to 400. In the first ten days of March alone it had sunk 600,000 tonnes of Allied shipping, operating with some impunity in the Mid-Atlantic Gap out of range of RAF and USAAF air attacks.)

No. 15 Group had nine squadrons, based as far west as possible, either in Northern Ireland or the Hebridean coast of Scotland, in order to be out of range of German bombers and in range of the eastbound convoys and their U-boat predators. Most of the Group's squadrons operated Short S.25 Sunderland flying boats and only two squadrons, 120 and 220, flew B-24 Consolidated Liberator GR1s and Boeing F-17E Mk IIA Flying Fortresses respectively. The Liberator and the Fortress had the longest range available to Coastal Command, the Liberator at 2,400 miles, the Fortress at just under 2,000 miles. In spring 1943 both squadrons were based at RAF Aldergrove, 18 miles north-west of Belfast, the only squadrons so located. I mention all this detail because:

It is at this stage in Francis's war that we come across his mysterious, unofficial visit to Northern Ireland to navigate a Liberator and a Fortress in the Battle of the Atlantic. As Sebastian Cox, Head of Air Historical Branch at RAF Northolt tells me, 'According to his personal record Chichester was then sent to HQ No. 15 Group in Liverpool, again for duties connected to navigation, although somewhat puzzling is the fact that the RAF List continues to show him in AMT's Directorate and not in one of the staff navigation posts at 15 Group. 15 Group was an operational group within Coastal Command, principally responsible for maritime air warfare against German U-boats in the north-west approaches to the UK and the North Atlantic. Navigation was, of course, of supreme importance to Coastal Command aircraft, which had to navigate for very long distances far out into the Atlantic.'

Francis himself is a little more forthcoming in his autobiography, where he writes about his sorties in a Liberator and a Fortress:

> *Convoy escorts and antisubmarine patrols were out for long flights with continuous manoeuvring, such as square searches to be plotted. I took part in one sortie, in a Liberator which was 11 hours and 40 minutes out. We proceeded to 25° W in the Atlantic, and after an oblong search of ships picked up a convoy on the return.*
>
> *Another day I joined a Fortress, for an eight hour thirty-five minutes flight into the Atlantic. I got into hot water with the captain of the aircraft for firing a burst from a .5 machine-gun I was interested in, just as a corvette was passing below.*

Putting all the pieces into place, it is not unreasonable to surmise that Francis's mysterious mission to Liverpool and then Northern Ireland was to brief Dickie Richardson personally on long-range Atlantic navigation practice, including the possible usefulness of the new American LORAN (long-range navigation) radio positioning system. As noted, these long-range flights needed either a Fortress, as flown by No. 120 Squadron, or a Liberator, as flown by No. 220 Squadron. Conveniently both flew out of Aldergrove near Belfast. No doubt Francis reported back to Dickie and no doubt, being Francis, he suggested ways in which matters could be improved.

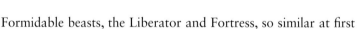

Formidable beasts, the Liberator and Fortress, so similar at first sight – long-range, four-engined Second World War American bombers, yet significantly different for the aircrews who flew – and died – in them. The armchair Air Marshals much preferred the Liberator. Not only could it fly faster and higher and longer and drop more bombs but it was far less expensive and time-consuming to produce and was remarkably reproducible: by July 1945 some 18,482 Liberators had been manufactured by five manufacturers, with the Ford Motor Co. responsible for half of them. But the aircrews much preferred the Fortress. The Liberator was known as the 'flying boxcar' because of its ungainly slab sides and the 'flying coffin' for its frailty under attack, its propensity to catch fire on attack and the near-impossibility of evacuating through the rear-only exit wearing a flying jacket and parachute after attack. They were also harder to fly in formation, with heavy and waffly controls – dead sticks, as the pilots called them. Somehow a 50/50 shot-up Fortress held together and made it home; a 50/50 shot-up Liberator crashed and burned.

I was keen to find out about Francis's wartime exploits and luckily there are examples of each type on display in the UK and enthusiastic curators willing to show me around them. John Delaney looks after the Imperial War Museum's B-17 Boeing Flying Fortress at Duxford and Andrew Simpson keeps the Consolidated B-24 Liberator at the RAF Museum in Hendon.

Let's start with the Fortress. Housed in Duxford's American Air Force Museum behind an ex-Desert Storm eight-engined B-52 Stratofortress and alongside a B-29 'Enola Gay' Superfortress, the B-17 Flying Fortress looks almost quaint. I ask John how Francis's Coastal Command B-17 would have differed from the United States Eight Air Force one we are walking around. He explains: 'Tricked out for Coastal Command, the planes were different enough from the bombers. The side gunners' slots were replaced by windows for observation and the underneath "ball" turret removed for smoother airflow. So more range. Bomb bays took depth charges. And of course the whole plane would have been painted a dull white with RAF roundels.' He opens a tiny hatch on the rear starboard side of the fuselage and we crawl in. 'As you can see, getting in is only marginally easier than getting out', he says, 'especially getting out falling through the air at 300 mph in a spin,

RAF Coastal Command Boeing B17

on fire, wearing a flying jacket and parachute'. The very thought does occur.

Once inside, behind the bomb bay, we can just about stand up but barely move around. 'And this is just with two of us', I say. 'How many did they carry?'

'On a bombing mission a crew of ten. Two pilots. The navigator and seven gunners. The top gunner was also the radio operator, the front gunner also the bombardier.'

'So Pilot Officer Chichester was spared gunning duties?' I ask.

'Two things here. Generally speaking, the navigator was the most educated person on board. In the USAF he had to be an officer. And he was a few years older. The rest of the crew were late teenagers, early twenties. The navigators maybe mid-twenties. And then, of course, they thought the navigator was too genteel to be in direct combat. And then, of course, they all wanted to get home. For which they needed the navigator.'

'So on Francis's sortie, what crew would he have with him?'

'Bear in mind the RAF were perennially short of manpower and Coastal Command even worse. The "Cinderella Service", it was called. Over the Atlantic they wouldn't have had to fight off Messerschmitts, so they would do without the side gunners. Their main problem would be Focke-Wulf Condors.'

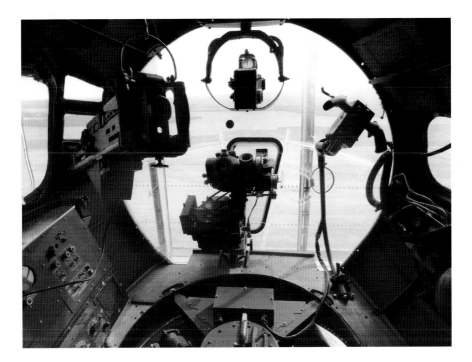

'Which were?'

'Like the Fortress, four-engined bombers converted for long-range reconnaissance, also over the Atlantic, looking for convoys. If a Condor saw an Allied plane it had battle orders to attack it. Our boys did the same if they saw a Condor unawares. So you had two four-engined bombers dogfighting like single-engine fighters.'

'So rear and front gunners only?'

'Yes, plus the top gunner-cum-radio operator. Let's go to the sharp end.'

As we crawl through the bomb bay to the navigators' station in the bubble in front of the pilots, the lack of space through which to squeeze static in a museum – let alone through which to bail out in full kit with a parachute – is made worse by sharp edges and unfolded chamfers. Within seconds I snag my new Christmas present cashmere jumper on an exposed nut.

'Now then', John says, 'crawl in backwards through there'. He is pointing to a 3-foot-square opening in between and in

Francis wartime action view, navigating from the bombardier's seat in a B17

front of the pilots. 'That's where your Francis would have been.' Suddenly an element of space and visibility opens up. On the port side is a small desk, about two foot square, and a chair: the navigator's station. In front of him the bombardier/front gunner's glass turret gives an uninterrupted view of what's ahead.

I ask John about life on board. 'Cold was the worst of it. Coastal Command would have flown lower, but for the Bomber Command crew at 20,000 it was minus 20 or 30. If you took your gloves off to touch something, you stuck to it. So frostbite was a massive early problem. By 1943 they had introduced electric heated suits, which you plugged in, but they were pretty ineffective. So he would have worn one of those under his flying jacket, fully lined boots and helmet, and navigator's gloves, which he would have swapped for proper ones when writing up the log or doing his workings.'

'And if he needed the loo?'

'There was an Elsan right aft, really a potty with a lid. To get there from here … well, you can imagine how undressed you wanted to get to squeeze through versus how warm – if that's the right word – you wanted to stay. Better to hold on if you could.'

'For eight hours.'

As we crawled, scrambled, squeezed, squirmed out of the rear again, thoughts of young crew desperately trying to escape the spinning, burning, hurtling bomber in full kit and parachute, the bravery of it all comes to mind. Even Francis's un-dangerous sorties in to the Atlantic were desperately uncomfortable – and still had the Condor uncertainty. 'Brave men all', John and I agree as we stand up, warm and straight, alongside the fully intact Flying Fortress.

It was with Francis's other plane, the B-24 Liberator, that I hoped to find out more about the navigation practices he was using. Luckily the Liberator and the records are under one roof, the RAF Museum at Hendon. It was lucky, too, that the museum's very helpful curator, Andrew Simpson, is under the same roof. I ask Andy about the navigation equipment Francis would have carried on board. 'In 1943 ... well, for sure a chronometer, in the form of an RAF-issue wristwatch; a bubble sextant – so a sextant with a spirit level basically; dividers; a Dalton computer – a very glorified circular slide rule; a Douglas square-sided protractor; a ruler, known as a straight edge; some pencils and a rubber. And of course an almanac and reduction tables for back-reading the sextant.'

Navigation was principally by dead reckoning and, where Atlantic cloud conditions allowed, bubble sextant. The theory and practice of dead reckoning were second nature to Francis. On the Fortress or Liberator he would ask the bombardier/front gunner to trade places for a few minutes, while he trained the drift wires on the bombsights on the prevailing sea lanes over the waves. If he took three drift readings from three different headings it was easy to work out the wind speed and direction; knowing the true air speed it was simple to calculate the ground speed and enter it in the log, this being done every hour.

RAF Coastal Command Liberator

On the Fortress and Liberator there is an astrodome between the pilots and the front gunner but I imagine astronavigation in the North Atlantic was limited by cloud cover. Optimally they would fly at 5,000 ft, high enough to spot convoys but not so high as to miss tell-tale signs of U-boat wakes.

'Francis mentions being out in the Liberator for eleven hours and forty minutes, reaching 25 degrees west. That's about a 2,000-mile round trip.' The crew quarters were only slightly less cramped than the Fortress but he was up there for three hours longer. 'It was cold too, of course, and noisy', says Andy, looking out at the inner port engine's prop just a few feet away from the navigator's perch.

The sorties excitements over, Francis had to moulder at the Air Ministry for only a few more months; maybe more smoulder than moulder, as in his own words: 'By the middle of 1943 I reckoned that I had written 500,000 words on navigation, and was becoming difficult to live or work with'. But relief was at hand: 'I was offered a post at the Empire Central Flying School at RAF Hullavington in Wiltshire, with no official status and the rank of Flying Officer, the lowest commissioned rank except Pilot Officer. I accepted what looked like an interesting job.' And so it proved to be; from now on Francis could say he had a good war. All that rankled was rank:

> *For my job at the Air Ministry I had been upgraded to the rank of Flight Lieutenant, but that was as high as I could rise. I was not officially allowed to fly, not officially allowed to navigate, and I was not permitted to wear pilot's or navigator's wings on my tunic. One of the results of this was that whenever I visited an operational mess, unless I knew one of the members of the mess personally, I would soon be quietly edged out of any group of*

operational pilots talking at the bar. I could only have an
administrative job.

In the National Archives at Kew I look through the Operations
Record Book for the Empire Central Flying School at RAF
Hullavington and can see what happened, operationally, on
every day of Francis's time there, starting with his arrival:

4.7.43 F/O (A/F/L) CHICHESTER (61089) *posted to*
D.D.T. (Nav) *for Navigation duties (supernumerary)*

D.D.T. was the Deputy Directorate of Training. One hopes they
meant supernumerary in the additional staff and not the unneeded
staff sense of the word. The school had been started in April
1942 to train Allied pilots, mostly from the Commonwealth, in
the latest instruction methods, so that they in turn could instruct
their own pilots. Its mission statement was 'To train instructors,
test individual aircrew, audit the Flying Training System, give
advice on flying training and provide a formation aerobatics
display team'.

The base was divided into two squadrons, the Handling
Squadron, which was involved in exploring the outer limits
of a plane's capabilities and writing remedial reports, and the
Examining Squadron, in which Francis served, instructing and
examining the pilots, all officers. Francis describes his duties thus:
'My job, principally, was to brief the pilots on the navigation of
their flights, and to devise navigation exercises for them.'

The intake of pilot students on Francis's first full course in
September 1943 was typical: '46 names in all, 12 Canadians, 3
Australians, 2 New Zealand, 3 US Navy, 1 Rhodesian, 2 South
African, 3 representatives from Bomber Command, 2 from
Fighter and TAF, 2 from Coastal Command, 12 from FTC, 1
Naval Officer and 1 Belgian'. Francis noted that:

We ran courses for officers such as Chief Flying Instructors with ranks from Flight Lieutenant to Group Captain. They were mostly pilots drawn from every arm of the Service and from every ally. In one course we might have Fleet Air Arm, Army and RAF officers, together with Australians, New Zealanders, South Africans, Poles, Frenchmen, Norwegians and Americans. We never had US Air Force and US Navy pilots at the same time, because they did not mix well.

The course was intensive in the air and on the ground. Every weekday night there was a lecture, mostly on aspects of flying machines and how to survive them: 'First Night Flight', 'Operational D.R.', 'Aircrew Duties', 'Cockpit Gadgetry and its Limitations', 'Bomber Flying Control', 'Command Synthetic Training', 'Met Flights', 'Western Desert Operations', 'Pathfinders', 'Luftwaffe Training', 'Coastal Command Navigation' (given by his old chief Group Captain Dickie Richardson), 'Low Level Attack and R.P.', 'Fighters in the Western Desert', 'Principles of Aircraft Recognition', 'Intruder Operations', 'Photographic Interpretation', 'Functions of an M.U.', 'Army Air Support in the Mediterranean', 'Medical Aspects on Ditching', 'Lack of Confidence', 'Glider Operations for D-Day'. These aeronautical themes were interspersed with lectures on current affairs: 'Russia', 'The BBC at War', 'America', 'Life in Occupied Belgium', 'Escape form Germany', and so on. Another old friend, the First World War ace Lord Douglas Hamilton from the Royal Aero Club and Francis's formative suicide squadron, was a frequent guest lecturer.

Flight Lieutenant Chichester gave three lectures: 'Plotting', 'The Value of Observer Navigation to Pilots' and 'Pilot Navigation Exercises in AP 1388a'; later – in December 1944, when the war was almost won – he could be more esoteric: 'Astro Navigation in the Pacific'. Saturday evenings were set asides for debates. Francis took part too:

*15.5.44 Motion: That alcohol is a help not a hindrance.
Proposed by F/L Chichester and S/L Airey, Opposed by
S/L Hay and Major Hayden Thomas
The motion was defeated.*

(Major Hayden Thomas, from the SAAF, was killed in night
training at Castle Combe a month later. The Operations
Record Book has frequent entries reminding us of the dangers
of advanced flight training, recorded typically with the words:
'Killed in Flying Accident, Multiple Injuries'.)

Another motion, three months later' was 'That in the opinion
of this house Flying is an Invention of the Devil'. It was carried
43 to 28.

It was the Handling Squadron that had a more amusing war.
Their duties included putting a long list of fighters, bombers and
trainers through their paces and then writing Pilot Notes. Their
jobs seem to have had the glamour of a test pilot's without the
obvious drawback. Francis remembered with enthusiasm there
being thirty-seven different aircraft types at Hullavington.

───❧───

Flight training still happens at Hullavington but on a much more
modest scale. It is now home to 621 Volunteer Gliding Squadron,
which has the very worthy intention of training Air Cadets
from the age of thirteen to fly for free. I am fortunate enough
to be shown around by Squadron Adjutant Flight Lieutenant
Nick Blake and Squadron Administrator Neville Cullingford.
Although not officially part of the RAF, many of the cadets go
on to join the RAF or Fleet Air Arm or commercial aviation. The
ethos of the squadron is very much RAF, with the emphasis on
discipline, teamwork and respect; I imagine it does the teenagers
the world of good. Run on an entirely voluntary basis by the
instructors and using long-serving Grob gliders that have seen as
many as 25,000 launches, in its own way 621 Squadron is just

as admirable an occupant of Hullavington as the Empire Central Flying School was sixty years ago.

The enormous runways are still remarkably intact considering their age and heavy use all those years ago, nowadays they're used by *Top Gear* for filming squirming super cars and various track day companies – in fact any commercial use above a car boot sale is welcome. The largest hangers are in commercial use too, by karting and storage companies.

The base is now divided in two: 621 Volunteer Gliding Squadron uses the runways and principal hangar while the Lutyens-designed buildings and parade and sports grounds belong to 9 Regiment Royal Logistics Corps. Only a rather jumpable fence separates the two. Station Staff Officer Peter Murton and his collie, Sam, are kind enough to show me around Francis's old wartime base.

Francis's HQ at RAF Hullavington

At first sight Hullavington is exactly as Francis would have remembered it. Being large and solid, the Lutyens buildings reflect a time when the forces weren't under constant budget attack by the Treasury. The mess building in particular is most impressive, with wood panelling and an eighty-place oak dining table and mahogany and leather chairs. The façade of the orchestra gallery is lined with the emblems of the services that Francis taught: in the centre the Empire Central Flying School and the Royal Canadian Air Force, and on either side the South African Air Force, Royal Australian Air Force, Royal New Zealand Air Force, Rhodesian Army Air Force, Indian Air Force and so on. One can almost smell the pipe smoke, hear the banter and see the flying suits. For a lover of aviation it must have been a paid paradise.

Beyond the dining room is the library, where Peter considers that the lectures and debates would have been held. Upstairs are the officers' rooms. No one knows in which one Francis spent his eighteen months there; but as they are all the same, I can say that there is more than enough room to swing a cat and still have a splash in the enormous basins.

What has changed a lot, and for the better, is that the 400 soldiers now have sufficient space for their families, so the base is now home to 1,200 souls. Of course the horrible modern buildings that house the families jar uncomfortably alongside their Lutyens counterparts, but space is space. When on home leave Francis tried to persuade Sheila to come with him back to Wiltshire, but that would have meant sharing a house with other wives – not really Sheila's thing; she preferred to take her chances with the doodlebugs in Essex.

Not that Francis wasn't amusing himself at work:

At the end of each course we used to have a navigation race with twelve light two-seater Miles Magister training planes in it. This was fine training for the sort of navigation that is really valuable to a pilot. We made it a kind of treasure hunt. For instance, in one race they had to fly to Stowe, the public school, and count the number of tennis courts there, multiply the number by x, and then fly in that direction for 5 miles to find another clue. These races were immense sport, and very popular.

Another of my jobs at Hullavington was to devise methods for teaching 'nought feet' navigation to pilots intruding into enemy territory when they would be unable to take their eyes off the ground ahead, and must be

jinking all the time to avoid anti-aircraft fire. It amounted to map-reading without maps, in other words all the map-reading had to be done on the ground before taking off. It sounds an impossible requirement but, with the right methods and plenty of drill, pilots could find a haystack 50 miles off while dodging about all the way to it.

By April 1943 there was a feeling in the air that the war was winnable and the impression arising from studying life at Hullavington is one of the last big push: the war was ours to lose,

Miles Magister RAF trainer and Francis's weekend warrior

not theirs to win. Consequently the rules were relaxed about Francis being grounded because his uniform was without wings, the chiefs realising that he could do a better job of teaching navigation if he could reconnoitre training routes first and so devise more testing drills and write more telling exercises. An added bonus was finding any of his lost ducklings:

> *If any of my students were lost on a navigational exercise I used to spend many hours in my light aeroplane searching where I estimated them to be.*
>
> *Two South African majors were lost on one exercise, and I hunted for days among the Welsh hills. Three months later, when we had given up all hope for them, word came through that they were prisoners of war. They had flown the reciprocal heading of their compass, south-east instead of north-west. When they crossed the English Channel they thought it was the Bristol Channel. They were grateful when an airfield put up a cone of searchlights for them, and it was not until they had finished their landing run on the airstrip and a German soldier poked a Tommy gun into the cockpit that they realised that they were not on an English airfield.*

As the war progressed he was even allowed to fly his Magister home at weekends:

> *I used to land at Fairlop, a mile from our house at Chigwell Row. One morning, just before I took off, a cryptic message came through from Air Traffic Control London saying that I must take great care while flying and look out for anything strange. I usually flew low, because it was more interesting, and I was surprised to see all the children dash across a playground and take cover from my little monoplane as I flew over. When this happened a*

second time, I realised that they were taking cover from me, and when it happened a third time, I wondered what it was all about.

Back home he soon discovered Pages had been damaged and the leaves blown off its trees by a doodlebug. The schoolchildren thought Francis's plane was an unguided missile. Actually, his war didn't finish with an explosion but rather petered out without comment from him or Sheila or any official record of him ever having left Hullavington. I note from the RAF list that he was discharged on 27 September 1945. But as we will see in the next chapter, he had his eyes on new horizons long before then anyway.

NOTES:

13. Mary Baker Eddy, *Science and Health with Key to the Scriptures*, p. 587.

I said, 'There's the shore; you can swim for it if you wish, but Gipsy Moth is racing on'.

CHAPTER 7

Gipsy Moth II

Seven years after the war I was attacked by an overpowering
urge for some practical navigation. So I decided to go sailing
or gliding, and plumped for sailing, because it was more
sociable; the family could weekend in a yacht, but hardly
in a glider. My first sail (as crew) was to the Baltic. That
cruise was not a success, but it did result in my becoming
an ocean racer.

I decided that sailing was going to be a misery for me if
I was going to worry about the weather all the time, about
getting caught out in a gale and being fearful of my gear in
a blow. If I was going to sail, I must learn to do it properly. I
thought that the Royal Ocean Racing Club sailors would be
the ones to learn from, because they raced in all weathers.

Thus in the summer of 1953, at the age of fifty-two, Francis
first took to the waves; even he would have been astounded to
have known that just thirteen years later he would be the most
famous sailor in the world.

He had spent those seven years since the war building up
his map publishing business, working and living at home, 9 St
James's Place, an elegant four-storey William and Mary house
tucked in behind the Ritz and Green Park: very much London
SW1. He later recalled that in 1944 his thoughts had turned to
what he would do when peace came:

I wanted to get into the air travel business. When on leave I marked off an area in the West End of London where I thought the air travel business would be centred after the war. This was a rectangle, with Piccadilly in the centre. I hired a taxi and drove through every street in the area noting down all the houses for sale. In the end we bought one in St James's Place.

The 'we' who bought the house was actually Sheila, as Francis was still without funds. As she remembers:

In August 1944 Francis came home on leave and said I ought to buy myself a house in London. This was at the height of the doodlebugs and London was pretty empty. He brought me to 9 St James's Place, I walked into this house and fell in love with it at once.

The Chichesters moved in: along with Francis and Sheila were George, by now 19 and about to join the Merchant Navy, Dimbleby the dog and Francis's fellow navigators, the bumblebees, whose hive was soon up on the roof.

It was a brave move – and typical of Sheila that she made it. Great property fortunes were won and lost during the war. The falling bombs were a form of Russian roulette. A walk around the St James's area now shows how many post-war buildings there are; in 1944 it must have looked rubble-ruined. Among the bombed neighbours was the Royal Ocean Racing Club at 19 St James's Place. Sheila gambled and she won – unlike my grandmother, who sold her house in Kensington for £500 in 1942; family folklore says that everyone thought the buyer was mad. But the house survived the bombing and the buyer proclaimed sane, even wise. It is now the Moroccan embassy.

There is not much to report from outside sources about those seven post-war years: Francis had demobbed and his service

Francis and his fellow navigators, bees, on the roof at St. James

records ceased and the press cuttings and friends' memoirs of later years had yet to start. Instead we have to rely on his and Sheila's respective autobiographies. Francis gives the seven years only a few paragraphs, mostly about Francis Chichester Ltd, his map and guide publishing business.

'A friend suggested that I should make jigsaw puzzles. There were 15,000 maps left over from my 'Pinpoint the Bomber' game. I bought a ton or so of cardboard, designed some cutters, and turned these maps into jigsaw maps.' He made a series of jigsaw maps, 'The Heart of London', 'The Heart of Paris', 'Shakespeare Country' and 'London Zoo':

> I set off on a sales campaign and sold the first 5,000 to big stores and other shops. I came back elated thinking, 'Hurrah! I'm in business', and promptly made 10,000 more.
>
> On my next sales round the buyers told me that the puzzles had not sold as well as they had hoped. I decided that this was due to using an old map, so I designed a new one. Then one day a man walked into my office and said, 'This picture map of London is the best I've seen; if you will take it off this lousy piece of cardboard I'll order 5,000'. And so I became a map publisher by accident.

He was 'the designer, producer and salesman, I typed all the letters, did the bookkeeping, invoiced the goods, parcelled them up and delivered them'. He was pleased to have fallen into map making, which was

> the right business for me, for I have been involved with maps ever since I made my first chart for my Tasman flight. My adventures with faulty maps when flying, and my search for methods of teaching fighter pilots how to meet map-read at nought feet without using a map, left

me with strong views on what should be put into a map
and, equally important, what should be left out.

However, the business was surviving rather than prospering, with Francis keeping one room for himself in which he slept, worked and lived, while renting out all the other rooms to provide an income for the family.

Where was Sheila all these seven years? Luckily, in her autobiography she is far more revealing. A Craven family friend, the Earl of Cardigan, had offered them Fisherman's Cottage, a water bailiff's shack on the River Kennett by Savernake Forest near Marlborough. Francis took to it immediately for the mile of trout fishing and 750 acres of rough shooting. Sheila noted that

the cottage had no drains, no water except by pump and
of course no electricity. At first we used to drive down,
Francis and I together and our dog Dimbleby, and camp
there. During that first winter we would make marvellous
blazing fires and were blissfully happy. We both loved it
there. I couldn't get over the peace, with no air raids. I
stopped worrying about money. I became a fatalist.

So blissfully happy were they that soon she felt 'a heightened pleasure in everything. The trees looked more brilliant, the autumn tints and sky looked brighter, everything seemed marvellous'. She was, of course, pregnant.

Giles was born on 29 July 1946. Typically, Sheila was far ahead of her time, opting for a natural childbirth at home under the auspices of Dr Pink, 'a priest as well as the doctor, a vegetarian, very gentle, very wise, he used to come and talk to me and from then on I was extremely happy'. At Christmas that year the three Chichesters and Dimbleby drove down to the cottage; only one Chichester drove back: Francis. Sheila and Giles – joined latterly by the au-pair, Siglinda – were to spend

Sheila, Giles, Francis and Dimbleby at Fisherman's Cottage

Giles's christening

the next six years living there more or less full-time – and more or less alone.

Sheila remembers Francis's visits wistfully:

He used to come down to the cottage at weekends, arriving on Saturday night looking very tired indeed. He used to sleep all day Sunday, and on Monday he went out shooting all day. It was rather lonely for me, but he felt desperately cooped up living in one room in London and needed this break of an out-of-door life.

I did feel rather cut off from Francis. Especially since I had become such a keen vegetarian, to see all the shooting and killing of game going on around was trying, but I had to make the best of it. It was difficult for Francis too, for men like to feel they're bringing home a nice present for their wife to roast. I don't think I really recommend husbands and wives splitting up like that. It is lonely for both, and you don't seem to see each other's point of view.

Towards the end of this semi-separation their autobiographies coincide. After his unsuccessful cruise of the Baltic in the summer of 1953 Francis decided to buy his own boat.

I said nothing to Sheila about this, because I felt sure she would disapprove when we were so hard up, and I was determined to get a yacht. I went round looking at various likely yachts for sale, and finally bought a day sailor with a horrible name of Florence Edith.

Francis paid £1,150 in September 1953 for the yacht and set about sailing her around her Essex moorings as much as he could at weekends. Sheila must have been feeling lonelier and lonelier in her river cottage in Wiltshire.

Pretty soon the day came when 'I had to break the news to Sheila. Expecting a terrific rocket for my extravagance, imagine my astonishment when she said, "Oh, I always wanted to sail. What an excellent idea!"' No doubt seeing something of Francis again only added to the excellent idea.

A few weekends later Sheila arrived to join Francis for her maiden voyage from Brightlingsea but no one there had seen or heard of the *Florence Edith* or Francis Chichester. At last an old fisherman told her, 'Oh you mean that there yellow boat? She be lying on Buxey Sands 10 miles out. 'Tis lucky 'tis fine weather, otherwise she'd be sunk when t'sea rises. What's more, there be thick fog coming up, and if she do get off the sands, it'll be a long time before you see her here again. My advice to you is to go home. She won't be in till morning. If then, with this dreadful fog.'

Sheila was staying with one of her more doughty cousins nearby and when she reported all this she was urged to get a divorce immediately; but, as Francis remembers, 'she decided to defer that'. Sheila had her sail the next morning, a particularly idyllic one, thank heavens, and she enjoyed it enormously. She was soon redesigning *Florence Edith*'s interior. Together 'they rebuilt the cabin, making berths for six, which cost as much as the boat'. Francis renamed her *Gipsy Moth II* after the brave little biplane that had taken him half-way round the world. Two *Gipsy Moths* later he would complete the journey.

Now change was in the air for the Chichesters. The east coast sailing meant that time in westerly Wiltshire was harder to find. More importantly, Giles was now seven and needed to go to a 'proper' school. Neither Francis nor Sheila had much truck with boarding schools: Francis's experiences were only forty years behind him and the scars were still sore; the homeopath in Sheila thought that parent-child separation barbaric. And then there's the seven-year itch; time for a change. And change they did.

Sometime between the unsuccessful Baltic cruise and buying *Florence Edith*, Francis stepped out of no. 9 St James's Place, turned right, then quickly right again and walked the few yards up the cul-de-sac of St James's Place to nos 19 and 20, the clubhouse of the Royal Ocean Racing Club. He asked about ocean racing and how to start. It was agreed that a young member, presently busy but free soon, would come to no. 9 in an hour to tell him all about the club and yacht racing. That young member then is my neighbour now, John Roome. John went on to become the Commodore of the RORC and an internationally influential figure in the world of ocean yacht racing. We are both members of the Royal Cruising Club and the Royal Yacht Squadron, as indeed was Francis and is Giles. Now in comfortable retirement next to the Solent, John is kind enough to delve deep into his memory of all things Chichester.

'He only lived around the corner and so I knocked on the door, introduced myself as being from the club. We chatted for an hour or so about racing, how to get started, who to crew for, crewing on the club boats, what boat works best, all that sort of thing.

'I remembered pretty soon that a few months earlier he had put a notice up on our board looking for a navigator's berth. Another member had told me that he was in fact an air navigator. Now air navigators were never very popular as they had a reputation for wanting to go from A to B in a straight line, putting members on the rocks. Probably unfair, but that was how it was.

'I think that's what prompted him to buy what became *Gipsy Moth II*, the fact that he couldn't find a berth of his own.

'To qualify as a member he would've had to sail 500 miles offshore. Same as now. He did a couple of channel races, crewing on our club boat *Griffin*.'

John shakes his head and laughs when I ask him about *Griffin*. 'Oh, she was an appalling boat. She had been given to the club by some members. She was incredibly heavy. Gaff cutter. She had no engine. Impossible to handle in light airs. Used to come a day late in most races, you know. But she was ideal as a club boat in many ways. She had twenty lines off the mast and she kept everyone busy. The tradition was to take twelve beginners. The captain could choose his two mates, the rest were beginners or miles builders. But she did a wonderful job of starting people off because there was always something to do. Of course there was no way to keep warm or anything resembling creature comforts. Paraffin stove cooking, so primitive, but hot and hearty, as we used to say.

'The worst was the 1956 Channel race when we had two gales. There was one wave she fell off and she never really recovered from that. We had to pump the whole time. Safe harboured in Newhaven of all places. As a result of that we retired her. Luckily Owen Aisher, amongst others, gave us *Yeoman III*, which was a suburb yacht and she became *Griffin II*. We continued with successor *Griffins* until the Fastnet of '79, when we lost *Griffin VI* in the middle of that terrible night.'

John has been kind enough to delve into the RORC archives and dig out some of the race programmes from the 1950s.

Francis's first RORC offshore race

'This looks like Francis's first race', he says. 'The 1954 North Sea Race. Started on the fourth of June. Seems like he came practically last, poor chap. Mind you, he had the smallest boat. Class C, we'd only just introduced it.'

2. North Sea Race (Class III continued)

Yacht	Owner	Division	Yacht Club	Pts.	Elapsed Time	Corrected Time	Prizes
					hr. mn. sc.	*hr. mn. sc.*	
SYLPHIDE	C. H. Costello	Open	Nav. (Port.)	22	47 11 40	31 39 12	
ALBATROS II	Kon-Mar. Y.C.	Open	Mar.	21	49 39 42	31 45 07	
LAERTES	Brig. W. G. Carr	Open	N. & S.	20	48 38 53	32 16 40	
BANJAARD	Capt. A. W. Joppe	A	Maas.	19	48 34 00	32 18 58	1st "A" Div.
ANN SPEED	John Lewis Partnership's S.C.	Open	Lew.	18	48 40 16	32 19 39	
NAIANDE	V. Powell	Open	Msa.	17	46 49 00	32 48 32	
PERIWINKLE	W. Johnston	Open	For.	16	47 07 20	33 05 21	
BANDOR	J. R. Grundy	A	Cch.	15	48 29 00	33 13 32	2nd "A" Div.
SYRINX	D. P. S. Fox	A	Msa.	14	47 56 23	33 35 29	3rd "A" Div.
PANACEA	Dr. F. R. Stansfield and M. J. Slater	Open	Har.	13	52 16 30	33 54 57	
CONCARA	Major H. G. Moore	A	Art.	12	49 08 30	34 28 58	
KALYPSO	Dr. Th. F. Bloem	Open	Maas.	11	50 54 44	34 29 35	
STORMMEEUW	Kon-Mar. Y.C.	A	Mar.	10	55 37 05	35 35 44	
HARVESTA	P. B. Frost	Open	Mal.	9	54 55 00	38 19 54	
GIPSY MOTH	Francis Chichester	Open	—	8	60 52 00	38 44 52	
MODALIMAR	Kon-Mar. Y.C.	A	Mar.	7	60 47 00	39 40 02	
ELIZABETHAN	Lt. Cdr. J. N. Wise	A	Esx.	1	Gave up		
QUINTET	R. R. Clifford	A	Med.	1	Gave up		

Class I, Haaks Cup—FOXHOUND
Class II, Goeree Cup—UOMIE
Class III, Maas Cup—MINDY

Francis rightly thought he hadn't done too badly for a near-beginner in one of the smallest boats: 'I had been in only one race before, and was the only member of the crew who had been in any. She was only 8 tons and 24 feet on the waterline, the minimum length permitted to enter for RORC races'. He added, rather touchingly: 'Sheila had so much faith in me as a navigator that she expected me to win, and was most disappointed when I telephoned from Rotterdam to say that we had come nearly last.'

A month later Francis was in the Solent for the Cowes to La Coruna Race. All we learn from John's records is that *Gipsy Moth* 'gave up'; Francis makes no mention of the race either, perhaps because, as Sheila recalls, they were dismasted off Guernsey and she took the opportunity to fly down there for a mini-break on board.

Two weeks later he was back in Cowes for the Dinard Race and some eerie excitement:

Unfortunately there was a weakness in the new masthead fitting which had been specially designed for her, and the top of the mast snapped off in the middle of the night in some dirty weather west of the Channel Islands. From the cabin it sounded like the crack of doom, and when I darted up into the cockpit there was a tangle of shrouds, halyards and wires wherever I shone the torch over the boat or in the water. Then one of the crew dropped the torch overboard with the light still shining, and as it sank getting fainter and fainter, it looked like a ghost leaving us for a better world.

Francis set up a watch system to get them through the night and awoke for his own turn to find the pre-dawn 'graveyard' watch fast asleep. In the daylight they cleared up the mess of shrouds and stays and lines from the broken mast, set a small staysail and headed for Guernsey. With this minimal sail and a strong current they were being taken towards the rocks. Francis noted:

*One of the crew was a very devout Roman Catholic,
and I noticed his lips praying nervously as we were being
carried towards the rocks. We cleared the point, sailed
into St Peter Port and tacked up to a mooring buoy by
carrying from one side of the deck to the other the boom
to which the staysail was attached.*

In that race *Gipsy Moth* really did come last – but in the next
one, from Brixham to Belle-Île, did one better: sixteenth out of
seventeen.

Francis was typically matter-of-fact about his new sport: 'In
my first season I sailed that boat 2,510 miles, including three
races. Our racing record was one of the worst in the club, but I
was learning.'

The 1955 season started with the Southsea to Harwich Race
in May. *Gipsy Moth II* finished ninth out of fourteen in forty-
four hours; the winner, *Foxhound*, only took ten hours less. No
longer last, or nearly last, Francis really was learning.

'You see here', John says, handing me the programme, 'The
Southsea to Harwich was won by *Foxhound*. She was a sister
ship to the famous *Bloodhound*. She was skippered by our
most glamorous member, the Hon. Ray Pitt-Rivers, who was
also a famous actress; most people knew her as Mary Hinton.
Eventually she became Vice-Commodore. A very striking figure
she was.' John smiles at a particularly vivid memory. 'She lived
in a big house to the north as you enter the Beaulieu River. I
expect you know it?'

'Lepe House, perhaps?'

'Yes, that's it. Maybe that's why he came to Beaulieu in the
first place? A lot of RORC boats were berthed there for the
Solent races.'

'Actually, it wasn't the reason', I reply. 'He had close family
connections in the area. His first cousin Sir John Chichester,
who would have been the eleventh baronet, had married Lord

Rare photograph of Gipsy Moth II, off Cowes

Montagu of Beaulieu's eldest sister, Anne. Sir John and Anne lived there and of course introduced him to the Montagu family.'

The line continues today as Sir John and Anne's son and the twelfth baronet is my friend and neighbour Jamie Chichester, who was only just born when Francis completed his first race. He attended the knighting ceremony at Greenwich on day release from Eton a dozen years later.

Actually the most fruitful Beaulieu-Chichester connection is not family but another neighbour, the ex-Buckler's Hard harbour master Bill Grindey. Bill lived for most of his working life in one of those picturesque shipwrights' cottages in Buckler's Hard that line the gravel slipway down to the Beaulieu River. Retired now for twenty years, he lives in rather the opposite, a modern bungalow in the modern town of Dibden Purlieu, just outside the New Forest limits. He and his wife Rene are clearly making up for all those years without a garden as a horticultural miracle awaits the visitor at the back of the house. To one side stands the smartest garden shed in Hampshire, complete with Union flag on a varnished pole and a Harbour Master nameplate above the door. As all about the Grindeys is so present and correct, I suggest that in this land-locked context the Union flag could be called the Union Jack; Bill remains unsure of taking such liberties with naval tradition.

Bill's earliest memories of Francis are from 1954. He had started working in the old Agamemnon boatyard as an apprentice in 1948 and then in 1952 he was sent to Egypt on National Service with the Parachute Regiment. He came back in 1954 and found *Gipsy Moth II* in the yard. 'I remember her in the yard as the engineers had to make a new stem shoe as he raced her so hard. She was an eight-tonner. He was a hard sailor.'

Francis rather whimsically recalls that time in the yard too:

I changed her from sloop to cutter rig. With her mainsail, staysail and yankee she carried 540 square feet of sail. I had one brilliant idea after another for speeding her up.

For example at great trouble and expense I streamlined her sharp-edged iron keel with a false wooden keel, bolted on below. It made not the slightest difference to her performance.

A week later Bill and I meet again at Buckler's Hard marina. Bill has commandeered the harbour master's launch for a tour of Francis's Beaulieu River moorings. On a mooring opposite lies Bill's own boat. 'Only two people have been given the Freedom of the Beaulieu River', he says, 'Sir Francis and me. I was harbour master in '58, 24 years old. Fifty years I served.' We motor for half a minute upriver, around the first bend to where the river twists west again.

'This is where *Gipsy Moth II* lay', Bill says, slipping the launch into neutral as we hover around the spot. 'He liked working on her on his own, could be down here for days on end. He used to row up to the hard: the marina was twenty years coming.'

'No outboard?' I ask.

'There was a British Seagull, but he could never get it started. No one could, those things.' We both laugh at the memory of recalcitrant British Seagull outboards and flaying starter strings and fraying tempers.

Bill's memories of Francis and Sheila cover thirty years, from Francis's lung cancer, likely caused from paint-stripping *Gipsy Moth II*, right here where we are floating, to the glory days of *Gipsy Moth III* – 'Sir Francis's favourite yacht, his most personal one' – to the trials and tribulations and eventual triumph of *Gipsy Moth IV*, to the last British waters passage of *Gipsy Moth V*. For now, he gives a passing memory of Francis and his time on *Gipsy Moth II*: 'He saw me passing by one day on the river. I don't normally drink during the day but we polished off Lady Chichester's sherry, which she never forgave us both for first time it happened. Happened more than once too. He used to say 'Drink up, Bill, Sheila will be descending upon us at any moment!'

The 1955 season finished with Francis's first Fastnet Race. He was climbing up the rankings with every outing, this time finishing tenth out of twenty in six days and eight hours, only thirty-six hours behind the winner, the American Dick Nye in his much larger yacht, *Carina*. But the constant stresses and strains on his fifty-four year-old body and the way he was continually pushing himself harder and harder were starting to fight back. At the end of the Fastnet he had to be helped out of the cockpit and went off to see a specialist. He was diagnosed with chronic arthritis. Visiting the hospital to be treated with the other arthritic patients only made him more distressed. After two months of this, Sheila insisted he see her nature-cure doctor, Dr Latto, who said: 'Ask your fellow patients how long they have been receiving this treatment and then decide yourself whether it seems likely to cure you.' Francis reflected:

> *That made me think hard, and as a result I underwent a severe course of nature cure treatment at Enstone. Fortunately the treatment succeeded; it seemed to take a long time, but by the next spring I was a fit man. I started a hard season's racing in* Gipsy Moth II.

Actually, the first race of the 1956 season wasn't so hard; not only that, but he won it! How so? Francis explained:

> *The first race of the season was the 220-mile race from Southsea to Harwich by way of the Hinder Lightship in the North Sea.* Gipsy Moth II *won this race outright. It sounds terrific, but the truth is that the going was very slow in light airs as far as the Dover Straits, and many of the other competitors gave up. One of our own crew said we must stop racing and put him ashore. I said, 'There's the shore; you can swim for it if you wish, but* Gipsy Moth *is racing on'.*

What is becoming clear by now is how much time Francis was spending on his yacht racing – and so how little time running the map and guide book business. It's all very well racing from Southsea to Harwich but then one has to get back from Harwich to the Solent. What with the day or two of preparation before the race, the race itself and the ceremony at the end, the voyage back and the packing away, a simple RORC 220-miler like the Southsea to Harwich would take the best part of eight days, light airs notwithstanding. But Francis took even more time off than this: the Southsea to Harwich was only the first leg of the North Sea Race from Harwich to the Hook of Holland. *Gipsy Moth II* came twentieth out of fifty. Even pressing on, Francis must have taken twenty days off; and this was still only May.

He made up time back in the office in June and July but took most of August off for the Cowes to San Sebastián Race, then a week in Spain followed by the second leg, San Sebastián to Belle Île. The plan was for Sheila and Giles to join him for a leisurely cruise back to the Beaulieu River. Neptune, however, had made another plan. As Sheila recalled:

It was one of my most frightening passages, partly because Giles was involved. The weather was so rough that we had to wait and in the end the rest of the crew went off, leaving Francis, myself, Giles and our crew Stormy Nichol to get the boat home. We left with a very bad weather forecast but Francis seemed frantic to get away. I could never argue with him and he just sailed. A friend of ours saw us leave and said 'That man wants his head looking to, sailing with the wife and child aboard'.

It soon blew up very, very nasty weather. We were out in the Bay of Biscay, water was coming over, and I felt very sick. Giles started being sick every few minutes which worried me very much: it is bad for a child of only eight.

Francis wanted to stay out to sea but as concession to his crew made for Concarneau. Sheila again:

> *The seas were running so high that whole place seem swollen. We were wet through and through. Giles was marvellous; I did admire the child.*
>
> *Next day I told Francis I was going to leave him and Stormy to bring the boat up to Dinard: Giles and I would meet him there. By great good luck I not only got a nice room in a hotel but a bathroom too. 'Very extravagant to have a bathroom', Francis said. I went out for a walk. When I came back, to my great amusement, there in my hotel bedroom was Stormy asleep on the bed and Francis wallowing in the bath, both very happy.*

Stormy then had to depart for work, leaving the three Chichesters to bring the boat home. For Sheila 'It was a ghastly business getting into St Peter Port, Guernsey. When we finally reached it, people said they were thinking of sending out the lifeboat. Finally Giles said, "I want to fly home, Mummy, I don't think I can go on." Sheila agreed: neither could she. 'Although Francis said we were disgusting to desert him and were a rotten crew, I stuck to my point that we must leave the boat. There are times when one must be disciplined and admit defeat.' A very Sheila-ish statement, that one.

So that summer was work mixed with play, weekdays in London and weekends on the Beaulieu River. By now his family friendships had led Francis to be a frequent guest of the Montagus at Palace House in Beaulieu, as frequent entries in the Visitors Book confirm. I sought out another friend and neighbour (sorry about all the friends and neighbours) Belinda, Lady Montagu, Lord Montagu's wife during the Chichester years and mother of more friends and neighbours, Ralph and Mary. Belinda now lives on a farmhouse in the heart of the New Forest, a few miles north of the Beaulieu River and the Beaulieu Estate. We meet on a lovely summer's morning, her enthusiasm for plants and flowers flowing from the garden to the conservatory to the sitting room. And pets: 'I'm always looking after other people's pets', she says as we wade through scurrying dogs and cats. The canary in the brass bell cage tweets in agreement.

'So many memories', she smiles. I mention that Edward has shown me the numerous Francis and Sheila entries in the Palace House Visitors Book. 'Yes, they used to come to Palace House all the time. Of course his *Gipsy Moth*s were always on the River. Edward gave him a free mooring and later the Freedom of the Beaulieu River.

'He came here because of Anne [Lady Chichester] marrying Johnny [Sir John Chichester]. Johnny was a sideways uncle of sorts. You know the Chichesters, all somehow remotely related!

'Sheila rather ruled the roost. She was strong woman, powerfully built too. She was a very avid vegetarian, and he loved a bit of fish when she wasn't looking. She was very strict about this and I remember having him to lunch at Palace House and he fairly wolfing down the fish with a naughty look of pure pleasure. Sea bass from our river, probably. Later she always said she cured his cancer with her avid diet.'

I asked if she had eaten on board any of the *Gipsy Moth*s.

'Oh yes, and one always offered to bring the picnic. One had to be frightfully careful not to have meat anywhere near it. No inadvertent ham sandwiches, we used to say. You always knew when you went on board it would be only vegetarian food cooked.'

'And who cooked?' I ask.

'Oh, Francis. I don't think she was very interested in cooking; eating yes, of course, as long as it was vegetarian.'

'In his accounts he was always frying up down below in even the most terrible storms', I recall.

Two unrelated spaniels yelp and paw for the digestive I'm dipping in my coffee. The canary strikes up; must have seen one of the cats. 'Oh, do shut up!' Belinda encourages the assembled throng.

'And what was he like as a skipper?' I ask.

'Oh, very easy going, very relaxed. Didn't shout or even raise his voice. I always felt it was a real honour to be asked to sail with Francis.'

'And Sheila, how was she on board? I'm mean about taking orders.'

'Funnily enough, she was fine. Sheila knew it was his realm.'

'Role reversal.'

'Yes, it was. She was captain on land, he at sea. So they sailed for fun too?' Belinda asks.

'Oh yes, very much for fun when out together. Francis alone was a different matter. It seems that for him sailing alone was always a trial, an ordeal. Always pushing himself. Something to be mastered rather than enjoyed. But with Sheila or Giles on board he relaxed.'

<hr />

The 1957 season started with the Cowes to Dinard Race. Unusually, Sheila was one of the crew. Francis remembered:

There was a fresh wind with a choppy sea, and I was cutting the corner fine at Guernsey, standing in as close to the rocks as I dared in the hope of avoiding a tack and the loss of time that it would cost. Mike [Jones, one of the crew] did not like being in so close, because he had been wrecked on these rocks in another boat, and Sheila was gossiping with him below about social nothings because, she told me afterwards, she thought the atmosphere was too tense. I barked harshly at them [a sure sign that the skipper is too tense himself] because I wanted to be ready to tack at a second's notice.

At that moment I saw a column of water shoot 20 feet straight into the air, where a wave had hit a submerged rock a cable's length [about 200 yards] on the beam. I said nothing to Mike, because I thought he would have a fit, but I laughed to myself and carried on – if the rocks were going to show up as clearly as that, I need not worry. We managed to scratch past without having to tack.

Sheila was presented with a cup by the handsome commodore of the Dinard Yacht Club, and I think nothing could have given her more pleasure.

In fact Sheila's pleasure at being presented with a cup was so great that she suggested to Francis that he should have a new boat, much as suggesting that he might want a new suit. She said: 'If you can win prizes pushing along this old thing, you ought to do well with a new one.'

'We haven't got the money to pay for it', Francis replied.

But once Sheila had made up her mind… 'It's a terrible strain on you with this one. I'm sure something will turn up if you order it. Have faith, and go ahead', she said.

Francis wrote:

I sketched on the back of an envelope the hull that I should like to have. This was passed to Robert Clark, who designed Gipsy Moth III *for us. Jack Tyrrell's boatyard in Arklow, Ireland, started building it. Throughout the year, worried about my business, I alternated between bouts of despair at the liability of the new boat, and waves of enthusiasm for it.*

While *Gipsy Moth III* was being designed and built in Ireland Francis raced hard through the 1957 season, at the end of which he concluded: 'At the end of *Gipsy Moth*'s fourth racing season she had started in sixteen RORC races and I had learned a lot

Jack Tyrell's yard in Arklow

about sailing; perhaps more important, I was aware how much more there was to learn'.

Francis had high hopes of being the winning crew in the last race of the season and of the Admiral's Cup series, the Fastnet Race, on board *Figaro*, another famous yacht of the period. Eventually they came third, well behind their sister ship *White Mist*. Francis was by now even more competitive than the famously competitive Americans and rather huffily put their poor showing down to the crew having been up all night in Cowes celebrating their victory in the New York Cup, causing them to be late and presumably rather groggy over the starting line. Worse, when Francis called for an offshore tack into the Channel, the captain overruled him for a less swelly tack inshore, costing them dearly. Worse still:

> *Another drawback was that the yacht was stuffed with experts. Everyone tended to exercise his own special expertise. One wanted to demonstrate his latest methods of jibbing, which cost us time unsnarling the spinnaker and repairing the damage. Another liked to harden in the foresails, unconsciously demonstrating how strong they were. They were marvellous sails, but often hardened in too flat for the best speed.*

The Fastnet finishes in Plymouth, and Bill Snaith needed to fly home to make some more money. He asked Francis to stay on as part of the crew to take her to the Port of London. Francis would, he said, as long as Sheila could come along for the cruise. Some cruise. It was freshening up to Force 6 then Force 7 westerly as they left Plymouth for a very fast run down the Channel. Past the Isle of Wight it blew up even further and Sheila remembered it as

> *The most terrifying storm I had been in up to that time. All that night we ran up the Channel on the bare poles. There was nothing much I could do so I got into my bunk hoping for the best. It really was a terrible night with the noise of the screaming wind and crashing waves. Next morning I woke up and looked out. 'Goodness,' I said to Francis, 'How green the cliffs look!' 'Don't be silly,' he said, 'those are waves you are looking at'.*

Cliffs or waves seemed to be the least of his worries as he sailed into that autumn. The map and guide business was in that limbo land that all entrepreneurs have to pass through: not profitable enough to employ fresh arms and legs and minds and needing all his energies to keep it as profitable as it was. But now he had other worries: *Gipsy Moth III* was being built in Ireland and had to be paid for on top of the costs of visiting the yards; *Gipsy Moth II* was proving hard to sell, as out-of-date racing yachts are; and to cap it all, he wasn't feeling too well within himself.

⌘

And so in early 1958 we come to Francis's cancer, although actually I think this whole cancer-and-cure story began four years earlier, when Sheila started attending her Open House faith healing and prayer groups. Francis's cancer no doubt had ideas of its own; but then it hadn't reckoned on meeting Sheila's wall of faith. In retrospect the cause became clear. Francis:

Every weekend I went down to the Beaulieu River and worked on Gipsy Moth II, *trying to tidy up the mess after the season's racing. I worked feverishly by myself, feeling that I could not afford to pay a boatyard to do the work. Sheila said this was nonsense. Bitterly, I accused her of failing to help me, and came down by myself. I worked furiously while the yacht swung to her mooring in the grey swirls of autumn mist on the glassy water. There always seemed so little time for work on the yacht, after I had cooked my meals and done the boat's housekeeping.*

One of my jobs was to remove some old paint on the forecastle sole [floor] with a strong chemical paint-remover, to dissolve the old paint. I worked on my knees, doubled up over the stuff on the floor, and the forehatch was closed above my head, because of the cold. I believe that the fumes burnt my lungs, and that my lung trouble started then.

Bill Grindey: 'He was always working on *Gipsy Moth II*. If you think yachts need a lot of attention now, you should have seen them back then. We didn't know exactly what he doing down below as he was shut in. So many jobs, anyhow.

'Later we knew he had been stripping paint off the forecastle sole with Nitromors or something similar. But everyone did then, we never knew about that, asbestos, all these health things we know now, even smoking. The fumes down there caught his chest and that was that.'

Sheila only knew: 'That winter my husband became very ill with bronchitis, pneumonia and goodness knows what. After Christmas he had X-ray tests which showed a most unusual condition superimposed on the sub-acute asthma'.

For the next four months Francis went through the conventional medical mill: one X-ray after another; two bronchoscopies; specialists; consultants with their students prodding and poking him; long coughing nights and endless bedsore days, 'suffocation by a thousand deaths'. Still the results were uncertain: pleurisy, asthma, pneumonia and bronchitis were all candidates for the cause.

All of us who have or have had cancer will always remember the moment they were told they had the disease. Mine came from an aloof and expensive doctor in South Kensington. A few months earlier he had told me rather breezily, as he was syringing my ears or some such, 'Of course I always think that cancer is a sign of failure'. I remember thinking, 'Gosh, I hope I don't get cancer, I would not like him to think me a failure'. Now he was telling me I have failed. 'The results are in. I'm afraid you have cancer.' Not just the words but the image of the occasion will always be a striking memory. (Prostate cancer, by the way, currently zapped into abeyance.)

For Francis it happened thus: one day as he was leaving the hospital he ran into the doctor who had done the latest bronchoscopy. He had heard that the doctor was antipodean and so knew that there might finally be a chance of some straight talking. What did the doctor reckon?

'Cancer', he replied.

'You can't be sure, can you?' Francis hoped.

'We are making these examinations all the time, and cannot possibly be mistaken.'

'I don't believe it. How can you tell?'

'I not only saw it, but cut off a piece and sent it off to the laboratory to be examined.

'What can be done?' asked Francis.

'I think it's already too late to operate', said the plain-talking Aussie. 'Your only possible hope is to remove one lung immediately.'

Reading Francis's account of his new finite reality also brought me back to a sense of déjà vu. For me it was a walk home through

Hyde Park with a newly intense feeling of inclusion in all of nature, a feeling that life would never be the same again. But at least I knew there would be life. For Francis, sixty years ago, when lung cancer meant certain death, the feeling was much more intense:

> *When I emerged from the hospital it was a fine spring morning in April. As I walked along, the sun shone in my face. I heard the gay spring-song of birds. Young pale-green leaves were beginning to tint the trees. Life had never seemed more wonderful – a priceless, desirable thing to lose. I had read about this sort of thing happening to other people; somehow I had never imagined that it would happen to me. I walked along slowly, wondering how long I had got before I was snuffed out from this lovely fresh spring of life.*

Back home it was time to tell Sheila and he did so with 'desolate sadness'. Of course she already knew and had been praying silently the while.

'What are you going to do?' she asked.

'I have done what they told me to do – booked a room for the operation next week', Francis replied.

Sheila was having none of that! 'How can you be so feeble as to agree? It's the wrong thing to do. You are too ill to make a decision.'

'Dammit', Francis replied, 'first of all the radiologist says he is examining pictures all the time, and can't possibly be mistaken. Then the surgeon says he has not only seen the cancer, but removed a piece of it. Then the chief surgeon said it was cancer. What else can I possibly do but agree to the operation?'

'It's wrong to operate', Sheila insisted, 'your lung is in such a state that you are bound to die if they operate.'

Sheila organised another opinion from a leading consultant in respiratory medicine. This specialist duly agreed with the others: lung cancer, operate urgently. By now five different doctors, surgeons or radiologists had given the same opinion. In spite of Sheila's protests and sympathy for her nature-cure ideals, Francis decided that he had to go with the majority of experts and re-booked himself into hospital for the operation a week later.

On his way there he rather ghoulishly went into the RORC clubhouse for a last drink. Talking to his friends in the bar, he felt intensely lonely and doom-laden. He did not say where he was heading, least of all why, so as not to spoil this one last moment of conviviality before he died. In this frame of mind he saw a notice on the club board that would change his life, and inspired him in the dark year ahead to fight for his life. It was posted by Lieutenant Colonel H.G. 'Blondie' Hasler DSO, OBE, RM, a popular war hero whose real-life story had inspired the 1955 film *The Cockleshell Heroes*.[14]

SINGLE-HANDED TRANSATLANTIC RACE

The object of the race is twofold: (a) sport and (b) to encourage the development of suitable boats, gear and techniques for single-handed ocean crossing under sail.

Start from Cowes on Saturday 26 July 1958

Finish at City Island, NY, by any route, but leaving Long Island to port.

Entries may be sponsored

800 mile qualification run required in 2 parts

Yachts may be of any size and type

For more details ask member H.G. Hasler

Francis thought, 'That would be a terrific race, shame the only other race I am likely to take part in is that with old Charon across the Styx'.

An hour later he was in hospital. He recalled: 'I was resigned to my fate. Not so my wife; she was now really in a fighting mood, and went into action.' Look out, world!

As we have seen, Sheila always had an intuitive interest in healing through faith and prayer. On her return to London from Wiltshire four years earlier she had enrolled with a prayer study group called Open Way that met every Wednesday evening in Harley Street. Lecturers included the famous Buddhist pioneer Christmas Humphreys and the Maharishi Mahesh Yogi in this pre-Beatles era. She had also become involved with the Churches Council of Healing, so by the time of Francis's diagnosis she had little faith in the medical doctors' prognosis and a lot of faith that, with others, she could pray his cancer away. She had never forgotten how, in her view, over-zealous doctoring had killed her mother; one thing for sure, over-zealous doctoring was not going to kill her husband.

A few days after Francis was admitted she made an appointment to see the surgeon. She was 'guided by some inner force; I had clear knowledge that this operation must not take place. I was scared to be opposing the decision of this very eminent man, but I could not change my destiny.' Or Francis's.

Sheila laid out her case: her nature-cure doctor had told her that statistically this particular operation had only a 10 per cent chance of long term success; her husband was so ill that the operation would certainly kill him; and above all – the clincher – he so liked flying and sailing that to remove a lung would be like removing a wing from a bird. In short, she would not consent to it. Never.

'Many people live with only one lung', the surgeon shot back.

'But not for long. His lungs are so septic it will kill him. I refuse to allow that.'

'You are the most extraordinary woman and you are wasting time.'

'I apologise, I realise you are a busy man', said Sheila.

'No, I mean the patient's time.'

But Sheila stuck to her guns and the surgeon had to agree to a further – final – test. Sheila had won time and set about organising the prayers that would replace the knife. Francis summed the Sheila/surgeon meeting up thus: 'I suppose that he, like me, had never met a woman like Sheila – someone who would carry the responsibility of refusing to allow an operation against the overwhelming weight of medical opinion.'

Sheila's study of prayer had led her to believe that praying was not about asking but about surrender – and hope and faith. That is to say, prayer is not asking God to change what is, but making Him aware of what is – and once He is aware, His grace will flow from that awareness. Prayer does not then mean claiming that grace as one's own but sharing it with others; and the greater the sharing, the greater the power. Her favourite muses were written by Brother Lawrence in 1666 in his *The Practice in the Presence of God*:

All things are possible for him who believes, but they are less difficult for him who hopes, and still more easy for him who loves, and still more easy for him who perseveres in the practice of these three virtues.

And from the Gospel of St Mark:

All things whatsoever ye pray and ask for, believe that ye have received them and ye shall have them.

For Francis God was an Englishman. For Sheila, if God was not literally an Englishman, he certainly had all of an Englishman's virtues – from what little I know about her God, a not unreasonable proposition.

Sheila now set about praying for Francis on an industrial scale. She had two strategies, praying next to him in the hospital and praying for him around the world. For the former she sent in the Jesuit Father Kelly, who, apart from Jesuit fathering, was writing a book about the early navigators; his Order had sailed with them as they were there only ones who could read and write. For the latter she had a prayer typed on index cards and sent them to family friends and prayer groups around the world. Luckily, another friend and neighbour, Joyce Rowlston, has kept one she found in her mother's trunk of papers:

> *Friend, this prayer will help Francis recover. Say it when you will but also together with all others every Sunday at noon Greenwich Mean Time.*
>
> *Lord, I give you your son Francis who is in pain and suffering. We offer him to Your grace and light and share with You his distress. We believe in You, we have hope for Francis and love for all Your creation.*

Poor Francis. His body was lying in a 1960s National Health ward, digesting 1960s hospital food: thin white bread with margarine, tinned soup, meat and two veg boiled beyond redemption, ditch-water tea and sweet biscuits. He described it thus:

> *Hospital routine; dreadful nights, lying for hour after hour, unable to sleep; sometimes choking and gasping for breath; not allowed to switch on a light, because it would wake up other patients in the ward. Patients coming in, having a lung removed, suffering bravely, leaving. Every day the surgeon on his rounds poked my neck with his finger as if to see if I was ripe for the knife. I felt degraded, defiled and deeply depressed.*

As if that was not bad enough, he had the strain of having to be at least part-way cheerful for Sheila every day and having to bear Father Kelly in frantic prayer next to him. He must have thought these were the last rites, and he wasn't even a Catholic; in fact, he was brought up to be the opposite, a hell-and-damnation Protestant. Sheila sent in two other priests as well, at which point Francis found the strength to rebel and she settled on Father Kelly praying beside him solo.

Francis particularly came to dread visits from friends:

> *I felt too ill to talk. I would make an effort, but felt I needed to conserve the vital spark, and not to fan it into flame. I wanted only to lie still in peace, and to defer the horrid moment when I would start coughing, and pass through the experience of feeling suffocated. I developed a terrified dread of that slow choking from within. I despised myself as I became an abject coward about dying that way. As each fresh crisis built up, I wanted to cry as if surrendering to that weakness that would give me respite.*

Meanwhile, Sheila was becoming decidedly shirty with the medical establishment; there was only ever going to be one winner in that battle. Her visits every day were becoming more fraught and frustrating. She wrote of

> *endless tests and x-rays. I asked them not use any more drugs. I must confess I felt a total lack of communication with the doctors in general. I very rarely saw any of the senior doctors and I fear I must have seemed a very strange individual, always questioning what they were doing.*

Away from the hospital, the worldwide synchronised prayers continued apace – and she was developing a Plan B.

Enton Hall, Francis's cure spa

Her nature cure doctor, Gordon Latto, knew of a health farm, then called a hydro, Enton Hall, near Godalming in Surrey. It had once been a Chichester relation's baronial hall; it has now been divided up into 'luxury apartments' but in the 1960s it was a self-styled health clinic. Slowly but surely Sheila mentioned Plan B to Francis, lying distraught on what to her must have seemed his deathbed.

Francis had defied her before when admitting himself to the hospital; dare he defy her again? The doctors with their 'endless tests and X-rays' were gearing up for the operation he knew must be any day now. He had never felt worse or more miserable. Then Father Kelly would arrive and misery and discomfort would take a different tack. Then his wife would arrive, a lone voice against the medical profession, and not a quiet voice to sooth the misery and discomfort. Now Francis was mired in the misery and discomfort of having to make the biggest decision of his life – and to do so utterly enfeebled and autophobic. Sheila or the system? The hospital or the spa? One lung or two – or none? Dr Latto's hands or the surgeon's knife? Science or faith? Enton Hall or St Bartholomews? Death foretold or death abeyed? Life restored or life abridged? Decision imminent or decision deferred? To his bedside they came: Sheila; nurse; Father Kelly; surgeon. You must do this; you should do that. Francis, torn this way and that, had to make a decision. Love, faith and hope won: he chose Sheila.

At Enton Hall at first Francis deteriorated rapidly. The staff told Sheila that he was too ill for a hydro, that he must go to hospital. In the meantime they had to move him from the Hall to one of their chalets as his coughing was keeping their other clients awake at night. But the chalets were cold and damp and he developed a further cough and a return of his asthma. In some desperation, Sheila administered the Laying on of Hands, standing over Francis and taking his head in her hands praying aloud:

> *In the name of God and trusting in His might alone,*
> *Receive Christ's healing touch to make you whole.*
> *May Christ bring you wholeness of body, mind and spirit,*
> *Deliver you from every evil*
> *And give you peace.*

Dr Latto arrived and said that Francis's heart could not take the strain of more distress and Sheila must give him hydrotherapy immediately. This was clearly a crisis, the low point at which Francis's body could easily expire if his spirit had not been determined to live. Thus in the cold, dark chalet Sheila and Francis fought for Francis's life through the night, applying hot then cold then hot then cold compresses to his back and chest. Sheila encouraged him with talk of the new boat being built in Ireland. Francis 'knew that they had given me up that night, and somehow it did me good. It infused the will to live into me.' By dawn he was still alive; a day later he was shuffling around the chalet, a week later shuffling around outside. 1958 was a glorious summer and Enton Hall had glorious grounds, taking Francis back to his nature-filled childhood. Survival was in the air, the sense not of if he would survive, but how.

Two months later he was well enough to return home. At least that was Sheila's view; Francis had not seen a medical doctor for weeks. But the return was not a success at first. He was still clearly very weak and the return to his home also meant return to the office, the business he had not seen for four months. Inevitably it had suffered, even though Sheila had stepped into the breech in his absence. And as she would be the first to admit, she was not a natural business person. As Francis analysed:

> My map business had been running steadily downhill. Finally Sheila could not stand it any longer, entered the office and took charge. She had never had anything to do with business before, and on top of that she's artistic, with a slow casual approach to an issue, which can be maddening to the business mentality. On the other hand, her perception is brilliantly acute, her judgment excellent for half the occasions, and her imagination amazingly fertile for new ideas. Her chief asset however, is that if she makes up her mind to do something, she will do it. She overcame the inevitable frictions, introduced some new ideas, which, if not successful as money-spinners infused some new life into the firm. The hive had a new queen, and came alive again.

As, indeed, did he. Forty pounds lighter, all folded skin and sticky-out bones, his confidence and personality battered, by early 1959 he felt strong enough to visit his mother in Devon 'before it was too late'. The visit was not a success and should never have happened; clearly Sheila's guard was down, perhaps now focused on her other sick charge, the map and guide business. In the cold, damp Devon farmhouse he caught bronchitis, which brought back his asthma. His mother called for a doctor; the doctor asked if his wife knew how seriously ill he was. 'With what?' asked his mother. Francis, lying down upstairs, couldn't help but overhear. 'Cancer', replied the doctor. Francis wrote: 'When I heard this it cheered me up: in fact I laughed. I don't suppose many have laughed on hearing that dreadful verdict, but I reasoned I must surely have been dead eighteen months ago if it had been a living cancer.'

Obviously concerned, Francis's sister Barbara telephoned Sheila with the news that their mother had had to call the doctor.

'What does he say it is?' Sheila asked.

'Cancer', Barbara replied.

'Don't talk such nonsense', Sheila barked back. 'He's got no cancer now. Let him rest, leave him alone. As soon as he is strong enough he will come home.' It was 11 April, Sheila's fifty-sixth birthday.

Back in London, Sheila was preparing to send Giles on a school trip to France. Francis returned to London and an X-ray giving him the all-clear. Spontaneously Sheila and Francis decided they need a break in France too. They packed quickly and took the Blue Train down to Nice. They were heading to Vence, a famous health resort in the foothills of the Alpes Martimes, known for its healing air since Roman times. After two days Francis had a relapse and needed oxygen. Sheila was at first unsympathetic, thinking that he had come to rely on oxygen as some sort of prop. But then she doubted herself, perhaps for the first and only time: 'Can I stand much more of this? Am I wrong?' she thought, 'yet at some deeper level I knew it was going to be all right'.

Which is how Francis met Dr Jean Mattei, the doctor with the oxygen. To Francis he was 'a remarkable man, a wonderful man, a

*Dr Jean
Mattei*

man's man: short, nuggety, fit, with terrific energy exuding strength
and activity, one of the cleverest lung physicians in Paris before
he settled in Vence'. After examining the patient Dr Mattei said,
'Ce n'est rien, rien, rien. There is nothing serious the matter with
you, you'll see. You will be fine, do not worry. If you follow my
treatment you will be climbing up those mountains in three days
time.' And Francis was: 'At 2,200 feet Baou Blanc may not be much
of a mountain, but it was the most wonderful climb I ever made.'

How did this remarkable new cure come about? Sheila
insisted that Francis was already nearly cured by her faith and
prayers and Dr Mattei merely put the final polish on her good

work. For Francis it was something more fundamental, the discovery of some part of his body that had somehow ceased to function that the doctor had found and repaired – perhaps a bit like a recalcitrant seal in a water pump. Sheila repaired to the local church to thank God for His delivery of Francis to good health: 'I felt that this recovery was very miraculous. Throughout I was controlled and directed by a power outside myself. I felt that these were holy matters and must be kept private, but this was not to be.'

Back in London in May 1959 Francis stopped by the RORC again and saw Blondie Hasler's notice for a single-handed race across the Atlantic still on the noticeboard. The proposed date of departure was nearly a year old; the race hadn't happened

Blondie Hasler

– yet it still might. He also noticed the chance to navigate *Pym* in the Cowes to Dinard and *Mait II* in the Fastnet. How good it must have felt to be breathing sea air again! To be pitting his navigation skills against others and elements! On *Pym* he had a slight relapse and found a local quack with a needle in Dinard to 'ginger me up'. On *Mait II* some nifty short-cut navigation avoiding the rocks entering Plymouth Sound moved them up the field. He was back doing what he loved best, ocean racing and all that that entailed.

But it was Blondie Hasler's notice on the club board, by now curling at the edges, that really fired his imagination. 'Good God,' Francis thought, 'I believe I can go in for this race.' And he did.

Mait II

NOTES:

14. Hasler conceived of and led the mission that took ten Marines in canoes 60 miles up the Gironde River to Bordeaux, where they sank several German steamers at the quayside. Only two of them returned alive.

I believe that this is the greatest urge to adventure for a man – to have an idea, an ideal or an ambition, and then to prove, at any cost, that the idea is right, or that the ambition can be fulfilled.

CHAPTER 8

Gipsy Moth III

Author's note:

As we head into the sailing exploits part of the story I am going to have to use some nautical terms, as life at sea cannot really be described in any other way. Port, for example, means the left hand side of the boat if you are standing at its rearmost part but the right hand side if standing at its sharp end going forwards; starboard, the contrary. So much more elegant to use stern and bow, and port and starboard.

I'll keep the sailing terms to the minimum but there is no other way to describe the sail plan. Working from bow to stern, Francis refers to the jibs as his small sails ahead of the main mast, genoas as his large sails and spinnakers as, well spinnakers. There are two masts, the main mast amidships off which hangs the mainsail and the smaller mizzen mast near the stern off which hangs the mizzen (sail). To reef a sail means to lower it partially. A cable is a tenth of a nautical mile, and that reminds me – a mile here means a nautical mile, being 1.15 normal miles, or 1.85 kms. A knot is a nautical mile per hour. Windward means the side of the boat facing the wind, upwind; leeward (pronounced lewod) the opposite, downwind. To tack is to change direction through the wind on the bow; to gybe to do so with the wind astern. To be on starboard tack means the wind is blowing from the starboard side; to be on port tack the opposite.

That should do it; believe me this could go on for pages!

EVERY SUNDAY MORNING, RIGHT IN THE CENTRE OF LONDON, some of the world's most sophisticated yachts take part in a regatta. Like a truly eccentric English round pond, the Round Pond, in the prevailing lee of Kensington Palace, is neither round nor a pond. It is rather a 200 metres by 150 metres by 5 metres deep, round-cornered ornamental lake. When George II built it in 1730 he had no idea that it would not be until 130 years later that it would find its true purpose, to be home to the Model Yacht Sailing Association, and five years later to the London Model Yacht Club. And every Sunday morning, 150 years after that, the LMYC yachtsmen are busier than ever tacking and gybing around the mute and whooper swans, the Canada and Egyptian geese, the mandarin and tufted ducks, all of which paddle away with avian insouciance and a complete disregard for the long-established rules of yacht match racing.

It was to the Sunday regattas at the Round Pond that Francis repaired during April 1960. He had a problem; the model yachtsmen had the answer. He reckoned that if a model yacht could self-steer herself 200 metres across the Round Pond, his full-size yacht, with full-size self-steering, could in theory self-steer herself in Blondie Hasler's race across the Atlantic.

The problem was far more than theoretical. There were problems all over the boat. The Transatlantic Solo Race was due to start in less than two months. *Gipsy Moth III* had only been re-launched on 3 April, after her winter lay-up at the Agamemnon Boatyard at Buckler's Hard. Francis, Sheila and Giles had sailed her over to Buckler's Hard from Tyrrell's yard in Arklow[15] soon after the 1959 Fastnet on *Mait III*. Apart from that gentle delivery trip from Ireland, an inconclusive shakedown in the Channel and some mild weather trials in the Solent, Francis knew practically nothing about sailing his new yacht. He only knew that he instinctively warmed to her: 'The yacht suited me. She was staunchly built, and gave me confidence. She seemed so powerful that I felt at first like a small boy astride a tall, strong, broad-backed horse which would not stop'.

Inevitably there was a snagging list that had to be unsnagged in the yard over the winter, or as Francis put it more poetically:

I think that there were several leprechauns still on board. One must have had his feet jammed in the rudderstock. By the time we reached the Solent I could only move the rudder by exerting my full strength with both hands on the tiller, and both feet on the cockpit seat opposite. However, Gipsy Moth III has always had a friendly atmosphere, as if she carried the goodwill of the craftsmen who built her, and I try to avoid strangers coming aboard for fear they might trample the Little People and drive them away.

But above all it was with the self-steering system that Francis was preoccupied. This is the single most important piece of kit for any solo yachtsman, without which life on board would be literally impossible. His old friend Allen Wheeler had by now become what Francis described as a 'celebrated boffin and aviation consultant' and had designed what must have seemed to Francis at first sight like a whizzo solution, a kind of autogyro-cum-weathervane with cordage working the tiller directly. Francis was full of a racer's enthusiasm for this competitive advantage. Then Wheeler bowed out. Undeterred, Francis bought some Meccano, built a rough approximation and showed it to another friend at the Sperry Corporation. This was by now January, with six months to go before the Plymouth gun. Sperry made a life-sized model and then in late February declared it unworkable except in a stiff breeze; this meant it was completely useless, as breezes are not always stiff, far from it. Three months to go.

Francis and Sheila already had an appointment to revisit Dr Mattei for a health boost in March and I suspect that it was while mountain high in Provence that he hit on the idea of going to the Round Pond for inspiration. Time was now desperately short; any solution would have to be right first time.

Just as it was for Francis, I think that a trip to the Round Pond might be fruitful in trying to understand what he was looking for. One sunny Sunday in July, with barely enough wind to muster a ripple, about two dozen yachtsmen are twiddling and twisting their radio control consoles while their charges flop about listlessly on the water. Somewhere between 1960 and now, model yachts had ceased to be vane-steered and became radio-controlled. Undaunted, I approach one of the sportsmen and unburden onto him my dilemma.

What is always so lovely about enthusiasts is that they are always so ... enthusiastic. Mike, the very first model yachtsmen I approach, can't himself help me, but 'You see that old boy over there, just to the left of the bench, with the bright green cap? He'll help you. He's got an old vane type he'll show you.' And he has; and he does.

Thus the following Sunday Gregor Halsley arrives with two yachts, one radio-controlled for himself, one vane-steered for me. I must say they were both beautiful. In fact all the model yachts had the graceful sheer and purposeful hull of a classic 12 metre racing yacht. I ask Gregor how the self-steering worked and what Francis would have been looking for to transfer to *Gipsy Moth III*.

'The principle is easy enough', says Gregor, taking vane-steered *Yonolla* out of its pram. 'It's just a sod to get right. Black art and dark magic all part of the game. I'm out of practice but imagine you want to steer to that weathercock.' He is pointing to the top of the east entrance to Kensington Palace. 'Today the wind is coming from over there.' He is now pointing to the park entrance by the Royal Garden Hotel. 'Forty-five degrees south off your target course. So you adjust the vane to point into the wind and the yacht with its tiller centred to point at the weathercock. Then you lock these two together. Should she steer off course either way, the wind will force the vane back into it and so make the tiller steer back on her course. The vane moves the tiller, the tiller moves the rudder, the rudder steers the boat, hey presto!'

We give it a go. There is just as much sticky sun and barely more wind than last week but enough to fill the sails and work the vane. Now I see why Gregor brought not just the yacht and its pram, but a broom with its brush end swathed in a bandage. *Yonolla* heads off on starboard tack but of course, with the steering locked to the vane, cannot tack herself to fashion a course towards the weathercock. Thus Gregor has to rush round on foot to intercept her at the shoreline and give her a good shove onto port tack. Then he has to walk briskly around the pond in front of her to do the same again onto starboard tack until ten minutes later she arrives approximately at her destination.

Miranda

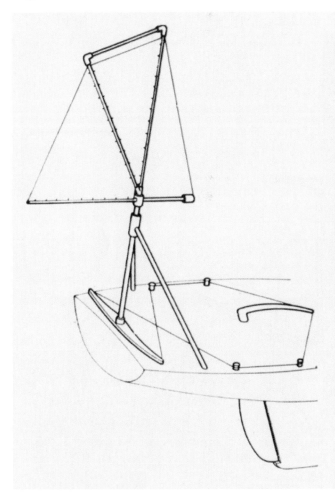

'Quite exhausting', I say.

'This is on a calm day', Gregor replies. 'On a brisk day you'd be running around the pond to reach her shore point before the yacht did.'

As a result of his research at the Round Pond and after studying a model yachting design book (which Gregor reckons must have been *Model Racing Yachts* by B.H. Priest and J.A. Lewis), Francis designed his self-steering system, which he called 'Miranda', thus:

From the book he learned that the vane – in *Gipsy Moth III*'s case actually a flat sail – had to be four and a half times the size of the rudder. As Francis rather ruefully admitted, 'I cannot describe how ugly it looked on the beautiful *Gipsy Moth III*'. But the design imperative was strength, not beauty, and the engineering challenge was to design a system that would be sturdy enough to withstand the worst of the Atlantic howlers, yet light enough to pick up the odd light breeze or even zephyr.

While *Gipsy Moth III* was having her leprechauns realigned in Buckler's Hard, Francis was in the library of the RORC studying the June, July and August editions of the British Admiralty North Atlantic Ocean Routing Charts. These give highly detailed historical weather patterns by the month and the precise locations that he needed to predict which course best to lay for *Gipsy Moth III* across the Atlantic.

He knew that they were going to be in for a rough ride:

> *Three thousand miles, plugging into the prevailing westerlies, probably strong, bucking the Gulf Stream current, crossing the Grand Banks off Newfoundland which were not only one of the densest fog areas of the world, but also stuffed with fishing trawlers. No wonder the Atlantic had only once before been raced across from east to west. That was in 1870, by two big schooners, the* Dauntless *and the* Cambria.

The Ocean Routing Charts showed him that the shortest route from Plymouth to New York, the Great Circle route, is 2,900 nautical miles but considered by navigators to be the worst option, neither fish nor foul. The more northerly route brings the promise of stronger winds but bigger seas and fouler weather, to include the certainty of fog and icebergs; the more southerly route shows gentler winds, flatter seas and fairer weather. In a fully crewed yacht of *Gipsy Moth III*'s size the northerly route would be preferred, whereas sailing solo the southern route would be more sensible. Naturally Francis planned to go north in search of speed; sleep would somehow take care of itself. He also knew that circumstances and forecasts at the time – hopelessly unreliable by today's standards –would probably make the actual decision for him. Which they did: Francis eventually sailed the direct Great Circle route and had a horrible, if fast, time of it.

In the bar of the RORC Francis was helping Blondie Hasler get the race organised. There was much to admire in the Cockleshell Hero.

> He was a quiet-speaking, interesting man; short, round and bald-headed with a red face. He never seemed to move a muscle while speaking. He steadily and quietly pursued his affairs. Blondie was also an expert ocean racer, and one year, with a novel type of boat for ocean racing, came top of the smallest class of the RORC for the season's racing.

The two never became friends, being such different characters. Whereas Blondie was quietly determined, still waters running deep, and discreet, Francis was overtly determined, mercurial by comparison, thin-skinned at times and quick to claim the credit. They fell out before the race when Francis questioned the entry requirements and after the race when, having won it, Francis failed to correct the public perception that it had been his idea all along.

One problem Francis did not have was Sheila fussing about him. Quite the contrary:

> I was fascinated to think of the entrants starting from the same port at the same time for the same destination, testing themselves and their boats against the loneliness of the ocean. I saw immediately that this would be the cure, the final cure, for my husband, that he need just this kind of venture.

But at this stage all was not well with the race. In spite of widespread publicity in the yachting press, only two tentative volunteers had stepped forward: Dr David Lewis, who sailed *Cardinal Vertue*, and Valentine Howells in *Eira*. Both yachts were the same size as Blondie's *Jester*, 25 feet, and *Eira*, being a Folkboat, was more or less *Jester*'s sister ship.

By the time Blondie and Francis met, the notice had been on the RORC board for two years. One or two club jokers had written discouraging asides on it. (Blondie recalls 'the Club Secretary was kept busy rubbing out the proliferation of unsolicited, usually adverse, comments'.) The race was just considered too outrageous, too difficult, too dangerous – as Francis said, 'too hair-brained' – for public acceptance or media interest. This then frightened off the sponsors. It also frightened off any organising yacht clubs, officially needed to record the racers starting at one end and record them finishing at the other. Then for the competitors there was the expense: not everyone could take six months off work, the time needed for the sea trials, the race itself, the regrouping in America and then the voyage home eastabout – all this before the expense of the specially equipped and victualled yacht itself. The race appealed to genuine Corinthians like Blondie, David, Kim and Francis, less so to anyone vaguely normal or confined by vaguely normal circumstances. At one point, when it looked as if our four heroes would just have to race each other, with no financial backing or yacht club sanction, they all agreed to put half-a-crown (£0.12p in today's money) into the kitty and the winner would claim the ten shillings (or £0.50). Thus they formed the Half Crown Club, to which every finisher was entitled to life membership.

However, Blondie's Cockleshell exploits had led him to know a fellow Royal Marine, David Astor, who owned and edited the *Observer* – in 1960 still a highly respected Sunday newspaper rather than the sorry hand-wringing wretch it has become today.

Initially, the *Observer* offered a first prize of £1,000 and £250 for each yacht competing. Then Astor's suits, sensing a PR disaster of sinking yachts and drowning heroes, warned him off. Luckily his Sports Editor, the Olympic champion and broadcaster Chris Brasher, warned him back on again. The *Observer* became title sponsor for the Observer Single-Handed Trans-Atlantic Race, OSTAR, with the kitty dressed up as a story option rather than prize money in order to stop the suits flapping. Now that the *Observer* was on board to take the worst of the flak if it all went wrong, the yacht clubs soon fell into line: The Royal Western to fire the starting cannon off Plymouth and the Joshua Slocum Society to blow the foghorn in New York.

Apart from working on the routing and helping Blondie get the race under way, not to mention running the map and guidebook business, Francis's main preoccupation was the struggle against the clock to make *Gipsy Moth III* race-ready. It was not until a month before the start that the yard had fitted Miranda – yet Francis was thrilled:

> *I crossed the bar at the entrance to the Beaulieu River, headed the yacht across the Solent and locked the vane to the tiller.* Gipsy Moth *started tearing through the water, sailing herself entirely. Her wake was almost dead straight; it was fascinating to watch. That was one of the most thrilling moments of my life. Gradually I found out that Miranda required just as much skill to get the best out of her as does setting the sails of a yacht in a keen race. Also it gave me the same pleasure to succeed.*

Sheila meanwhile had more important plans for *Gipsy Moth III*, her official blessing. For this they called in their long-standing friend, a very well-known figure at the time, Revd 'Tubby' Clayton. Tubby had achieved fame during and after the First World War with his refuges for soldiers and parishioners. He never went anywhere without his retinue of boy disciples and three of them joined Tubby, Lord and Lady Montagu and Francis and Sheila on board *Gipsy Moth III* for the blessing.

Luckily for our story, Belinda, Lady Montagu, remembers the occasion well: 'Earlier that day we were playing with Edward's [Lord Montagu's] new speedboat at the top of the river. It was early in the year, so quite cold. One of Edward's friends was waterskiing. They all had new wetsuits. Very flamboyant, as you can imagine. I was in the boat and Edward always did everything in double-quick time, so he turned it very sharply and we nearly toppled over, upside down. Out I went into the river. Of course I was then completely soaking wet, made worse because I had earlier been waterskiing in my duffle coat. It really was quite a sharp morning.

'We all went to Buckler's Hard to change into something dry and a bit more solemn as Tubby Clayton was arriving to bless Francis's new boat. Tubby always had a couple of young men to look after him and he always had his dog, Chippy, with him.

'We all crammed into the cabin. Tubby robed himself in the forepeak. It was a really strange party. We all stood around in the cabin and sang verse after verse of 'Those in Peril on the Sea'. There was no accompaniment; it was really quite hard work. And of course none of us were blessed with wonderful singing voices. But Tubby insisted we go on and on right through every verse. And then he said a prayer of blessing.'

Francis takes up the story:

When Tubby imperiously demanded to be disembarked, I found that Giles had gone off with the dinghy. So, somewhat fortified with 'Liffey Wather' [Scotch whisky], I offered to motor the yacht down to the jetty at low water of the spring tide, with mud banks showing horribly on each side. Turning thirty yards below the jetty we went onto the mud, where we were presently heeled over 45 degrees. To run aground within an hour of the ships being blessed must be a record.

I find two other local memories of those final, frenetic days before the race. Growing up in the area in the 1960s – I was eleven when all this happened – we all knew the Martin family at Buckler's Hard. Mr Martin, Bill, ran the marine workshop and fuel pumps and Mrs Martin, Rhoda, ran the village shop. Luckily another friend and neighbour, Mary Montagu-Scott,

Francis and Gipsy Moth III on the Beaulieu River

Edward Montagu's daughter, not only runs the Maritime Museum at Buckler's Hard but is a keen chronicler of local characters and their folklore. Before Mrs. Martin died she was interviewed about her life at Buckler's Hard. From the tape, concerning Francis:

'I knew Sir Francis very well. Did his stores for going round the world you know. I've got a couple of books autographed by him. He was really a friend. I used to de-eye all his potatoes and preserve his eggs. It was very interesting. He pickled them to keep them fresh at sea. One day he said to me when he came back, "Mrs. Martin, I've got eggs you preserved for me that are good now but eggs I bought in Plymouth that have gone bad". I did it with liquid paraffin, no it was Vaseline. All over the shells. He was a vegetarian too so it was very difficult.

'He took tinned cake and tinned marmalade and tinned jams. I used to have to get these specially made for him. Oranges and grapefruit he was very fond of, but not so many as they didn't keep. But the potatoes always amazed me as they all had to be de-eyed as they sprout so quickly in the dark. Chocolate he had to have, lime juice.

'Lots of vegetarian food, baked beans and cheese. Long keeping milk'.

Both Mr and Mrs Martin are long gone but luckily their son, David remembers Sheila organising *Gipsy Moth III*'s victualing with his mother. 'She was what's known as a piece of work, but Mother had her measure. He was good as gold, Francis, always had time for us. Old-school gent. But I remember giving her a wide berth. Mind you, we were only young.' We were. I remember David and his parents but I didn't run into Sheila. Sounds as if I might have remembered her if I had!

Bill Grindey, the Buckler's Hard harbour master, whom we've met before, remembers ferrying out the supplies in his launch; he also remembers Francis's hundred number formula: 'He used to say a hundred all round. So a hundred pounds of potatoes,

Mrs Rhoda Martin, Buckler's Hard's and Francis's shopkeeper

a hundred fresh eggs, a hundred apples, a hundred onions, a hundred carrots and a hundred oranges, and so on and also a hundred bottles of Guinness. And some whisky and sherry, I've no doubt!'

The last local memory from the hectic days before the first Transatlantic comes from another friend and neighbour, Ken Robinson. At the time Ken was Lord Montagu's go-to man for just about everything. One day they were pottering down the river on their way to Gull Island to 'borrow' some gulls eggs for lunch. 'On our way down we passed *Gipsy Moth* and saw signs of life on board. On our way back we stopped by, knocked on her hull and Edward shouted up something like "Francis, would you like a couple of gull's eggs for lunch?" So Francis took them, thanked us and off we went. A few days later we did the same. Again, we saw signs of life on board and naturally we thought it was Francis busying himself as usual. So on the way back we knocked on the hull again and Edward said, "Francis, more gulls eggs for you". But this time it was Sheila! She was furious. "Don't you know he's a vegetarian? Of course he doesn't want gull's eggs!" And off we went, smirking and giggling like children.'

———— ᨏᨏᨏ ————

After a quiet sail down from Beaulieu to Plymouth, Francis, Sheila and Giles tied up *Gipsy Moth III* alongside the three other British entries, like four brothers of the lonely sea. Their surroundings were much more workaday than their adventure, perhaps foretelling the ill fortunes to come: all were tied up to a decrepit old landing craft-cum-workshop in Millbay Dock.

The Chichesters had of course met Blondie Hasler many times before but it was Francis's first chance to meet the others and to see Blondie's boat, *Jester*. When Blondie had put the original notice for the race on the RORC noticeboard nearly three years earlier, he emphasised that 'the race had two purposes: (a) sport and (b) to encourage the development of suitable boats, gear and techniques for single-handed ocean crossing under sail. (When Francis first introduced Sheila to Blondie, she asked him what was the purpose of the race. 'To cut down the chores in sailing', Blondie replied. Sheila wrote: 'I immediately fell in love with this and thoroughly understood it'. This part of the aim bypassed Francis completely.)

The sport side of this was self-evident as the four competitors lined up to race 3,000 or more miles to New York. The second aim though, was open to interpretation: *Jester* was Blondie's vision of supreme simplicity, a 25-foot Scandinavian Folkboat with an unstayed mast and a Chinese junk-style sail – and just four ropes with which to control the sail, all from the security of the cockpit. He told Chris Brasher that he considered his main problem on the passage would be boredom; to relieve same he had on board the last fifty issues of the *New Yorker*, which he had not had time to read this last year.

Blondie was a quiet and discreet hero and we can only surmise what he thought about the 39-foot, 13-ton *Gipsy Moth III* as he looked at her across the dock. Whereas *Jester* had one sail, the cutter-rigged *Gipsy Moth III* had eight, three of which were likely to need adjusting at any one time, more or less constantly. He would have looked at Miranda too, a 14-foot high complex of bars and ropes needed to drive *Gipsy Moth III*'s rudder directly, then looked back at his own self-steering invention, a neat servo-assisted device driving just a trim tab attached to *Jester*'s rudder.

If *Jester* was the apogee of the spirit of Blondie's rules and *Gipsy Moth III* quite the opposite, the other four competitors were lining up with Jester's philosophy. *Eira*, Valentine Howells' entry, was also a Folkboat but with increased sail area to pick up more breeze on the southern route Val intended to take. Of the four other competitors it was this boisterous Celtic Viking, the man-mountain Val, that Francis warmed to most personally and feared most competitively. Here was a man who not only sold his farm to finance taking part in the race, but whose 'Live-Long' grog was as fearsome as the man himself. The recipe? Smash up two dozen whole eggs, including the shells, stir in juice from six lemons, leave it to do whatever it does for two days, pour in two bottles of Pusser's British Navy Rum. Two cupfuls a day to Live-Long.

The other British entry was also only 25 feet in length, a Laurent Giles-designed Vertue, *Cardinal Vertue*. Vertues were already renowned for their seaworthiness, and if in reality they were no more seaworthy that the lighter, simpler Folkboats, they we certainly more 'sea kindly'. Sailing her was Dr David Lewis, 43 years old, already an experienced solo yachtsman and one interested in the medical side of loneliness and endurance, of which he had already written a paper. Blondie's race was for him as much an exercise in psychological self-experiment, a chance to be his own guinea pig, as it was a dash for glory to New

York. He was a bit too cerebral for Francis's taste, not being a traditional man's man; Francis suspected he would come plum last. In fact he finished third.

On the night before the race these four musketeers were joined by a 40-year-old Central Casting Frenchman, Jean Lecombe, on board an 18-foot bathtub with sails, *Cap Horn*. Little did anyone at Millbay Dock realise that he was to be the opening salvo in the French domination of endurance ocean racing that

All four competiors on board Gipsy Moth before the off at Plymouth

was to come. He was due to leave three days late, after his radio was fitted and supplies brought on board; he was sure he would catch the others up soon enough.

———— ✺ ————

Which route to New York would each one take? The race instructions were deceptively simple: 'Leave the Melampus Buoy to starboard and thence by any route to the Ambrose Light Vessel, New York.' Francis's time studying pilot weather charts in the RORC library had been inconclusive: there was no summer trade wind route sailing west across the Atlantic, only the weighing up of least worst options. His natural inclination was to aim for the shortest route, the Great Circle route, and react to whatever uncertainties the weather gods threw at him. The Great Circle route may well be the shortest but it has its own demons: it passes through the landmasses of Newfoundland and Cape Race, and the fog off the former and ice floes off the latter. To give the fog and ice too much respect by running south of them would take the yachtsmen out of the favourable Labrador current and into the foul Gulf Stream, running there at about 2 knots against them.

Blondie and Val let their yachts make the decision for them. The disadvantage of *Jester*'s junk sail was her reluctance to sail into the wind: equally, she fairly flew along with the wind astern of her. Blondie aimed to sail north to pick up the seasonal North Atlantic depression and use the resulting easterly wind at the top of it to slingshot him towards New York. (Winds travel anticlockwise around a low-pressure area and clockwise around high pressure – that is, in the Northern Hemisphere, the reverse being true south of the Equator).

Val's plan was to use *Eira*'s enhanced sail area to pick up another seasonal weather system, the Azores High, to do the same further south. He forsook the fogs and icebergs in exchange for warmer climes in which to enjoy his Live-Long, if nothing else. Like Francis, Dr Lewis was planning the try his luck with the Great Circle route and take it from there. Jean Lecombe claimed, with the usual shrug, that he was more or less just setting off towards America and hoping for the best. But the reality was that all were guessing and gambling which way the Atlantic winds would blow for the next month; only in New York could the winner take the credit for being the wisest man, for knowing all along.

⚬⚬⚬

And so on 11 June 1960 at 12.00 GMT, off they set into a pure headwind and a choppy sea. Grey clouds lurked above. For the first three days the weather was rough, with gales and no respite in which to rest, let alone sleep properly. For the four yachtsmen it was their baptism by sea water.

Now we don't know exactly when Francis realised that *Gipsy Moth III* was totally unsuitable for single-handed racing, but I suspect it must have been with Plymouth still on his starboard quarter [aft flank], in other words still in sight. It was hardly her fault; she had been built as a bigger and better version of *Gipsy Moth II*, to take part in the RORC coastal races, with a crew of three – or four on the longer races. To race cross the Atlantic she should have had six crew working the watches. Francis had only ever sailed her alone, in calm weather, and had no idea of the trials and effort involved in handling the racing rig and Miranda in rough, tough weather. This is how it soon looked to Francis:

> *As I drew away from the land the wind freshened and the seas got rougher, and I was soon wet through with sea water and sweat reefing the mainsail. The difficulty was to get the sail to roll easily on the boom without someone at the aft end to haul out the creases and folds.*
>
> *For the first three days, the weather was rough with gales. Heavy seas burst on the deck, and I reckoned that it*

took thirty seconds after a sea had broken on deck before the water finished running out of the lee scuppers.

I envied my rivals the comparative ease with which they would be able to change the smaller sails of their boats. In rough water my bigger boat should be better off, but I was losing too much valuable time over my sail changing. It took me up to one and a half hours to hoist the mainsail and to reef it in rough water. I know it sounds inefficient, but my 18-foot main boom was a brute to handle when reefing.

I had to balance on the counter and slacken off the main sheet to the boom with one hand, while I hauled on the topping lift with the other hand to raise the boom. Meanwhile, it would be swinging to and fro, and I had to avoid being knocked out by it. While hoisting the mainsail, I could not head into wind for fear of the yacht's tacking herself, and causing further chaos. As a result, the slides would jam in the track, the sail would foul the lee runner, and the battens would hook up behind the shroud as I tried to hoist the sail. All this time the boat would be rolling to drive one mad, and bucking.

With heavy rain falling, and wave crests sluicing me, I would feel desperate until I got into the right mood, and told myself, 'Don't hurry! Take your time! You are bound to get it done in the end.'

Once, after all this, I had just got the mainsail to the top of the mast when the flogging of the leech started one of the battens out of its pocket. So I had hurriedly to lower the sail and, after saving the batten, go through the whole procedure again. At the end of this unpleasant three days I was only 186 miles south-west of Plymouth.

For non-sailing readers, Francis's problem was this: a sailing boat heading into wind needs to have her sails balanced if she is to steer a steady course. A yacht's sails work in much the same way as an aircraft's wings, by using the air passing over them to create a lifting effect. The mainsail is the powerhouse sail and if not drawn in enough will not 'bite' into the wind – hence the old adage 'a flappy sail is not a happy sail' – but if drawn in too tightly will overreact by trying to steer the yacht into the wind, the so-called 'weather helm'. The foresail's job is partly to encourage the air to flow enthusiastically over the mainsail and partly to create lift of its own. If left to flap it will not be working either and if drawn in too tightly it will offer too flat a face to the wind, catch too much of it and the yacht will be steered away from the wind, the so-called 'lee helm'. When they are both trimmed to complement each other, the yacht will be balanced.

So, having set the sails to balance the yacht, she should in theory carry on in a straight line without any steering needed. In practice it is very hard to achieve the perfect balance for more than a few minutes at a time except in flat water. At this stage the self-steering can be set to maintain the correct course and, as long as the wind doesn't change direction, the boat will crack along nicely on that course for ever. But the wind will change direction and to maintain the original course the foresail, the mainsail and the self-steering device must now be adjusted. On a fully crewed yacht, no problem: one person for each task, all done together, nice cup of tea, thank you very much. Now throw in a typical complication. The wind doesn't just change direction, it blows up a bit too, and a bit too much for all the sails already up. The crew needs to reduce the sails, to reef. Naturally this means rebalancing the foresail and mainsail and re-adjusting the self steering. Again no great drama with a crew, happens all the time, just takes a little longer.

Then Francis had an additional complication: *Gipsy Moth III* didn't have one foresail but two, so his adjustments would normally require a crew of four, if racing. Trying to do it all alone became somewhat fraught in choppy weather but when he hit his first serious Atlantic howler two weeks into the race:

I ran into big trouble on 25 June. The wind had backed steadily during the night. I retrimmed the sails and Miranda before starting to prepare the twin headsails for running.

It took me two and a quarter hours to get the twins rigged, and drawing on the right heading. I thought this was good going, because it was only the second time I had run with twins since the yacht was built, and there was a lot to do.

On every trip from cockpit to foredeck I had to transfer the snaphook of my lifeline four times. I had to unlash the two spinnaker booms from the deck. Then each of them, 14 feet long and 18 inches in girth, had to be hooked to the gooseneck 7 feet up the mast at one end, and to a strop at the clew [aft lower end] of the sail at the other end; then hoisted up by a topping lift, while two guys from the middle of the pole down to the deck kept it from swinging fore or aft.

The tiller had to be freshly adjusted after each sail was hoisted, because the sailing balance was then changed. When both headsails were drawing, it took me a quarter of an hour for the final adjustment to the self-steering gear.

What he doesn't mention is that he was doing all this in the dark, with breaking seas soaking him through and *Gipsy Moth III* wallowing around and not under control. Then, two hours later:

I had been below for two hours after setting the twin headsails, when I noticed by the tell-tale compass attached to the cabin table that the course was erratic.

I found that the clamp which locked Miranda to the tiller was slipping, and I knelt on the counter [flat area at stern] to begin fixing it. The boat was yawing to one side or the other, and each time one of the sails would crack with a loud report.

I turned round and grabbed the tiller. We were going at a great pace, and the following seas would pick up the stern and slew it hard to one side. The yacht would start broaching-to with one headsail aback, promising serious trouble ahead if I did not check it.

I could not leave the tiller, and wondered what I should do. Fortunately I became so sleepy that I could not keep my eyes open, and realised that I must get the sails down.

I thought hard for some time before making up my mind how to tackle the job. At a favourable moment I made a rush for the foredeck, after slacking off one sheet from the cockpit to let the spinnaker pole forward, and to decrease the area of sail offered to the wind.

As soon as I stepped on the deck I realised that I was in for big trouble. I found a 60 mph wind, which I had not noticed in the shelter of the cockpit with the yacht bowling downwind. My sleepiness had been partly to blame, but the storm was blowing up fast.

When I slacked away the halyard, the bellied-out sail flapped madly from side to side. The noise was terrific, and the boat began slewing wildly to port while the great genoa bellied out and flogged at the other sail with ponderous heavy blows. I was scared that the forestays would be carried away.

I rushed back to the tiller and put the yacht back on course, and then forward again to grab some of the genoa in my arms and pass a sail tie round it to decrease the area.

Next, I slacked away the halyard to let the lower half of the genoa drop into the sea, while I struggled with the spinnaker pole on that side.

I had more trouble with the jib, because I could not get the sail clew free from the spinnaker pole; the sail was like a crazy giant out of control. In the end I twisted the foot of the sail round and round at the deck, and finally I got control.

It was dangerous work, and I was grateful and relieved to find myself whole in limb and unsmashed at the end of it.

I realised that I had a serious storm on my hands. I spent five and a quarter hours on deck without a break, working hard.

After lashing down the spinnaker poles, I next started on Miranda, which was already breaking up. The topping lift had parted, letting the spanker drop, and the halyard of the little topsail had gone.

I could easily have got into a flap; it was now blowing great guns, and I had to stand on the stern pulpit while I worked with my hands at full stretch above my head at the wet ropes jammed tight. Miranda's mast was 14 feet high, and free to rotate with the wind.

I was standing with stays and wires all round me, and could have been swept off the pulpit horribly easily if the wind had suddenly changed direction.

I told myself that it would be much worse if I had iced-up ropes to deal with; not to fuss; and to get on with the job. There seemed fifty jobs to do, but I did them all in time.

I lowered the mainsail boom to the deck, and treble-lashed it there. It was only after I had finished that I became aware of the appalling uproar, with a high-pitched wind was now 80 mph.

By the time I got below at 4 o'clock in the afternoon I was still able to cook myself a breakfast, a fry-up of potatoes, onions and three eggs. I reckoned that the wind was now 80 mph. I went to sleep reading Shakespeare's Tempest.

At 8.30 in the evening, I woke to find the sea getting up, and the ship taking an awful pounding. Some seas, like bombs exploding, made the ship jump and shake; she was lying beam-on to the blast, which was from the north-north-east and was moving pretty fast, about 3 knots.

I knew that I must try to slow her down, so I dressed in my wet oilskins.

First, I tried to head her into wind, but no matter where I set the tiller she refused to lie other than broadside to the wind.

I had a big outer motor tyre for a sea anchor, and I shackled this on to the anchor chain, paying out 10 fathoms of chain over the stern; I also paid out 20 fathoms of 2½-inch warp [heavier rope] over the stern. It did not seem to make the least difference to the speed.

I put the wind speed now at 100 mph. The noise was terrifying, and it seemed impossible that any small ship could survive. I told myself not to be weak – what was a 90 or 100-mile wind to a man on Everest?

As night came on I tried to sleep, but waiting in the dark, for the next crash made me tense, and I kept on bracing myself against being thrown out of the bunk.

I was afraid; there was nothing I could do, and I think that the noise, the incredible din, was the chief cause of fear. The high-pitched shriek from the rigging was terrifying and uncanny.

Two hours before midnight I came to think that we were headed into the eye of the storm. I dressed reluctantly, feeling dry in the mouth whenever I started to do anything, but better as soon as I began to do it.

With difficulty, I climbed out into the cockpit. It took strength to hold the rudder full on, but slowly the ship jibbed round. She seemed easier on the east-south-east tack.

When I went below again I could not help laughing; all the same books, clothes, cushions and papers were back on the floor.

I dozed, but could not sleep. I lay tense and rigid, waiting for the next sea to hit. Nothing mattered to me now except survival.

My main fear was that one of the spinnaker poles would break loose and hole the hull. I found that by shining a torch through the cabin ports I could see the poles where they lay on the deck, and I was relieved to find the lashings still holding.

Some of the waves were breaking clear over the ship; one filled the ventilator and shot a jet into the cabin, but everything in it was already wet.

I jibbed round on to the west-north-west heading. I reckoned that the wind had dropped to 80 mph, but the seas were rougher and would be rougher still later on. The angle of heel indicator came up against the stop at 55 degrees, and I watched it do so time after time.

It was difficult to stand up or to move about the cabin, but the queer thing was that the Aladdin heater went on burning steadily throughout; it just did not seem to care a damn for any storm, and was a great comfort.

All night the ship ploughed ahead at 2 to 3 knots, towing the sea anchor and the warp. Next morning the wind had dropped. It was still Force 9 but I went on deck relaxed and grateful to be alive.

The wind was still north-north-east. The turbulent, impressive seas, like mountainous white-capped country, rode down on to the ship. The waves were not regular. Looking down from a crest to the trough below, I estimated the height at about 25 feet.

With the wind abated, I could now hear the striker seas coming. There would be a lull as the ship was deep in *the trough, and I would hear the sizzling sound from the comber before it struck.*

I wondered if I could set a spitfire jib [tiny, heavy cloth jib for storm use] aback to ease the deadly rolling, which made it dangerous to move about below.

Well, admirably heroic, of course, but also – I can't help but feel – all rather necessary. We learn from Blondie's account that he rode out the storm, assuming it was the same one, by simply double reefing his single sail from his cockpit and going below – presumably to catch up on all those old *New Yorkers*. Not a drop of water was on his oilskins, if indeed he used oilskins. We also learn that by the end of the storm they were more or less equally in the lead, albeit with Blondie several hundred miles to the north of Francis.

(If I sound a bit disdainful of Francis's heroics it's only because I'm writing these words on my own yacht, *Vasco da Gama*, currently cruising in the Sea of Corinth. *Vasco da Gama* is a more or less a full size *Jester*, at 40 feet a foot longer than *Gipsy Moth III* and 15 feet longer than *Jester*. Whereas *Jester* had one unstayed mast [so no wires from mast to deck] and one sail, we have two of each; whereas *Jester* had one junk-style sail, we have two windsurfer-style sails; and whereas *Jester*'s sail could be controlled by one halyard [sail hauling up rope] to pull it up, one sheet [sail pulling in rope] to pull it in and two reefing lines [sail partial lowering ropes] to shorten the sail area, we double up on these. The only reason to double up on *Jester*'s rig is size: a single sail big enough to power a 40-footer would be unmanageable, therefore all single-sail boats over 35 feet have two sails and masts, so are ketches. I can't claim to have been in a Force 10 Atlantic gale like *Gipsy Moth III* but my wife Gillian and I have been in many lesser gales, including a particularly bad-tempered Force 8 in the Bay of Biscay. At no time have we had to leave the cockpit to double-reef the sails, and in the

Biscay gale to lower the mizzen sail completely. Like Blondie, we stayed dry and calm – if weary and tense – throughout.)

Anyway, back to the race. At the midway point Chris Brasher's headline in the *Observer* was:

ATLANTIC RACE IS NECK-AND-NECK
One Lone Yachtsman Still to be Sighted

He then reported that *Gipsy Moth* III and *Jester* had both sailed 1,500 miles, with *Jester* 300 miles to the north of *Gipsy Moth III*. Val Howells' gamble to take *Eira* south had failed and he was in light winds and 400 miles behind. Dr Lewis had suffered a broken mast soon after the start and had to return to Plymouth for repairs, re-joining the race three days later. He was the 'One Lone Yachtsman Still to be Sighted'. Lastly, we read that our French friend Lecombe had started five days after the others and had taken the sensible option of heading for the Azores and crossing in the sunshine; as a result, *Cap Horn* was 300 miles behind *Eira*.

⸙

Apart from reading the *Observer* accounts, I am lucky to be shown *Gipsy Moth III*'s log in pride of place in the Holborn headquarters of GAPAN, the Guild of Air Pilots and Navigators, of which Francis was a prominent – and its most famous – member, and to whom he donated his logbook. Nowadays the need for navigators is negligible, so GAPAN has become The Honourable Company of Air Pilots and is the largest livery company in the City. I'm very grateful to the Company's historian, the retired British Airways pilot Peter Bugge, for spending so much time researching Francis's and GAPAN's times together.

So, I learn that Francis always kept very detailed logs. It seems that no event was too small to record in his own shorthand, which, translated could be:

1149 made tea; still 4 knots – 287°

1205 napped

1243 awoke sails flap, adjust main sheet, now 4.5 knots – 294°

1318 adjusted course 301° – 3.5 knots,

1328 napped

1348 tired, back on deck…

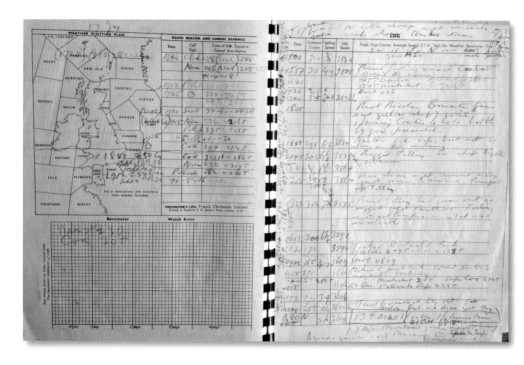

The log had two roles, navigational and narrational. As we will see, in the pre-satellite days navigation was done by dead reckoning, with confirmation by sextant as and when the clouds cleared for a sun, moon or star sight. As the world's greatest navigator, this was second nature to Francis. Then the log was never meant to be seen by anyone but him and it doubled up as an aide-mémoire for the fuller account that would follow in a book or lecture. Consequently the excitement of finding Francis's Rosetta Stone is tempered by the prospect of unscrambling his hieroglyphs.

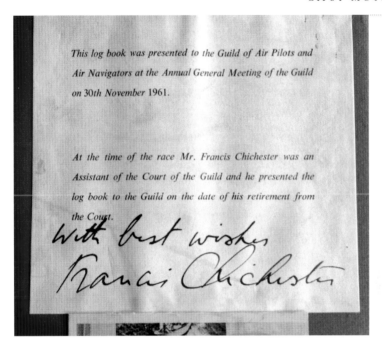

This log book was presented to the Guild of Air Pilots and Air Navigators at the Annual General Meeting of the Guild on 30th November 1961.

At the time of the race Mr. Francis Chichester was an Assistant of the Court of the Guild and he presented the log book to the Guild on the date of his retirement from the Court.

With best wishes

Francis Chichester

In these satellite days of us each knowing within a few metres where we all are all the time and telling each other about it too, it is hard to appreciate the excitement in Chris Brasher's next headline:

ATLANTIC RACE; THE FIRST RADIO MESSAGE
Yachtsman Sails 2,100 Miles From Plymouth in 27 Days

Then the copy:

Francis Chichester in Gipsy Moth III *contacted Cape Race radio station and reported he was 50 miles south-south-west of the Cape. Cape Race is the extreme south-east tip of Newfoundland and about 60 miles south of St. Johns.*

All previous reports received had been from vessels which had sighted the yachts, and it had been feared that the yachts' radio sets had been out of action by the very heavy weather of June 12 and 13.

Chichester is making extremely good progress. He has covered approximately 2,100 miles in 27 days since leaving Plymouth on 11 June. He has 800 miles still to go to New York, and if he keeps up his present average of 78 miles a day he should compete the voyage on 19 July. This would be considerably faster than anyone else who has sailed single-handed from Europe to America.

However, he is still in the ice area off the Newfoundland coast and the United States Navy says that several ships have been diverted from the area because of icebergs.

Francis found it all rather exciting too:

On 8 July, excitement; after twenty-seven days of calling in vain on my R/T, I had an answer! It is true that I closed the land to within 40 miles of Cape Race, Newfoundland, but I got through a message to Chris Brasher in London.

It was a Saturday morning and I felt that he would urgently need some news for the next day's Observer. *I had an odd feeling of excitement in speaking to someone after four weeks' silence.*

Now on the home run, Francis became more philosophical, aware from the coastal radio station that in spite of all the dangers and efforts, the soakings and exhaustion, at the end of this third week he had not sailed as far in a straight line from Plymouth as Blondie had. Although his northerly course meant that Blondie was still 85 miles further from New York than Francis, it must have been discouraging. Furthermore, the late-starting Dr Lewis in his 25-foot *Vertue* was catching him up and was now only 350 miles astern. Still,

Everything seemed to go wrong in that week. I ended it up on the night of 2 July by freeing Miranda and leaving

the yacht to sail herself through the night. I refused to struggle any longer with one sail change after another.

During the next week's sailing I came to terms with life. I found that my sense of humour had returned; things which would have irritated me or maddened and infuriated me ashore made me laugh out loud, and I dealt with them steadily and efficiently. Rain, fog, gale, squalls and turbulent forceful seas under grey skies became merely obstacles. I seemed to have found the true values of life. The meals I cooked myself were feasts, and my noggins of whisky were nectar.

I was enjoying life, and treating it as it should be treated – lightly.

Tackling tough jobs gave me a wonderful sense of achievement and pleasure. For example, on 5 July I was fast asleep, snug among my blankets at 9.30 at night. I woke with a feeling of urgency and apprehension.

A gale squall had hit the yacht, and I had to get out quickly on deck to drop sails. This is one of the toughest things about sailing alone – switching from fast sleep in snug warm blankets, to being dunked on the foredeck in the dirty black night a minute later.

Then I was standing in the water in the cockpit, and from there pressing against the gale. I made my way to the mast, and wrestled with the mainsail halyard with one hand, slacking it away as I grabbed handfuls of mainsail with the other hand and hauled the sail down. The sail bound tight against the mast crosstree and shroud under the pressure of the wind, and the slides jammed in their tracks.

The stem of the yacht was leaping 10 feet into the air and smacking down to dash solid crests over my back. The thick fog was luminous when the lightning flashed, but I heard no sound at all of thunder; it was drowned by the thunderclaps from the flogging sails. I scarcely noticed the deluge of rain among the solid masses of sea water hitting me.

When I got below, my oilskins off, sitting on the settee in glorious comfort sipping a bowl of tomato soup, I had a wonderful sense of achievement.

It was a positive, but perhaps a simple thing, dealing with a difficult and tricky job in a thrilling, romantic setting.

If the first three quarters of Francis's race had been alternatingly arduous and dangerous, the last quarter must have been exhilarating and terrifying. He was now sailing fast in seas of ice and fog. Reading his account I was reminded of the time we were following Dame Ellen MacArthur's round-the-world record attempt in the winter of 2004/5. She too was in iceberg oceans and just carried on regardless at 25 knots, right through the nights. She couldn't see the icebergs on the radar and she couldn't see them with her eyes. She just knew they were out there and that if her trimaran hit one the boat would break up and she'd have to take to the icy waters in her lifeboat. But racers are racers, normal calculations of risk/reward don't apply and like Ellen Francis ignored the risk, gloried only for the reward and cracked on into the invisible:

By this time I was over the Grand Banks, and in fog nearly always, thin fog, thick fog or dense fog, always some kind of fog.

Before I started I had intended to heave to and keep watch in fog, but in the event I never slowed down; I was racing, and what difference would it make if I was stopped anyway?

I had expected 300 miles of fog, but actually I sailed through no less than 1,430 miles.

My reason told me the chance of being run down in the broad Atlantic was infinitesimally small; but my instinct said you must be a fool to believe that.

Then there was ice. I dreaded icebergs, though there were many times more trawlers to hit on the banks than icebergs.

Once a cold clammy air entered the cabin, and I thought there must be a big berg nearby. I climbed into the cockpit to keep watch, but found dense fog on a pitch black night. I could not see 25 yards ahead with a light. Gipsy Moth *was sailing fast into the darkness.*

I decided that keeping watch was a waste of time, went below and mixed myself my antiscorbutic. The lemon juice of this wonderful drink not only keeps physical scurvy away, but if enough of the right kind of whisky is added to it, mental scurvy as well.

I have made up my mind that it is reasonable to press on. I shall put my trust in the Almighty, who, I am convinced, has it all arranged.

The Grand Banks seem wrapped in romance after the turbulent Atlantic.

Next day ended the fourth week of the race. Gipsy Moth *had sailed as she should, like a horse picking up its heels and going full stretch'.*

It was during this last stretch that by a combination of the bravery we have seen, hurtling unseen and unseeing into the ice and fog, and outstanding – almost otherworldly – navigation that Francis won the race. During the fourth week he made 700 miles directly towards New York, leaving just 850 miles still to run. His spirits were high, literally on one occasion:

During this passage I had a narrow escape. I was sitting in the cabin with the last bottle of whisky aboard on the swinging table. Gipsy Moth *suddenly performed one of her famous ski jumps.*

She would sidle up the side of a wave and roll sharply at the top before taking off the other side, and landing with a terrific crash in the trough. This was more than the swinging table could cope with, the bottle of whisky shot up into the air, turned a somersault, and was headed for the cabin floor neck first. I was faced with tragedy – my last bottle of whisky. My hand shot out and I fielded it by the neck on the way down. I could not have been more pleased if I had brought off a brilliant catch in a Test Match.

And now we come to the navigation. Of all the aspects of sailing that have changed since Francis's adventures, navigation must be the foremost. In fact we don't really navigate at all now. I'm of the generation that spans the old, if not the very old, and the new. When I learned to sail, the very old, the sextant, had just been replaced by the old, radio beacons. This made life a lot easier, albeit by today's standards still hopelessly difficult. I remember going to a boat show and with great excitement buying something called a Lokata. There we were having a demonstration on the flat sea that is the Earls Court Exhibition Hall floor and it worked perfectly, with pinpoint accuracy. Weeks later, on a bucking, cold and wet English Channel, it was so hard to get a steady reading from the coastal stations that we nearly missed the Cherbourg Peninsula altogether.

And the new? A few nights ago we made a full moon overnight passage on *Vasco da Gama* from Corinth to Galaxhidi. Next to me as I write is a 15-inch navigation screen. All I have to do is put the cursor over where I want to go, press enter, and it tells me how to get there. If I want to, I can even tell the autopilot to take me directly there, although for that part I still like to make my own decisions. On passage other symbols tell me who else is

out there and if we need to take avoiding action. When we arrive
it tells me where the channel is and I just press buttons on the
autopilot to keep the yacht within the screen image. Navigating
has in effect become a video game.

(The best example I had of this was as a pilot's observer on a
bulk carrier in the Mississippi River. I was writing the last part
of my Mark Twain travel trilogy; he was a riverboat pilot on the
Mississippi before he became Mark Twain. The New Orleans
and Baton Rouge Pilots Association was kind enough to show
me what piloting the Mississippi is like now. We boarded a bulk
carrier just south of New Orleans and took her up towards
Vicksburg to load her with soya beans destined for China. On
the bridge the Bangladeshi officers had an array of all the latest
satellite navigation and radar screens you can imagine, but my
pilot whisked out his iPhone with its Navionics app and took
her the 30 miles up river on that.)

Of course the advantage of never losing oneself also means
there is no longer any satisfaction in finding oneself. You always
know within a few metres exactly where you are; and at the press
of another button, so can the rescue services. When one was not
nearly missing the Cherbourg Peninsula one would occasionally
make a perfect landfall at dawn, purely by old-fashioned dead
reckoning, taking into account tidal streams, leeway and all the
rest of it. Those days and this satisfaction – and danger – are
gone forever.

I once wrote a book about the Portuguese navigator Vasco
da Gama and his place in the Age of Discovery from Dias to
Magellan. The Portuguese had the world's first waterborne empire,
one born out of their extraordinary navigational skills. As they
were working their way down the west coast of Africa, looking
for the sea route to India. For example, each navigator would
erect a large cross on high ground to inform the next navigator
where he had been. After two months at sea, including navigating
by unfamiliar southern stars, Vasco missed the one he was aiming

for, in what is now Namibia, by just 50 kilometres. He then went on to 'discover' India; in fact he did discover it, as a sea route from Europe, and went on to become Emperor of India – twice.

But that's another story. What remains of this story is that some people, like Vasco and Francis, have an extraordinary ability to know where they are right now and where they should be heading next. But the abilities of these two men seem to me to be differently derived, as their aids to navigation were so completely different. Commenting on his navigational skills through the Nantucket Shoals, which would put the seal on his winning the OSTAR a few days later, Francis said: 'If one could rely on accurate information, navigation would be a simple science, whereas the art and great fascination of it lies in deducing it correctly from uncertain clues'. In other words, for Francis navigation was a process of investigation and deduction, a process of inexorable logic with a final twist of hunch. Vasco's navigation, however, was otherworldly, sixth-sensual, inexplicable to logic, like an Arctic tern or a monarch butterfly – or as he too was seaborne, a whale, salmon or turtle.

A few months later, back in London, Francis would be invited to give a lecture to the Institute of Navigation. During the race Blondie's chronometer had broken, leaving Francis to reflect on what he would have done in those circumstances. He called the talk 'An elegant variant of the lunar distance method of determining longitude at sea without reference to Greenwich Mean Time'. Introducing him to the audience, the Institute's Executive Secretary, Michael Richey – himself later to sail *Jester* with great distinction – explained what made Francis a great navigator. He spoke of the qualities of preparation, of dedication, of precision, of discipline and of persistence – and of when all of these had been exhausted and the point reached where logic can go no further in deciding the course to steer, a little something inexplicable, this final shrug of a hunch, that will invariably make the right decision.

But back to Francis's navigational *coup de grâce*, threading his way through the Nantucket Shoals:

I was approaching the Nantucket Shoals, about which the Admiralty pilots say, 'These shoals extend 40 miles south-east of Sankaty Head Lighthouse, and render this one of the most dangerous parts of the Unites States coast.'

At first I hoped to sail round them to the south, without having to tack, but the wind veered, and headed me straight for the middle of the shoals. I was racing, and did not want to tack. I studied all the charts I had to see if I could thread a safe passage through them, bearing in mind that I had seen no landmark or seamark of any description since the Eddystone Rock 3,700 miles behind me.

The night was pitch black, and there were no lights to aid me. I could not get soundings, and radio-beacon bearings are unreliable at night.

None of the radio fixes I got agreed with one another, and the dead reckoning differed from them all. I passed over one shoal, but I knew that there was enough depth and sailed on into a squall.

My track should have taken me, by my reckoning, within 2 miles of a Texas radar tower built on legs on the shoals, but I never saw it, for as soon as I was near the middle of the shoals a thick fog rolled up.

I was not happy; I could not get a radio-beacon fix because the three usable beacons [Nantucket Light Vessel, Cape Cod and Pollock's Rip] were all in a line with Gipsy Moth. *However, I kept on taking bearings from them and formed an impression of where I was.*

Three-quarters of an hour later we were still moving, but still had 20 miles of the shoals to cross. I could not think of anything else I could do, so I went below and turned in for a siesta.

When I woke it was 9.10 and I found the ship going well at 5 knots. I felt that I had been lucky.

He had no idea where he was in the race. He still feared the Celtic Viking in his beefed-up Folkboat and Blondie's northern route gamble. One thing he did know was that there would soon be company and Sheila wouldn't stand for him arriving scruffy, forty sometimes desperate days and nights at sea alone or not.

Next morning I sighted my first mark – Block Island at the north entrance to Long Island Sound. I embarked on an orgy of cleanliness. Sheila had made a strong statement that it was quite unnecessary for a single-handed sailor to turn up looking like a tramp with a dirty boat, so, after I had washed the cabin floor, the stove and everything washable including my shirts, I set to work on myself and threw in a haircut.

Half a day later, there she was:

At 3.50 pm I was met by a fishing-boat. Sheila waved to me, looking very smart in her Mirman hat. Great wavings from friends aboard.

I thought to myself, 'This is very fine but what about the race? They know, I don't. How can I find out without appearing too pushing?' I thought of something, 'What news of the others?' I asked. Someone said, 'You are first', and those words were honey sweet.

I crossed the finishing line at 5.30 pm, 40 days 12 hours and 30 minutes after the starting gun, having sailed 4,004½ miles to make good 3,000 miles on the Great Circle Course.

It was 21 July. For twenty-six of the forty days he had sailed into the wind, fighting Atlantic gales unceasingly. He had set and taken in the 380-square-foot mainsail 23 times and changed the headsails 40 times, numbers that take no account of the constant trimming, reefing, shaking out reefs, Miranda adjustments – nor the constant battle to reject sleep in order to be on deck fighting for every cable of sea across the great ocean. He would later reflect that he had found himself in the midst of all the struggles: 'I quite understand why people go in to retreat. During a month alone you become a real person and you are concerned only with the real values of life.'

Sheila meeting Francis after winning first single-handed Trans-Atlantic race

That heroic last leg dash through the invisible dangers of icebergs and fog and the navigational prowess through the shoals had won Francis the race; and in the end he won it comfortably. Blondie had run out of wind at just the wrong moment, as did the good Dr Lewis, the two of them finishing a week apart after Francis. Val's challenge just disappeared when he called into Bermuda to have his chronometer repaired. The eccentric Frenchman Lecombe eventually made it in his 18-foot bathtub four weeks later.

There followed a week of interviews and celebration, and a further ten days partying with successful Chichester relatives in Cape Cod. Now Francis's thoughts turned to taking *Gipsy Moth III* home. Sheila insisted on joining him and on 21 August they left New York, just as Lecombe in *Cap Horn* was being towed in. The plan was to rely on the Atlantic weather gods and take the sunny, soft, southern route to the Azores, have a break and refill there and then sail home to Plymouth and Buckler's Hard.

It all started swimmingly, in fact it was so hot on board that Francis fashioned a swimming pool from an old sail and he and Sheila took it in turns to splash around and cool down. In Sheila's words,

> *We had glorious sunshine and beautiful blue seas. It was a lovely lazy, happy existence. The nights were really wonderful. I used to go and sit in the cockpit with the moon shining brightly and all the stars out, the sails just billowing out and the ship sighing as she went on her way. I enjoyed watching the dolphins playing around the bow and also saw a shark which was the colour of brandy, accompanied by its pilot fish. We saw a few steamers but on the whole we usually had the whole scent to ourselves. This sort of weather went on for days and Francis became somewhat frustrated.*

Francis's wish for a bit more of a blow was soon answered. As they reached the Azores the gods got bored and sent them a howler. They tried to tack into Horta with just a storm jib and trysail [mini main sail] but then hit a foul current. Most unusually – and certainly only because Sheila was on board – Francis decided to start the motor. But the motor decided it wouldn't start.

Now I don't know how my readers are on the seasickness front in rough weather – I'm always all right as long as I'm on deck. Below deck I get a bit queasy; reading below deck, even looking at a chart or pilot book, is enough to make me actively nauseous; to be anywhere near the bilges I'm certain to puke; but worst of all – almost air ambulance time – is to try to be fixing anything in the engine room. And as for alcohol or a hangover and seasickness, nothing worse has ever been invented – apart from being upside down in a bucking and heaving, oily smelling engine room.

So, how about this from Francis?

I decided to start the motor, but I could not get a kick out of it. This made me angry. The motor had been temperamental before I left England, and the boatyard at Buckler's Hard had put in a lot of time on it; then it jibbed in New York, and the City Island boatyard had worked on it.

This time, I said, I would damn well find out for myself what was the matter with it. It was no picnic, with Gipsy Moth *bucking about in the short steep sea kicked up by the gale, and presently I was lying at full length under the cockpit to get at the bottom of the petrol tank. Every few minutes I had to pop up and tack the ship.*

But I found the trouble: the petrol tank was made of iron, and there was ¾ inch of rust sludge at the bottom, which kept on choking the carburettor.

After I cleaned the pipes I could get it to run only for a few minutes before the sludge choked it again. Finally

I said to Sheila, 'Do you mind if we heave to and wait outside the channel till dawn?' She was relieved.

I backed the storm jib, and we jibbed about in the lee of Fayal while I fished out a bottle of Californian wine and we had a good dinner. Next morning we beat up the channel against a Force 8 wind.

They spent two weeks in Horta, mostly spent waiting for a new copper fuel tank to be built. Horta was not in good shape. An earthquake had broken the island's plumbing, so no chance of the dreamt-for hot baths and it hadn't done the restaurants much good either. They could not leave until 3 October, at which point local wisdom, and not a few locals, told them it was too late. Sheila was inclined to believe them and thought about taking a steamer back to Lisbon and making her own way back from there.

These were in the days before accurate forecasts. No doubt Francis looked at the clear sky and flat sea, licked his finger and held it up to the wind, and decided now was a good a time as any. Within an hour they were in a Force 9, with steeps seas breaking over *Gipsy Moth's* decks.

Francis was in his element, a man at peace with himself while all nature raged outside:

We were fifteen days on passage from the Azores to Plymouth, and on nine of them we were under storm sails. There were impressive seas, magnificent and monumental, but not malicious. It was exhilarating to watch those mountains of water creeping up and passing. The whole passage was a grand sail. As soon as it blew up to Force 7, I could set the storm rig and retire below to prepare a good feast with a bottle of excellent American wine.

Sheila was now quite happy with big seas in a gale...

This doesn't quite tie in with Sheila's version:

> *Within 51/2 hours we were hove-to under bare poles,*
> *with huge seas. I must say I was scared, and I don't think*
> *Francis liked it either. However, he cooked a hearty lunch*
> *of eggs and fried potatoes while I took the helm, feeling*
> *I was going to be pulled into the sea at any moment, we*
> *were rolling so heavily. There were huge seas running, like*
> *black mountain ranges. Waves were crashing on the boat:*
> *they were about 20 feet high, I'd say, with foaming tops.*
> *This rough weather continued day after day.*

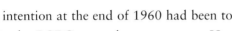

The intention at the end of 1960 had been to race *Gipsy Moth III* in the RORC races the next season. However, a bad back and then hepatitis that put him flat on his back early in 1961 put paid to that. Francis had already agreed to be the guest navigator for Cowes Week and the Fastnet Race on *Stormvogel*, a 75-foot racer of great renown at the time, and didn't feel he

Stormvogel in action

could or should drop out of that. Sailing on *Stormvogel* with her seventeen-strong crew, including a cook, was rather the opposite of sailing solo on *Gipsy Moth III*, and during the long hours when other people were doing all the work, Francis set to thinking about his 1960 Atlantic race.

Before the start he hoped, no matter how unrealistically, to equal the time *Gipsy Moth III* would take had she been fully crewed by six people working watches. He calculated a typical RORC race average distance and speed and added them up to equal an Atlantic crossing. Then he subtracted the foul Gulf Stream current and reckoned a RORC race-crewed *Gipsy Moth III* could cross the Atlantic in thirty days. He was disappointed in his forty and a half days, irrespective of the fact that most people thought it was mighty heroic.

And that was another thing, these 'most people'. The ones that mattered to him, his yachting peer group, his fellow RORC members, were divided as to who had really triumphed: Francis coming first or Blondie coming second. That rankled him. Perhaps Chris Brasher in the *Observer* best summed up the yachting fleet's sentiment:

> *The winner had paid the penalty of near exhaustion by driving his boat down rhumb [direct] line for 40 days with numerous sail changes and reefs, all of which require long hours soaked on a sloping and slippery deck. There was no doubt in the minds of those who saw the competitors arrive that Blondie had won in terms of effort expended and technical development, the prime aims of the race.*
>
> *To the second man in any race goes little glory. But to Blondie Hasler to become the second man to finish in the single-handed transatlantic race he devised will go immense satisfaction. If this race had been run on handicap lines he would undoubtedly have won it.*

But others were impressed, particularly the Royal Yacht Squadron, then as now the most select yacht club in Europe and, with the New York Yacht Club, the most exclusive in the world. They made Francis an honorary member in May 1961 and from then on he always sailed with their White Ensign.

The lesson of his achievements being decried in comparison with Blondie's had sunk home with Francis, who by now was determined to race across the Atlantic again the following summer. This time he would have only one competitor, time, thirty days' worth of time. Once more he had the bit between his teeth: 'I believe that this is the greatest urge to adventure for a man – to have an idea, an ideal or an ambition, and then to prove, at any cost, that the idea is right, or that the ambition can be fulfilled'.

As good luck would have it, also on board *Stormvogel* was the famous yacht designer John Illingworth; in fact, Illingworth had designed *Stormvogel*'s rig. During the Fastnet Race he and Francis shared ideas on how to make *Gipsy Moth III* less of a handful – and so also faster. John suggested a shorter metal mast and recut mainsail and a much shorter boom. This decrease in the mainsail area was to be offset by larger headsails, but ones that would be easier to handle, on dedicated stays. Francis also wanted to get rid of 'the lethal runners, which had seemed animated by a mad lust to brain me'. Miranda, too, had a major makeover and so would become Miranda 2. By the end of the Fastnet they had a plan, no doubt much helped by looking all around John's rig on *Stormvogel* as she romped home first and just missed breaking the race record by 100 minutes.

Francis now had to raise some sponsorship. The first port of call was the *Observer* but the nature of a 30-day dash didn't suit a Sunday-only newspaper. Francis knew the yachting writer John Anderson, then the *Guardian*'s yachting correspondent. One can't imagine the *Guardian* today sponsoring anything as competitive and elitist as a yacht race, even one against time, but like the *Observer* it was once a proud and stalwart rag that jumped at the chance.

With the *Guardian* on board came a technical challenge which today we take in our stride but which caused much boffin head-scratching in 1962: how to transmit Francis's progress daily from the mid-Atlantic back to the *Guardian*'s readers. In those days all radio transmissions were controlled by the government via the General Post Office; surprisingly, the Post Office was keen to become involved with this long-range experiment. Marconi, who made the actual radio equipment, were more obviously enthusiastic. Such ground-breaking radio hardware did not come small or light. Francis's account reminds me of the first mobile telephones, including my Nokia 'brick':

> *At the beginning of March, work started with a meeting of technicians on* Gipsy Moth *at Buckler's Hard. Place had to be found for four heavy banks of accumulators in acid-proof boxes, with Atlantic-proof tops; also for a special charging motor, which might seem light to them, but was heavy to me; and for a radio-telephone of half a man's weight, which had to be high above the water line.*
>
> *All this weight would put the stern down, increase the rolling movement and decrease the sailing power, but the brilliant technical bandits were merciless to* Gipsy Moth. *My chart table and navigating department had to be partially wrecked to make room for the telephone.*
>
> *There followed trouble with the transmitting aerials, trouble with the receiving aerials, trouble with the earthing arrangements, trouble with electrolytic action, trouble with noxious fumes from the batteries being charged.*
>
> *Fortunately Marconi's were really keen that the R/T should transmit, and the GPO men were determined that it should be received.*

Delays, delays, delays. After the first transatlantic Francis vowed never to race without proper sea trials again – and here he was, wading into the same trap. The Agamemnon yard was due to launch *Gipsy Moth III* at Buckler's Hard at the end of March but she did not get into the water until the end of April. The deal with the *Guardian* was for the attempt to take the whole of the month of June, so starting on the 1st with the climax on the 30th. Francis only had May to try out the new rigging, try to understand the vagaries of short-wave radio transmission, victual *Gipsy Moth III* (now forsaking whisky for new sponsor Whitbread's Pale Ale), get himself physically prepared, deal with the *Guardian* and other media, sail her to Plymouth by 27 May and start the race Bristol fashion.

I don't intend to report in detail on Francis's second and record-breaking transatlantic solo voyage of 1962, partly because his source material isn't particularly inspiring and the risk of repetition is as obvious in the telling as in the deed. Although he crossed solo westabout faster than anyone previously, he just failed to meet his own thirty-day target. If he felt that the extra three and a half days were a disappointment, the rest of the world realised that to sail across the Atlantic alone in thirty-three days was a stupendous achievement, and a full week faster than his winning time of two years previously.

On arrival he was met by the BBC's top man in America, Alistair Cooke, who gave Francis this telegram:

> *I would like to extend my hearty congratulations to you on your successful new record-breaking crossing of the Atlantic Stop Your skill and gallantry as a sailor are already well known but this new achievement will certainly cap your career Stop And we are particularly pleased that you have arrived in the United States on 4 July the great*

historic day in United States history when we celebrate our independence = President John F. Kennedy.

Then the following day came another telegram, this from HRH Prince Philip:

Delighted to see that you have achieved your ambition to beat your own record Stop All members of the Guild and millions of other admirers send their heartiest congratulations on a magnificent achievement = Philip.

But for Francis the greatest complement came not from the powerful and illustrious but from that old warhorse and pleasure palace, the Cunard liner *Queen Elizabeth*:

Later in the morning I was proceeding up the East River under motor with Sheila on board. The Statue of Liberty was abeam, and at that critical moment the Queen Elizabeth *passed close on her way out of New York Harbour. She saluted* Gipsy Moth *with three blasts, we dipped ensigns to each other and that was one of the great moments of a lifetime.*

The other interesting part of the voyage is that for the first time I have the impression that Francis actually enjoyed sailing. It sounds strange I know; most of us who sail do so because we love it – well mostly – enough of the time to make us come back for more.

But reading Francis's exploits of his time on board, one is reminded that he only chose sailing as a means to practise his first love, navigation. Seven years after the war, when he suddenly had the urge to navigate again, he was undecided between gliding and sailing, knowing aeroplane flying was unaffordable. It was Sheila who insisted on sailing, so that she could take part too. No, I can't imagine Sheila in a glider either. When Sheila decided on sailing, Francis first sought out a navigator's role with the RORC and it was only when none was forthcoming that he bought the yacht that became *Gipsy Moth II*. From that point the only time when he waxes lyrical about sailing is when navigating a much bigger boat for someone else in one of the famous races. Not until we read this, as he approaches New York for the second time, do we sense that he enjoyed sailing as much as most sailors do:

This is the sailing that sailors' dreams are made of, across the misty mysterious Grand Banks smooth as the Solent with water gliding along the hull gurgling and rumbling. The magic of the voyage was in my blood. It was sheer joy to set or trim a sail to keep Gipsy Moth *sailing at her best; it was sport getting over difficulties. I laughed at incidents like coming across a steamer on the Grand Banks. It began to seem as if life was a joke, and should be treated as one. I was bursting with fitness and joie de vivre that seemed to build up after a few weeks alone. Perhaps it had taken three weeks to shed the materialism of ordinary living. I had become twice as efficient as when with people; my sensations were all greater; excitement, fear, pleasure, achievement, all seemed sharper. My senses were much more acute, and everything was much more vivid – the shape and colour of sky and sea; feeling spray and wind, heat and cold; tasting food and drink; hearing the slightest change in the weather, the sea or the ship's gear. I have never enjoyed anything more than that marvellous last 1,000 miles sailing along the eastern seaboard of North America.*

I'm also not going to spend too much time on the voyage home back across the Atlantic, now *Gipsy Moth III*'s fourth crossing, except to note that Francis and Sheila were joined by Giles, by now sixteen and on summer holidays from Westminster. Both Sheila and Giles were uncomfortable and seasick for much of the voyage in heavy weather up to Force 9. Francis of course loved every moment, especially the quick time: 'As we crossed the line of Plymouth breakwater it was five seconds past noon GMT and we had made the passage from Pollock's Rip in 26 days, 12 hours 14 minutes. Even from west to east it was a fast passage short-

Francis, Giles and Sheila celebrating another Atlantic crossing

handed'. And once Giles had got used to the rigours: 'Before the end of the voyage he was a first-class foredeck hand. Giles had started the voyage as a boy, but finished it a self-reliant man.'

It was at this point in his life that Francis wrote his autobiography, *The Lonely Sea and the Sky*. It became a best-seller and has never been out of print. It finishes with these words:

> *Now I am impatient to return to the Beaulieu River and start my sailing trials. All my new ideas must be proved right or wrong before the spring of 1964. The single-handed race across the Atlantic starts on 23 May, and I believe that there will be a formidable entry for it. It seems to have fired the imagination of many yachtsmen, and so it should, if it is the greatest of all yacht races. I feel sure that my rivals will all be out after my title. However, I believe that with luck Gipsy Moth can go a good deal faster yet, and I look forward to a thrilling, fascinating race. What is more, I shall take my green velvet smoking jacket again, hoping that my new handling methods will be efficient enough for me to dine in style one night while keeping Gipsy Moth racing at her full speed.*

Which neatly brings us on to his next and final race across the Atlantic, but not before I finally get to meet his favourite yacht, *Gipsy Moth III*.

It took some detective work to discover what had happened to *Gipsy Moth III* since 1963, when Francis took delivery of *Gipsy Moth IV*. Her story from glory to neglect to glory involved her being rescued by her current owner, Piers Le Marchant, from a rough life in Plymouth and brought to her current surroundings, in pride of place on her mooring outside his villa in the lovely Kouloura Bay in north-east Corfu.

When Piers's wife, Silvia, learned that we were sailing in Greek waters she immediately invited us to sail over to Corfu, anchor in their bay, join them for lunch and have a look around what she calls 'one of Piers's moments'. Thus three months later Gillian and I find ourselves anchored in turquoise waters alongside a very satisfied-looking *Gipsy Moth III* lying to moorings. First we notice this plaque hanging off her stern:

GIPSY MOTH III
Designed by Robert Clark and built in 1959
By John Tyrrell of Arklow, Ireland for

SIR FRANCIS CHICHESTER

In 1960 he sailed her to victory in the first
Transatlantic Race for Singlehanders

Between 1960 and 1964 he crossed the Atlantic
Ocean six times, setting a new record for
Singlehanders in 1962 and taking second place
in the Singlehanded Race of 1964

'I put that up to ward off the endless questions', says Piers. 'And sometimes to remind myself what she has done.'

My first impression on board is how small she is. Today's yachts are so much more voluminous than those of fifty years ago because now they have to fulfil two roles: passage-making and holidaying – and often the passage-making is not much further than to the next marina. In *Gipsy Moth III*'s day, passage-making was all that counted; firstly, there were no marinas and secondly, the concept of yachting for leisure rather than racing had not yet arrived.

She also feels cramped because two months ago I sailed *Gipsy Moth IV* in the Solent and *IV* is so much larger than *III*, yet *IV* feels it is the right size for single-handing – maybe I've just got used to bigger boats. A look around any anchorage will

show that the average size for a yacht is now 40 feet, the same as *III*, whereas in the early 1960s *III* would have been much larger than the standard length of 32 feet.

The author on board the revived Gipsy Moth III in Corfu

I suppose it's also because I have spent the last two months on *Vasco da Gama* researching and writing this chapter, mostly, it seems, about Francis's heroics in the endless Atlantic gales. When he describes hanging on as the counter (at the very stern of the boat) rises and falls 20 feet, I had an image of him standing, bracing himself and hanging on to something solid like a rail or post; in fact the counter is so small that he could grab it with both hands. At first this scaling down somehow diminishes his heroics; then, when the image of him hanging on the gale-swept counter is applied, it magnifies them.

Piers has restored *Gipsy Moth III* to her specification of 1964, when, as we shall see, Francis came second in the second transatlantic race. Down below, he has kept the original heads and galley and most of the layout except for the navigation station, which has been modified for today's electronics. Everything you cannot see has been replaced and made modern: all the electrics, plumbing, tanks and power train. What is surprising in view of the narrow hull is the headroom at 7 feet; they had deep and heavy keels fifty years ago – again a boon in a rough going but a pain – almost an impossible pain – when trying to manoeuvre in a modern marina. On deck he has simplified the sail plan for ease of handling, just as Francis should have done.

Over lunch we chat about how all this came to pass.

'It was as simple as seeing an advertisement in *Classic Boat*. I had my first sights on retirement and thought that at that stage I would like sailing trips. My son Edward is a wonderful sailor and of course I wanted to encourage him. Something we could do together', he says.

'But you chose the hard way, restoring a classic rather than buying new fibreglass.'

'I just have always been into classics. Done a lot of classic car racing. And I just about grew up with the Chichester era, so it was connecting history in a way, I suppose. I couldn't resist. I had what Silvia calls one of my moments. It was an impulse buy but a considered impulse, if that makes sense.'

'So how long did it take? When did you start?' I ask.

'The restoration took nine years, I've had her sailing three years, so I must have bought her twelve years ago. 2002.'

'So you sailed her here directly from there?'

'No', Piers replies, ' I still have a day job'. He is high up at JP Morgan. 'We tried at first keeping here in the UK, on the Beaulieu River near you. But then we did the maths of keeping a boat in England and the Med. I don't want to sound skinflint, but...'

'We did the maths too', I agree. 'The difference in mooring fees pays for an awful lot of easyJet flights. So a crew sailed her down.'

'Yes, I was a grown man crying when she rounded the point and sailed into the bay.'

After a long lunch we somehow take the dinghy back for more photographs in better light. It is wonderful to see *Gipsy Moth III* live and alive after so many words and imaginings, to pull the tiller – still too heavy! – to haul on the rigging, which Francis grappled so enthusiastically, to kick back in the saloon where Sheila and Giles crossed the Atlantic too. What is so fine is that she has been so sensitively restored, so that she is not yet a venerable old lady floated out for show, rather a good old soul who can still put in good watch, but now has the pleasure of a family besporting themselves on and off her decks in ideal waters.

The 1964 Single-Handed Trans-Atlantic Race was a very different animal from the first one of 1960. The first race, with only four entrants, had struggled to catch the yachting and public attention until it actually started. The 1964 race drew fifteen entrants: eleven were British – including all four from 1960, two were French, one was Danish and there was one Australian. Whereas the 1960 race had been positively Corinthian, by 1964 sponsorship was everywhere – including on *Gipsy Moth III*. The *Guardian* had agreed to sponsor Francis in return for daily radio reports, the technology of which had also advanced to the point of reliability during the intervening four years.

Francis never said so, but I suspect he knew the game was up the moment he saw the French yacht *Pen Duick II* at Plymouth. If not then, then when he first saw her skipper, Éric Tabarly. Although *Pen Duick II* was the same size as *Gipsy Moth III*, she had been specially designed for this race; philosophically she was *Jester* writ large. Her mizzen mast was actually in the cockpit, so relieving her skipper of half his deck duties. Her foresails were permanently rigged on their stays. She carried no heavy long-range radio – and therefore no obligation to spend time composing and sending reports. She looked as if she had won the race before it even started. Then there was Éric himself, a serving French naval officer with official French government support, thirty-two, trim, fit and muscular – and already a well-known yachtsman.

They battled it out across the Atlantic but unless she sank *Pen Duick II* was always going to win. And she did, in twenty-seven days. It would likely have been twenty-three or twenty-four days had not Éric lost his self-steering after eight days. Francis at least came second and had the satisfaction of achieving his goal of breaking the thirty-day crossing – by three minutes – an amazing achievement in itself for a 63-year-old recovering from cancer sailing a yacht designed to be sailed fully crewed.

The purpose built racer Pen Duick II, Gipsy Moth III never had a chance

The archives from the *Guardian* don't make particularly informative reading, as the daily reports only ever mentioned those yachts with radio equipment, the only ones able to report their position. Thus it seemed as if Francis was going to win again until the day before the finish, when the US Coastguard spotted *Pen Duick II* and it became clear that all the headlines had been guesswork. The conditions had been the most favourable yet; the gods still threw in the odd gale as a sop to Francis but the times were fast and the crossings, by comparison, uneventful. Francis's own reports to the *Guardian* don't reveal much that we didn't already know: he was happiest in what most people would consider hardship and danger and unhappiest when conditions were balmy and undemanding. The final sentence of Gavin Maxwell's review of *The Lonely Sea and the Sky* comes to mind: 'I can feel nothing but admiration for his intense vitality, no matter what he's trying to prove to himself'.

But the implications of the race are more interesting than the race itself. In 1964 France was going through one of its grumpiest periods: the aftermath of the loss of Algeria was still divisive, as was guilt from the Second World War capitulation, the economy was stuck, the *gloire* of France lost in the modern world. There was open talk of a military *coup d'*état. Yachting as a sport or pleasure was élitiste and hardly existed; Britannia, it seemed, still ruled the waves, big or small.

Then all of a sudden, out of nowhere, a French officer in a French boat won a famous French victory and it was if someone, somewhere, had flicked a switch. The newspaper *Paris Jour* led with 'Thanks to Éric Tabarly, it is the French flag that triumphs in the longest and most spectacular race on the ocean, which the Anglo-Saxons have long considered their special domain'. General de Gaulle immediately awarded Éric Tabarly the Legion d'Honneur and he and Jean Lacombe – by now in a 23-footer – returned home to a hero's reception.

The purpose built racer Éric Tabarly, Francis never had a chance

Pen Duick II's victory fired a nation into yachting. Since then, long-distance ocean racing has been dominated by French boats and sailors, many of them superstars in France – even the exception, Ellen MacArthur, was based in France, speaks good French and has become a *héroïne*. Moreover, the French yachting industry now produces nearly half of all production yachts in the world and France is the biggest marine market in the world outside the US. French yacht designers are the most prolific and respected in the world. It seems that every French port and harbour has a marina, often subsidised locally, and crammed full of yachts, many of them British, escaping rapacious marina fees back home.

If *Pen Duick II*'s victory inspired the French yachting boom, *Gipsy Moth III*'s loss seems to have heralded the start of Britain's yachting decline. In 1964 most yachts in UK waters were still locally built. British designers like Francis's duo Robert Clark and John Illingworth, as well as Laurent Giles, Peter Brett, Arthur Robb and C.E. Nicholson were the most famous yacht designers in the world. But their traditional customers could afford the low-volume or one-off designs; when yachting became popular and the demand for volume grew, the British boatbuilders simply could not compete with the French – let alone the Germans or Americans.

The result is that whereas France claims to have eight million active sailors today, Britain has less than two million. In sense this is just as well as there is hardly anywhere affordable to keep a boat. Marinas are few and absurdly expensive – the reason why many British yachtsmen keep their boats cross the Channel and one of the reasons we keep *Vasco da Gama* in Greece. Like Piers le Marchant, we have done the maths and the 50–75 per cent savings of keeping a boat outside UK waters more than pay for the cheap flights out there.

Britain needs a new Francis or Éric – step forward Sir Ben Ainslie – but without affordability, yachting will never become a popular pastime in the UK as it is in France.

NOTES:

15. Still going strong with the fifth generation of Tyrrells, John and Billy, and now called Arklow Marine Services Ltd.

I hate being frightened, but, even more,
I detest being prevented by fright.

CHAPTER 9

Gipsy Moth IV

A few days shy of New York, when it had become obvious that Tabarly in his specially built *Pen Duick II* was going to beat Francis to win the race, two other Chichesters shared a phone call. One was Sheila; the other was a cousin, Lord Dulverton, grandson of Sir Edward Chichester, the ninth baronet of Youlston and heir to the W.D. & H.O. Wills tobacco fortune. Tony Dulverton was very rich and equally sporting and a great philanthropist of imaginative projects.

'Look here', he asked Sheila, 'why didn't Francis have a new boat to beat this ghastly Frenchman?'

'Two reasons, Tony,' Sheila replied, 'time and money.'

'Well, the French are backing their chap all out. If British industry won't back Francis, I jolly well will! Tell him I will provide him with a suitable vehicle for the next race. I want you to tell him that I want to come round and see you both.' Click, one imagines.

But during those long and lonely transatlantic days and nights Francis's thoughts had turned beyond the next OSTAR – and on to something far more ambitious: a record-breaking solo circumnavigation of the world. He mused on following the old eastabout clipper route around the capes of Good Hope, Leeuwin and Horn. The tales of rounding Cape Horn in particular intrigued and scared him in equal measure: 'Of the eight yachts I knew to have attempted it, six had been capsized.

Lord
Dulverton,
distant
cousin
and closer
sponsor

It not only scared me, frightened me, but I think it would be fair to say that it terrified me'. Then he added, tellingly: 'I hate being frightened, but, even more, I detest being prevented by fright'.

While being nursed back to health from his cancer by Sheila and her prayers, Francis became inspired by reading about the Australia-bound voyages taken by nineteenth-century wool clippers. He began to collect stories for what would become his next book, *Along the Clipper Way*. The clippers took an average of 123 days to make their passage, so Francis set himself the target of making the passage in a hundred days. At first sight this would seem impossible. The maximum speed of a yacht is directly related to its length in the water: a sailing boat for the attempt would be around 50 feet (16 metres) long, whereas a clipper ship such as *Cutty Sark* is 212 feet (65 metres). And there's the small matter of one old semi-sick man as crew versus several dozen strapping hearties working watches.

I decided that when the time came I would give out that
I was trying to equal 100 days, a good round number,
which people could understand. What I was really after
was a voyage round the world faster than any small boat
had made before; but I did not want to say anything about

this; I still had the feeling, inherited from the early flying days, that disclosing a particularly difficult objective was to invite failure.

What was the best time that I could hope to do this in? In 1964, in the second solo race across the Atlantic, I was beaten by Lieutenant Éric Tabarly of the French Navy, who had a boat specially built for the race; his speed was 105½ miles per day for the east-west crossing of the Atlantic. On the west-east passage home after the race I had my son Giles with me, and we averaged 126 miles per day. I reckoned that the clipper way would be more like the west-east passage across the Atlantic than the east-west. On the other hand, a passage of 14,000 miles was a very different proposition from one of 3,200 miles. However, I reckoned that 125 miles per day was a fair target, at least one that I could aim for, and hope to hit.

On his cancer recovery Fastnet sail on *Stormvogel* in 1961, Francis had sailed with the racing yacht designer John Illingworth. Illingworth's own *Myth of Malham* had been its own revolution and Illingworth himself was at the height of his reputation. After the Fastnet he had redesigned *Gipsy Moth III*'s mast for the 1964 OSTAR and as they got to know each other he showed Francis a sketch for what amounted to a British *Pen Duick II*: a purpose-built single-handed racer Illingworth and his partner Angus Primrose called *New York Express*. Nothing had come of it; Francis was the only realistic customer and there wasn't time, let alone money, to build and commission her before the 1964 race. But still, Francis reflected as *Gipsy Moth III* pounded her way towards New York, *New York Express* could be the basis of a *Gipsy Moth IV*.

In New York after the finish, Sheila told Francis about cousin Tony's offer. Back in London Francis told Tony about his new clipper route round-the-capes-round-the-world plan. Tony was enthusiastic and agreed to finance it, under one condition: *Gipsy Moth IV* must be built by Britain's premier yacht builder, Camper & Nicholson at Gosport, who had – after all – built his grandfather's yacht. Francis was in no position to refuse; in any case he had no reason to suspect that this alliance of the elite – Camper & Nicolson, Illingworth and Primrose, Chichester and Dulverton – would not produce the perfect girl child in which to follow the clippers around the world, and beat them too. In the fallout that followed, it's worth remembering that the designers faced an almost impossible task with the technology available in the early 1960s: to design a boat that was long and light enough, and full sailed enough, to be handled alone at speed by a man of sixty-five in the Roaring Forties and around Cape Horn.

The fact that at the first meeting Dulverton magnanimously announced that money was not to be an object only made matters worse, as it removed all sense of responsibility for time and money from the designers and builders. Without these constraints the impulse to fiddle and tweak became irresistible for people who love nothing more than an unbudgeted fiddle and tweak. At the second meeting Camper & Nicholson gave Dulverton their cost estimate, based on all their experience and the design in front of them at the time. Somewhere in there was the word 'approximate'. Even as Dulverton opened the envelope, the designers and builders were dreaming up modifications that would render any estimate – and the word 'approximate' – useless. While they were throwing away Tony's money, they were also throwing away Francis's time.

Building was due to start at the end of 1964 and to be finished by September 1965, ready for autumn and winter sea trials in the Solent – masquerading as the Southern Ocean. But almost immediately the squabbles started: Illingworth wanted her to be long and light, Francis wanted her to be a smoothed-out version of *Gipsy Moth III* ; Illingworth designed a single-skin hull, Campers insisted on a six-ply laminated cold

moulding; Illingworth drew an enormous and heavy self-steering installation, Francis pleaded for a simpler and lighter Blondie Hasler model; Francis had specified a flush deck to help the southern ocean rollers on their way; between them Illingworth and Campers had committee'd up all kind of sticking up appendages; the mast was supposed to be only slightly heavier than *Gipsy Moth III*'s, instead it was twice the weight – and that overweight was in the worse place, on high. Sheila had designed the interior to be sea kindly and sensible, Campers lost the design and quickly threw together a landlubber's special, with flying-open drawers and slippery surfaces; Francis knew how much mainsail area he could handle, Illingworth decreased it and increased the foresails; Illingworth's design called for a short, deep central rudder, while Francis saw himself broaching

Gipsy Moth IV at Camper & Nicholson for the rebuild (UK Sailing Academy)

in the Roaring Forties and insisted on a full keel. Sheila summed up the chaos of the endless roundabout meetings: 'I did my best to keep everyone coordinated and regretted very much that no one agreed it would be a good idea to make notes of the meetings of these highly expert men, who gave their views and said they'd remember it all'. They didn't take notes; and they didn't remember what they'd disagreed about.

Thus the summer of 1965 dragged on, the build stopping and starting with each design argument, the costs spiralling in the background, the winter sea trials becoming an impossibility. Every week Francis would stride from St James's Place to Waterloo, then take the train back and forth to Gosport.

Eventually, six months behind schedule, in March 1966 the yacht was ready to launch.

Now sea folk are a superstitious lot, seeking explanations in the fanciful for the inexplicable vagaries of Nature's seafaring temperament. These superstitions start before a ship has sailed. Thus when launching, two bad omens must be avoided at all costs: the bottle must break on the bow when the ship is named and she must flow smoothly down the ramp, of her own volition.

Yes, you've guessed it, both bode inauspiciously. It was Sheila's task to proclaim 'I name this yacht *Gipsy Moth IV*!' and smash the bottle on the bow. Unfortunately, she listened to the Camper manager, who told her: 'It's all perfectly engineered, just let the bottle swing from the holder and it will break on its own.' Of course it didn't. Francis 'was horrified; my heart sank; I thought, "What a terrible omen"'. An awkward shuffling of feet, knowing looks at the clouds and pursing of lips spread around the gathering. Next time Sheila did it herself, giving the champers an almighty chuck and the bottle spread its good luck shards against the bow. Now was the time for the foreman to wield his mallet against the holding chock, followed by *Gipsy Moth IV* sliding gracefully down the rollers. Whack! Off the chock flew – but the yacht stayed stubbornly in her cradle. Francis 'had a cold despair of

Two ill omens: top, champagne needs two attempts to wet the bow and bottom, ramp needs two attempts to slip the keel.

premonition in me' but jumped down from the quay and leaned his shoulder against the cradle. Others joined him and s-l-o-w-l-y she slid down the greased ways.

But worse was to follow. Superstitions may be whimsical but there was nothing whimsical about the way the hull floated on the water, a good two feet higher above the waterline than looked natural. Francis wrote: 'Then, two or three tiny ripples from a ferry steamer made folds in the glassy surface, and *Gipsy Moth IV* rocked fore and aft. "My God", Sheila and I said to each other, "she's a rocker!"'

Looking horribly tender, Gipsy Moth IV on first sea trials

But even worse was to follow. The first sea trials were a disaster. The rigging called for applying and unapplying levers and rockers with each change in direction, something Francis had specifically asked them to avoid. He quickly deemed the yacht unsailable singlehandedly. And then, yet worse:

> *The next thing that happened, far more serious, was that a puff of wind, only Force 6, heeled the boat right over, so that the masts were horizontal, parallel with the water surface. I kept watching the mast and never took my eyes off it as I particularly wanted to see how far over she would go. Campers' men told me that she lay over with her toe rail under water when on her mooring in a moderate puff of wind. Here was a boat which would lay over on her beam ends on the flat surface of the Solent; the thought of what she would do in the huge Southern Ocean seas put ice into my blood.*

Drastic surgery was needed and the team decided to cut into the keel to make space for 1,000 kilos of lead. No one mentioned this to Tony, assuming that he would keep paying away quite happily in the background.

Francis seemed to go from woe to woe. He had requested a flush deck so that the rollers would sweep right off it; but she had all kinds of superstructure in the way. On one of these was a skylight. Francis was sailing in a Solent chop with just mizzen and foresail and the boat leaned over 45 degrees as usual. He slipped and came down a real cropper. As is so often the case, the damage was not apparent until the next morning:

> *I noticed that this purple-black patch was spreading, and that it was down below my knee, and up into my buttock. Now the pain began, and I found my foot half-paralysed. Like a fool I did not go to my doctor: the truth was, I was*

*frightened that he would try to stop my voyage. I worked
hard with exercises, trying to get back the movement in
my foot and leg. It was a bad handicap because I could not
move easily or do my daily exercises which are essential
to keep me fit. Indeed, it was to be fifteen months before
I could begin to walk enough to get real exercise from it.*

When *Gipsy Moth IV* was re-launched she was more stable but
still horribly 'tender', as yachtsfolk describe a boat that fails to
make a lasting impression in the passing wind and waves. But
now that the most glaring problem was partially solved, Francis
began to notice all the others: the main cabin was cramped and
uncomfortable, the deck leaked onto the bunks, the navigation
table was far too small, the water fouled in the tanks, the fuel
leaked into the bilges, the basins and heads pumped backwards,
the engine had to be moved and so used up even more space, the
fumes backfired, the headsail was not able to power her alone,
the sail combination was incoherent – in fact, Francis felt, every
system on the boat was either poorly designed or poorly built.

Well, that all sounds like a bit of a disaster, so I think I'd better
see for myself and take a sail in the old girl to see if she really is
as wobbly as Francis made out. But first some back-story.

A year after taking Francis to his knighting in Greenwich,
so in July 1968, *Gipsy Moth IV* was back there being hauled
out and put into a dry dock cradle next to her inspiration, the
tea and wool clipper ship *Cutty Sark*, where she was opened
to the public. But by 2004 thirty-six years of exposure to air
and trampling feet had rendered her unsafe and she was closed
to visitors. Dry rot and woodworm seemed to be her fate until
Paul Gelder, editor of the sailing magazine *Yachting Monthly*,
launched an ambitious campaign to save her. First he had to buy
her from the Greenwich Maritime Trust. The price? £1 and a gin

and tonic.[16] How ambitious? She would not only be rekindled by the craftsmen at Camper & Nicholson, many of them coaxed out of retirement, but to celebrate the fortieth anniversary of Francis's voyage and a hundred years of the magazine, she would sail around the world again – this time for pleasure and education.

Her second circumnavigation was eventful. Managed by the UK Sailing Academy (UKSA) in Cowes, which still looks after her now, she set off on a multi-leg voyage in collaboration with the Blue Water Rally and *Yachting Monthly*. Each leg would have a different skipper, mate and four young crew from UKSA's training programme. All went well until one them managed to put her aground on a reef en route to Tahiti. Salvaged, she was taken to Auckland, New Zealand where Grant Dalton's America's Cup team generously enabled her second restoration. Two months after hitting the reef she was sailing again.

Back in the UK she rather lost her way and in 2010, with bills mounting and interest waning, the UKSA put her up for sale. The *Sunday Times* reported that a foreign sale seemed the most likely outcome. Luckily for us all, that Sunday the Cambridge Weight Plan business team Rob Thompson and Eileen Skinner bought the paper and were motivated into rescuing her. Keen amateur sailors, they were determined to keep the yacht that had inspired their generation of sailors to take up the sport in British waters. A deal was struck with the UKSA to keep her in commission at Cowes. They formed the Gipsy Moth Trust, a charity with the twin aims of encouraging disabled and disadvantaged children to take to the seas and keeping the old girl fit for sailing. And this is how she now plies her trade, chartering from Cowes for the greater good. Francis would be happy enough with that.

So, on a particularly perfect Solent sailing day, I take *Gipsy Moth IV* out for a jolly. With me on board is her regular skipper Richard Baggett, Bill Tate, who hopes to show me how Francis navigated by sextant, and two UKSA students, who are going to haul the ropes and generally rush around. The weather was the very opposite of Cape Horn's: full sun, flat calm and pleasant sea breeze of 12 knots running with the current. Still, I'm grateful to stand where Francis had stood, helming *Gipsy Moth IV*'s tiller as he had helmed it.

I find some clear water and hoist all three sails – well, I don't personally but you get my drift. For those of you who don't know, the perfect point of sail is called a beam reach, that is, when the wind is directly on the beam. The wind holds the yacht down into the water, the sails are full and free and offset at 45 degrees and if the sails are perfectly trimmed the hull will track straight through the water with no adjustment at the helm. I set about setting the sails just so. Too tight main or mizzen sail and the hull will tend to round up into the wind, so-called 'weather helm'; too tight foresails and the bow will blow off, so-called 'lee helm'. I start with the main, letting the mizzen and foresail almost loose, just short of flapping – as noted before, a flappy

The author sailing Gipsy Moth IV off Cowes; not a Cape Horn in sight

sail not being a happy sail. A well-set main will bring the hull just – and only just – into the wind. Time to let the main out a touch and haul the foresail in until the bow just – and only just – takes her course off the wind. Then tighten back the main, loosen off the foresail and hey presto, no hands on the tiller. At that point I bring the mizzen into play until it is full enough to look happy but not too full to be stressed. *Voilà! Gipsy Moth IV* is sailing herself 'straight and level', as Francis would have said flying his first *Gipsy Moth*, or 'full and by' sailing his subsequent ones.

Now I put her through a simple figure of eight, whereby we have to tack through the wind, pass through another beam reach and then gybe. Tacking and gybing are no drama, albeit with the crew hauling on the ropes and me just offering encouragement.

So *Gipsy Moth IV* sails sweetly enough in perfect conditions – but her behaviour in perfect conditions was hardly among Francis's complaints. We need some waves to throw her off balance. Looking over to Portsmouth, I see a large motor yacht heading towards Cowes at some speed. At the same time the red and white Cowes to Southampton car ferry is nosing out of the harbour. I estimate where the two washes might meet and head off towards it. The ferry's wash, even though hardly boisterous, is enough to bounce the bow overly into the waves. The stinkboat's wash did really unsettle her, far more than would seem compatible for a 55-footer. So even now, after all the mods and tweaking over the years, she is still inherently tender.

But it is down below that Francis's complaints seem most justified. The saloon is cramped, stark and uncomfortable. Most of the problems, like flying lockers and backfiring loos, have been solved over the years but the straight-backed, sharp-edge design is inherently unwelcoming. Weight saving was clearly the design priority and by today's carbon fibre Spartan standards Francis got off lightly, as it were. But today's racer is designed for young, fit crews, not 66-year-old cancer remissives sailing alone in the Southern Ocean; some concession of comfort would not have made much difference to speed and would have done wonders for morale.

Like Francis, I am bemused that a second heads, or loo compartment, had found its way on board. He kept quiet about the anomaly, knowing that it would be a good place to dry out sodden oilskins, something the designers had not otherwise thought about. The galley, the boat's kitchen, is down on the starboard side next to the stairs from the cockpit and I can almost hear Francis swearing as his casserole takes another dowsing. The navigation station is tucked away behind the cabin access and so invisible from the cockpit. Even on a calm Solent day it is clear the design is fundamentally flawed below decks and, judging by the way today's crew have to leap over protruding obstacles, flawed on deck too. If Francis was right about these, I'm sure he was also right about her behaviour in conditions I can barely imagine on this perfect sailing day.

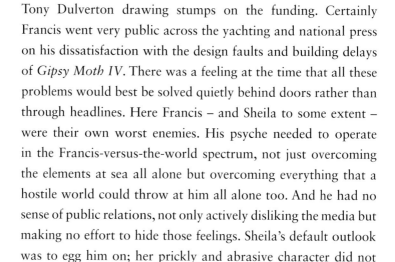

It's hard to say how much Francis was the cause of his next disaster, Tony Dulverton drawing stumps on the funding. Certainly Francis went very public across the yachting and national press on his dissatisfaction with the design faults and building delays of *Gipsy Moth IV*. There was a feeling at the time that all these problems would best be solved quietly behind doors rather than through headlines. Here Francis – and Sheila to some extent – were their own worst enemies. His psyche needed to operate in the Francis-versus-the-world spectrum, not just overcoming the elements at sea all alone but overcoming everything that a hostile world could throw at him all alone too. And he had no sense of public relations, not only actively disliking the media but making no effort to hide those feelings. Sheila's default outlook was to egg him on; her prickly and abrasive character did not suffer fools gladly and from her armchair she saw Illingworth,

Primrose, Camper and Nicholson as incompetents and cousin Tony a damn fool for paying for it all. No doubt Dulverton read about Francis's complaints in the press and heard about Sheila's disdain through the family grapevine. Either or both ways, he pulled the plug and told Francis the overspent monies would have to come from Francis's own efforts.

Thus Francis had to spend the summer of 1966 not on the sea trials he and *Gipsy Moth IV* so desperately needed, nor on trying to repair his damaged and non-repairing thigh, but on raising money. Luckily Colonel Whitbread of the eponymous brewing company came to the rescue, topped up by the International Wool Secretariat and major equipment suppliers who waived costs. The *Sunday Times* and *Guardian* chipped in as media partners with running costs, too, and eventually Francis had the funds to take on the voyage, if not the time to prepare properly for it.

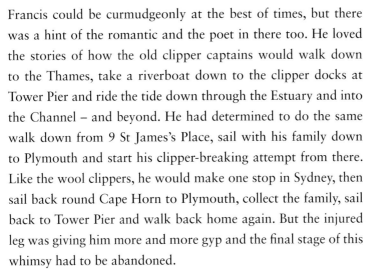

Francis could be curmudgeonly at the best of times, but there was a hint of the romantic and the poet in there too. He loved the stories of how the old clipper captains would walk down to the Thames, take a riverboat down to the clipper docks at Tower Pier and ride the tide down through the Estuary and into the Channel – and beyond. He had determined to do the same walk down from 9 St James's Place, sail with his family down to Plymouth and start his clipper-breaking attempt from there. Like the wool clippers, he would make one stop in Sydney, then sail back round Cape Horn to Plymouth, collect the family, sail back to Tower Pier and walk back home again. But the injured leg was giving him more and more gyp and the final stage of this whimsy had to be abandoned.

Instead, on 16 August 1966, the three Chichesters were joined on board at Tower Pier by Revd Tubby Clayton for a blessing. Also in the cockpit were Erroll Bruce, who had sailed her from Gosport with Francis and Giles, Monica Cooper from

the map business, the Port of London chief Dudley Perkins, and
Lady Dulverton. Tubby had made a composite of Psalms 33 and
107 for the occasion:

> *He gathereth the waters of the sea together. And lay them
> up as in the treasure house. Thy way is in the sea. And thy
> path is the great waters. They that go down to the sea in
> ships and occupy their business in the great waters, these
> men see the work of the Lord and His wonders in the
> deep.*

Tubby had been there at Sheila's insistence and she herself had
been preparing prayer cards. On one side was a reproduction of
Dürer's *Praying Hands* from 1506 and on the other, two prayers:

*Dürer's
Praying
Hands, 1506*

*O Lord God, when thou givest to thy servants to
endeavour any great matter, grant us also to know that
this is not the beginning, but the continuing of the same
until it be thoroughly finished,
Which yield if the true glory;
through him that for the finishing
off my work a down his life, our
Redeemer, Jesus Christ.*

(Sir Francis Drake, 1540–1590)

*O Thou, Who sittest above the
water floods, and stillest the raging
of the sea, accept, we beseech
Thee, our supplications for this
thy servant Francis Chichester,
who in yacht Gipsy Moth IV, now
and hereafter, shall commit his
life unto the perils of the deep. In
all his ways, enable him truly and*

Godly to serve Thee, and by his Christian life to set forth
Thy glory throughout the earth. Watch over him on his
departure and on his landfall, that no evil befall him nor
mischief come nigh to hurt his soul and bring Thy comfort
to those who wait his safe homecoming. And so through
the waves of this troublesome world, and through all
the changes and chances of this mortal life, bring of Thy
mercy to the sure Haven of Thine everlasting Kingdom,
through Jesus Christ our Lord.

(The Old Prayer of the Merchant Navy, seventeenth century, adapted)

It is not surprising that in her autobiography Sheila remarked that Francis's circumnavigation was 'a great spiritual adventure, a sort of pilgrimage'.

The Lord's weather certainly shone on them down to Plymouth; once there, they tied up at Mashfords Boat Yard for the final preparations. The archive film footage of his departure on 26 August shows it to be surprisingly low key, certainly compared to the great brouhaha that greeted his return there almost exactly nine months later.

It wasn't until he had been at sea for a week that Francis felt his voyage had begun. That first week had seen horribly choppy weather and seasickness, as well as crowded shipping lanes and the residue of the anxiety of the preparations and the excitement of the off. On 1 September he was far enough south to enjoy lunch in the cockpit; after lunch he had his first wash and shave for a week. Things were so primitive fifty years ago. Nowadays he would certainly have a water maker and could shower – hot shower too – whenever he liked. Francis's washing regime depended on emptying a bucket of sea water over himself, lathering up with special salt-water soap (since regular soap does not lather in salt water) and rinsing off with another bucket. It follows that his frequency of washing depended on the latitude: on the Transatlantics and later in the Roaring Forties only when things were getting pretty rank, one imagines; around the Equator several times a day, even if only to keep cool.

The warm weather and distance from the shoreside anxieties also helped him sleep. A few days later he reported: 'I had the first good sleep of the voyage, the first good sleep, it seemed, for months. I slept well for four hours without my leg waking me up. Of course this four hours sleep was not the only sleep I got; I would drop off for a few minutes from time to time, and sometimes for an hour or so, usually just about dawn. But four hours at a stretch was a wonderful relief'. He woke up to sluice himself down with some Madeira sea water and a lunch of bread, cheese, salad and beer.

Francis always enjoyed his tipple on passage, reflecting another change in attitudes over the last fifty years. I can just about remember driving in 1966 – it was probably the year I passed my driving test. Everyone seemed to drink and drive as a matter of course – the main concern being not to spill the drink while driving. I clearly remember driving as a teenager being so drunk I was weaving all over the road. A police car stopped me and the officer asked me if there was anything wrong with the steering. Barely able to stand, I must have mumbled something about everything being in perfect working order and off I drove.

Nowadays I drink like a fish ashore but not at all on a passage. Don't sail and drive is as ingrained as don't drink and drive. Francis enjoyed a beer at lunchtime, a whisky in the evening and a brandy when stressed. In fact a major source of stress was to come in two weeks time, when crossing the Equator. There was unlimited beer in the keg – courtesy of Colonel Whitbread – but no way of getting to it, due to a carbon dioxide leak. Luckily there were other kegs and more carbon dioxide to keep him lubricated along the way.

Soon, actually on 9 September, Francis was to have his first taste of one of *Gipsy Moth IV*'s less wholesome habits: broaching. By now well past the Cape Verde Islands, half-way between the Tropic of Cancer and the Equator, they picked up an unexpectedly decent breeze. He hung two poles off the mast, one off the port side for the jib, one off the starboard side for the genoa, so in effect making one large billowed sail to catch as much wind as possible. Inevitably when these sails both fill it effects the steering and on an inherently well-balanced boat there would be enough time between setting the sails and adjusting the steering; but this boat's flimsy self-steering mutinied at the slightest slight, swerved to starboard, backing the jib, which, now on the same tack as the genoa, swung the yacht round to port – not just any old port but right round across the wind and, worse, the waves.

For the casual sailor, too, this broaching is a dangerous situation. It happens when sailing with the wind astern. Let's say there's a nice 14-knot breeze astern pushing the yacht along at 7 knots. On board the wind feels like 7 knots. Slowly and imperceptibly the wind increases and an hour later it's 20 knots, the yacht is sailing at 8 knots and it still only feels like 12 knots' wind on board. Then the thought occurs: if I was sailing the other way at 5 knots, that 20-knot wind would feel like 25 knots. Time to reduce sail, but how? Sails won't come down easily when full, so the only way is to turn the yacht into the wind, at some stage turning through the wind full on the beam with the sails full and across the waves. It's a frightening manoeuvre with a prepared crew waiting for it to happen; alone and unexpectedly even more so. For Francis, though, there was something worse: the realisation that if she broaches this easily in a stiff tropical breeze, how will she fare in the Roaring Forties and beyond?

A week later, on 17 September, nearly at the Equator, Francis celebrated his sixty-fifth birthday with a one-man party.

First things first: the great luxury of a freshwater wash. Second things second: he was now fit and ready to open Sheila's present, 'a luxurious and most practical suit of silk pyjamas'. Third things third: 'drinking a bottle of wine given me by Monica Cooper and other members of our map-making firm for a birthday present'.

As the day wore on a clearly drunken Francis became more lyrical and – I never thought I would write this unFrancis word – sentimental. Firstly his thoughts turned to Sheila: 'I shed a tear to think of her kindness and love, and all the happiness we have had together since 1937'. Looking out at sea later in the afternoon, he felt an inner glow of satisfaction:

> *Here I am, right in the middle of this wonderful venture, just passed by 100 miles the longest six-day run by any singlehander that I know of, and a great feeling of love and goodwill towards my family and friends. What does it matter if they are not here? I would not love them as I do in their absence, or at least I would not be aware of that, which seems to be what matters.*

A wash and brush up in the tropics

By evening he felt the need to change for dinner. Almost as a good luck charm he carried his green velvet smoking jacket with him on all his voyages. It was a pre-Sheila item, made for him by Scholte of Savile Row, and in six Transatlantics on board *Gipsy Moth III* it had never come out of the cupboard. Tonight was its night, along with 'my smart new trousers, clean shirt and black shoes. The only slip-up is that I left my bow tie behind, and have had to use an ordinary black tie'.

Soon he was back in the cockpit writing his log:

Well here I am, sitting in the cockpit with a champagne cocktail, and I have just toasted Sheila and Giles with my love. I will turn on some of the music Giles recorded for me. I meant to ask him to get a recording of Sheila and himself talking together, but forgot, which is not surprising. That first voyage home from America with Sheila, just the two of us, keeps on recurring to me, all the little episodes, and the joy and comradeship of it. The same with the third passage back, with Giles. I wonder if I shall ever enjoy anything as much.

This was followed by a very Francis thought:

I see that action appears a necessary ingredient for deep feeling.

But why worry, with my bottle of the best presented by the Royal Western Yacht Club, my dear Coz Tony's brandy to make the cocktail, a lovely calm evening, hammering along at a quiet 7 knots on, extraordinary pleasure, a calm, nearly flat, sea.

Later, as all us drunks know, it was time to go from sentimental to maudlin:

*People keep at me about my age. I suppose they think that
I can beat age. I am not that foolish. Nobody, I am sure,
can be more aware than I am that my time is limited. I
don't think I can escape ageing, but why beef about it?*

*Our only purpose in life, if we are able to say such
a thing, is to put up the best performance we can – in
anything, and only in doing so lies satisfaction in living.*

*Is it a mistake to get too fond of people? It tears me to
shreds when I think of Sheila and Giles being dead. On
the other hand, I keep on thinking of the happiness and
pleasure I have had at various times with them, usually
when doing something with them.*

*This sort of venture that I am now on is a way of life for
me. I am a poor thing, incomplete, unfulfilled without it.*

As the day closed on his sixty-fourth year he wrote:

*It is too dark to see any more. Think of me as the sky
darkens, music playing, the perfect sail, and still half a
bottle of the satyr's champagne to finish. For all that
darkness came too soon, that was a magic evening.*

*I had much to celebrate, not only my birthday, but my
record run of the previous week. How often does a sailing
man sit drinking champagne while his craft glides along
at 7 knots?*

By mid-October he was well into the Southern Hemisphere.
What comes across reading his log, which thank heavens for
us he kept meticulously, is the constant search for speed, the
non-stop fight for every cable gained. Let's say a cruising sailor
is barrelling along at a healthy 6 knots in 12 knots of wind.
Suddenly you notice the wind has upped to 13 knots. The cruiser
will notice, say thanks to the wind gods, and go back to watching

the world go by. The racer will burst into action, trim and tweak the sails and see the speed is now $6\frac{1}{2}$ knots. What's half a knot? Twelve nautical miles a day, 84 miles a week, 1,344 miles in the sixteen weeks from Plymouth to Sydney. So when we read of a typical early morning in Francis's voyage, in this case just as he was about to head east and join the Roaring Forties, we should not be surprised, if a little exhausted:

> *0605. Port pole and sail down and pole housed. Speed 5.4 k.*
>
> *0610. Mizzen staysail down. Speed 4.2 k.*
>
> *0627. Gybed. Speed 5.1 k on other gybe.*
>
> *0643. Mizzen staysail hoisted for opposite gybe. 6k.*
>
> *0705. Big genoa rigged on starboard side dropped. I had to drop it because five or six hanks were off the stay. Changed sheet to port-rigged genoa and hoisted that.*
>
> *0747. Starboard spinnaker pole rigged and sail rehanked. One damaged hank repaired. Sail hoisted O.K., but difficulty with self-steering. Took some time trimming it before it would hold the ship to course. The load on each tiller line has to be adjusted carefully.*
>
> *0807. Mizzen staysail dropped and rehoisted because of twisted tack pennant. Poled-out sail trimmed.*
>
> *0810. Gybing completed. I hope a wind change does not require me to do it all again! Now a sun sight, and then I hope for some breakfast, for which I am full (or empty!) ready.*

This is far from untypical; the impression gained from reading the log is racing for every fraction of an advantage all the time, at least the waking time. Sleep was in twenty minutes' naps and he averaged about five hours sleep in every twenty-four.

It was in the Roaring Forties that more of *Gipsy Moth IV*'s faults were laid bare. The broaching problem described above and first experienced in a relatively mild tropical storm was now a constantly recurring disaster waiting to engulf her and him. In the Southern Ocean the winds whipped up bigger seas and against these the constantly suspect self-steering couldn't cope. He really was at the mercy of events he couldn't control.

But there was worse to come. In a really big blow, the skipper will take down all the sails and use just the wind on the mast and rigging to give enough speed to control the yacht. But sailing under 'bare poles' *Gipsy Moth IV* would only lie broadside to the wind and waves, ready to be rolled over at any time. A clearly alarmed Francis wrote:

> *I was now convinced that she could not be made to run downwind under bare poles in a seaway. The rudder could not control her without a storm jib on the foremast stay. This was a serious setback; it meant that her slowest speed running downwind in a gale would be 8 knots. I had never even considered that such a thing could happen!* Gipsy Moth II *had steered easily downwind under bare poles, or even with the wind on the quarter.*

And there was even worse broaching news to come. When Francis pressed on with the wind directly behind him, she wouldn't surf down the following waves but insisted on broaching across them, now at high speed. As he wrote,

> *Broaching-to was the danger that was most dreaded by the clippers. Slewing round, broadside on to a big Southern Ocean storm, they would roll their masts down, and, if the sails went into the water, they were likely to founder, as many did.*

The only solution was to cut down on the amount of sail – but at the cost of speed.

———⊗⊗⊗———

Things were not much better down below. Leaks had appeared all over the cabin. Francis made a list of them:

- *Doghouse [raised roof of the cabin] post over sink.*
- *Doghouse post over Primus*
- *Doghouse join about Primus v bad*
- *Post above head of quarter berth*
- *Cabin hatch lets water in freely, both sides (according to heel)*
- *All bolts holding hatch cover*
- *Foot of quarter berth under outboard edge of the cockpit seat*
- *From deck beside head of portside berth in cabin*
- *Starboard forward locker—everything wet through*
- *Seacock in cloakroom*
- *Both ventilators when closed*

No sooner had he vented his spleen on the leaks than he broke his tooth on a piece of mint-cake. Luckily he didn't swallow it. His dentist in London, Nigel Forbes, had given him a dental repair kit for just this sort of emergency. Francis took the tooth chip and scraped and cleaned it as per instructions. Next he had to dry it thoroughly, which must have caused him a wry, damp smile with spume flying outside the cabin and water showering in from the innumerable leaks. Undeterred, he hid it away and did what any sensible Englishman, half-toothless, wet through, cold and tired in a Roaring Forties gale, would do: 'I made myself a cup of tea and turned in'.

The next day he sat himself down, took out the repair kit and became a self-dentist. Firstly he placed a piece of cotton wool inside his gum to keep his tongue away from the cement. Then he mixed the cement, scooped some onto the tooth and pressed the chip onto it. Five minutes later he relaxed the pressure and looked in the mirror: there was cotton wool in the repair. He decided it was harmless enough and left it there.

> *Alas, my tooth-repair did not hold. I tried it out at suppertime, and it was no good – the broken bit simply came off again as soon as I tried to bite. Perhaps the best dentists do not mix cotton wool with their cement. I had another shot at cementing, this time without cotton wool fragments, but the repair was no more successful. In the end I got a file from my tool kit and filed down the jagged edges of the piece of tooth still in my jaw, and left it at that.*

⸗⸗⸗

The *Gipsy Moth IV* disaster that had been brewing finally came to the boil on Thursday, 15 November. Like many good disasters it provoked a heroic outcome, to my mind Francis's greatest acts of seamanship and ingenuity. Here he sets the scene:

> *I woke to a 40-knot wind – a heavy weight of wind, but no worse than the rough weather over most of the past weeks. The burgee [mast top flag] halliard parted, but that was small beer. At 12.15 I went aft to make what I thought would be a minor repair to the self-steering gear, and found that the steel frame holding the top of the steering blade had broken in half.*
>
> *There were two steel plates, one on each side of the top of the blade, to hold the blade and to connect it to the wind vane. Both had fractured. The oar blade was attached to the ship only by a rod used to alter its rake. It was wobbling about in the wake like a dead fish held*

by a line. I expected it to break away at any moment, and rushed back to the cockpit.

He knew he had to take all the strain off the self-steering immediately and so with a few quick flicks released the sails to slow the boat down and buy himself some thinking time. He retrieved the broken parts, laid them out on the cockpit floor – and froze with fear. The breaks were much more than mere fractures: they were major structural failures, failures that could only be repaired in a well-equipped yard. Dolefully he reviewed his options. His record-breaking attempt to Sydney was clearly scuppered as he could barely steer himself for more than half the time, and then exhaustedly. He was still 2,750 miles from Sydney. Even reaching there was in doubt, meaningfully. The one hundred days it should have taken would now become two hundred – and would take him into a different sailing season. And then there were water and food: could they be eked out too? Hardly.

No, pressing on solo, steering himself to Sydney was not any option. Then he felt something strange, a sense of relief, as if the failure had lanced some sort of boil, proving to the world that he had been right about *Gipsy Moth IV*'s fallibility all along: 'If I had had a normal boat I could have trimmed her up to sail herself, but experience so far had convinced me that *Gipsy Moth IV* could never be balanced to sail herself for more than a few minutes'. He looked up and around at the raging sea and 40-knot winds. 'The self-steering gear could not be repaired on board – I was well and truly in trouble. I went below and stood myself a brandy, hot'.

He knew the answer to his next question before he opened the chart: Fremantle in Western Australia had to be the new destination. That was still 1,160 miles, or three weeks' steering solo. He pointed slightly to north and shaped a new course to Freemantle. This was also where Sheila, on board the liner *Oriana*, was heading as *Oriana*'s first port of call before cruising round to

Melbourne and Sydney. That thought, an earlier rendezvous with Sheila, at least gave him some comfort.

The next few days were unpleasant and frustrating as Francis steered when he could and tried various methods of having *Gipsy Moth IV* self-steer when he couldn't. Then on the fourth night to Freemantle, something revelatory happened.

> *It was a stinking night, and I was called out several times to find the boat headed west instead of east, with all the sails aback [filled from the wrong direction]. On one of these occasions I lay drowsy in my berth, reluctant to get up again, and I noticed that although the sails were aback, the boat was forging ahead slowly and a most important fact – she kept a much steadier course than when she was sailing in the right direction with the sails all drawing. At the time I took these facts in without really being aware of them. They imprinted themselves; as it were, on my subconscious self.*

Francis had accidently discovered a new point of sail, which we might call 'heaving-to plus'. Regular heaving-to is a much loved practice of short-handed sailors and works like this: if you turn the yacht through the wind without touching the sails, the jib will fill with wind from the other direction, while the mainsail will remain full of wind, albeit from a different direction.

The great advantage of this tactic is that it slows the boat right down, while maintaining control and stability; it buys resting or thinking time in complete safety. As an added piece of finesse, if the skipper heaves-to with the wind from the starboard, so on starboard tack, he or she also has the right of way, so brewing that cup of tea or heating up that old curry below becomes even more restful.

After a great deal of experimenting on a bucking deck on a semi-directionless yacht in winds of 40-plus knots and lashed by Southern Ocean spume, Francis found this 'heaving-to plus'. Off the front of the main mast are four wires on which to hang the sails, arranged in two pairs of two. On the one nearest the bow he hung the largest genoa and flew it fully for maximum pull and speed. Left alone, that would soon have turned him off the wind, then through the wind from behind, lots of banging and slapping ropes, then off the other side, then back again and so on. To counter this he rigged his smallest sail, a storm jib, to back into the wind by fixing the end on the other side, the windward side.

He now needed to find a way of using this system to steer him more or less precisely in the right direction instead of just generally more or less in the right direction. This is the clever part. Kneeling on the slippery, crashing deck, battered by the ocean and with the boat only vaguely under control, he rigged a combination of pulleys from the end of the jib back to the tiller.

Francis wrote with a sense of eureka:

After a lot of trial and error, the result was as follows: When the yacht was on course, the sail was aback, and wind pressing on it pulled the tiller sufficiently to windward to counteract the tendency of the boat to turn up into wind. If the boat did begin turning off course into wind, the pressure on the sail increased, with the result that the pull on the tiller increased, making the boat turn off the wind again. If, on the other hand, the boat started turning downwind, this steering sail would presently gybe, as it were, and the wind would press on it from the other side, thereby exerting a pull on the tiller in the other direction to leeward, with the result that the boat turned towards the wind again.

Having won the day, his thoughts now turned to the next day, when Sheila was due to land in Freemantle. He needed to contact *Oriana*, which must be only a few hundred miles ahead of him, to get a message to her to wait for him in Freemantle rather than carry on to Sydney as planned. He fired up the Marconi wireless and made a contact of sorts: the liner's radio operator seemed to be able to hear him better than he could hear *Oriana*. He kept on repeating: 'I am on my way to Freemantle. I am putting into Freemantle'. The contact was too bad to explain why. Ever thoughtful – uniquely thoughtful – where Sheila was concerned, he logged: 'Poor Sheila, she will wonder what is happening'.

On board *Oriana*, as they neared Australia, Sheila was given the freedom of the bridge. Meanwhile, the crew and the passengers became absorbed in Francis's passage. Night after night the radio operator tried reaching *Gipsy Moth IV* but without success. Then, on 19 November, success. Sheila recalls just about hearing Francis's voice through 1,000 miles of the atmospherics and crackles: 'I'm going to Freemantle. I'm going to Freemantle'. She registered her disappointment; she hated changing her plans. 'Don't tell anyone on the ship about this', she told the radio operator. 'Things may change.'

Whether by Francis's ingenuity or Sheila's astral will-power, change they did. Those 24 hours around calling Sheila he had made 81 miles towards Freemantle. Not too bad. With every hour he finessed in his improvised self-steering system. The next day he made 105 miles. The following day he decided he could make Sydney after all, record or no record. And it would be no record; that much he now knew.

Now his concern was reversing the message to Sheila: don't get off in Freemantle, stay on to Sydney. Night after night he tried to get through. Frustratingly, there was no way of knowing if he had or not: the fact that his tiny receiver couldn't hear *Oriana* didn't mean that she couldn't hear him. Later Sheila told him that one of the messages had got through; she awoke to find a slip of paper from the radio operator under her cabin door – 'It's all right. He is going on'.

Up on deck Francis was joyful in adversity. His ingenuity had conquered the impossible; not only that but *Gipsy Moth IV* was cracking on famously:

> *I felt happier than I had been at any time previously during the voyage. I had been waiting for the self-steering gear to fail, and apprehensive all the time that I should be helplessly stuck with a badly balanced boat. That I had been able to rig up gear to make her sail herself was deeply satisfying. I hate turning back; I hate giving up; and I hate being diverted from my course; it was a seaman's job to get over difficulties.*

With good reason he felt he had proved himself to be the consummate seaman. I must say that as an observer I feel he had reached some other level too. For me Francis had always been primarily an otherworldly navigator and a tough-as-old-boots, hang-on-and-hope-for-the-best type of seaman. But it cannot be gainsaid that his seamanship in the final 2,800 miles to Sydney was quite exceptional.

He reached Sydney in 105 days and 20 hours: not a record but a wonderful circumstantial achievement, in which he took pride. In the first launch to meet him were a troop of journalists and photographers; wanting an ever-closer close-up, its bow hit *Gipsy Moth IV*'s stern and bounced off. Francis, who was about to hate the media even more than he did already, shouted 'Fuck off!' The reports next day had toned this down to 'Wander off!' and 'You bloody Sunday driver!' In the second launch was his first son, George, who by now had lived in Australia for twenty years, with his wife, Gay. In the third launch were Sheila and Giles; they scrambled aboard and *Gipsy Moth IV* was towed in to her haul-out berth at the Royal Sydney Yacht Squadron. An hour later, in their Billiards Room, Francis held a chaotic press conference with ninety-five media outlets hurling questions at him. It was at that time the largest press conference ever held in Australia.

He started hesitantly: he had, after all, spoken to no one directly for over three months and was now speaking to all the world at once. But the film shows him warming to it as he himself warmed up. By the end he was giving as good as he got:

'When were your spirits at their lowest ebb?'

'When the gin gave out.'

————oooo————

Press conference just after three months alone

The Billiards Room now has a deluxe series of showers and changing rooms, and the berth where *Gipsy Moth IV* was hauled out has been pontooned and given the latest in haul-out technology. Apart from that, the Squadron clubhouse and grounds remain recognisable, except for the entrance lobby, which has been turned into a Chichester shrine.

Above an oil-on-wood painting by John Alboor of *Gipsy Moth IV* rounding Cape Horn is her propeller, bronzed and mounted, and above that, in pride of place, the wind-torn burgee from the sister club, the Royal Yacht Squadron. Luckily the club is as welcoming to visiting yachtsmen now as it was then, even if in my case the visiting yachtsman arrives by ferry from no further than downtown.

Home from home: The Royal Sydney Yacht Squadron clubhouse

Sheila had checked all the family into the Belvedere Hotel, where Giles and George, twenty years apart in age, met properly for the first time. The three-storey building still stands on the corner of Kent Street and Bathurst Street, thanks to Sydney's

Heritage Protection programme, but it is now a rather seedy Greek-themed pub/restaurant/lounge. George, by now forty years old, was still sickly; in fact, he died a year later. The family decided to divide their energies: Francis would repair his yacht, Sheila would deal with the press, Giles would help Francis, George would help Sheila. George was particularly happy to have found a brother. In a letter to Geoffrey Goodwin he wrote: 'The most rewarding feature of the visit for myself was meeting Giles, who I find a most level headed and interesting person. Gay and I had dinner with Giles and Sheila at their hotel. Sheila was at her best and although worried by reporters, I think she enjoyed it'. He ended with: 'It is quite extraordinary how the voyage has caught their interest of people here.'

The Belvedere Hotel, scene of the knighthood phone call, as it is now

The Royal Sydney Yacht Squadron had invited Francis to haul out at their own dock and he accepted gratefully. He felt that the best help in the world was to hand in the forms of Warwick Hood and Alan Payne, the designers of the America's Cup racers *Dame Pattie* and *Gretel* respectively. At the time of his visit the club was at the centre of Australia's 1967 America's Cup challenge; the challenger, *Dame Pattie*, had the bad luck to come up against the New York Yacht Club's defending *Intrepid*, a breakthrough design by Sparkman & Stephens. She lost and was forever known as 'Damn Pity', beautiful though she is. Working for them were the yard manager Jim Perry and his team of shipwrights, who between them would repair and strengthen *Gipsy Moth IV*'s self-steering gear, staunch the deck leaks – of which Francis had counted twenty-two – as well as right the long list of various wrongs.

The designers quickly told Francis what he did and didn't wanted to hear, in equal measure: that *Gipsy Moth IV* was fundamentally ill designed and unfit for purpose. Their prognosis exactly confirmed his misgivings all along – and worse, because of their knowledge of the Tasman Sea, they pronounced her incapable of righting herself after capsizing. With an element of grim I-told-you-so-it is, he recalled: 'I told Warwick [Hood] how she had been built specially strong with a view to surviving a capsize and roll over. "Yes", he said, "but she might not come up again with that shape of hull". I said nothing'. Meanwhile Francis couldn't resist firing off a telegram to his UK designer Angus Primrose: 'I have found a proper designer to design a new keel profile.' Unimpressed, Primrose shot back: 'Just get on with it. If you've reached Australia you are barely run in'.

Knowing that he would ignore their pleas for him to abandon the circumnavigation attempt, the shipwrights set about making what improvements they could in the time to hand. Francis's deadline to leave Sydney was 29 January, in order to round Cape Horn by the end of February or early March, midsummer, its most benign – or least objectionable – month. They added a

Dry dock at Sydney

steel extension to close the gap between the keel and the rudder and simultaneously simplified and strengthened the rigging, the Achilles heel in what they felt was the inevitable capsize. They did their best down below too, centring the weight and beefing up the locker and drawer fastenings to stop the contents flying around the cabin when the inevitable capsize came.

Meanwhile, Sheila was having a rough time with the media doom-mongers. Two photographs of Francis had sped around the world. The first showed Giles and Francis hugging on their

reunion: Francis, who had after all been alone at sea for three
months and had hardly scrubbed up for the landing, looked older
than his sixty-five years, while the strapping young Giles seemed
to tower over him. It was an image of father and son in protective
role reversal. The second front-page photograph showed Francis
stepping ashore: the overhead camera angle showed him being
helped on to the dock by a policeman holding one arm and Giles
the other. I must say that he looks very frail indeed. The Old Man
of the Sea looks like an old man who had sailed one mile too many.

Of course Francis being Francis, he didn't confine his
feelings about his yacht to the boatyard and these public
thoughts on *Gipsy Moth IV*'s poor design, and the public
photographs of a frail, wraith-like Francis, soon brewed up a
storm of naysaying. Distinguished yachtsmen wrote to the main
sponsoring newspapers, *The Sunday Times* and the *Guardian*,
urging him to discontinue. Yachting correspondents the world
over weighed in too, pointing out that he was too old and too
frail and *Gipsy Moth IV* too unseaworthy to attempt rounding
Cape Horn. One of them, from the (Australian) *Sun*, received
an earful from Sheila for his troubles. He had suggested that
'with such a monstrously small yacht' Francis Chichester 'was
asking a little too much of God'. 'You don't ask anything of
God', Sheila shot back; 'that is not prayer. You offer up the
person you pray for, you hold them with your own strength and
love.' No more peeps from the chastened *Sun* after that.

Of course every naysay only made Francis dig deeper into
his determination. The higher the odds against him, the more he
thrived; the shriller the perceived wisdom advised him, the more
he delighted in proving them wrong. Slightly more worrying
was a telegram from cousin Tony Dulverton saying that on
no account must he continue. Tony was, after all, the actual
owner of the boat, Francis the peppercorn rent tenant. Francis
telegraphed back advising him to ignore the newspaper reports,
thanking Tony for giving him the chance to pull out if he wanted

to without losing face. He ended the telegram: 'Anyway I am sailing'. Tony knew better than to reply to that one.

Meanwhile, back at the Belvedere Hotel, Sheila was doing her best to ward off the press:

> There was a general atmosphere of 'Prepare to Meet Thy Doom' type of warning, and I had hundreds of letters and some very nasty Press at home, which surprised me. I have come to the conclusion that the world is more full of No-People than Yes-People and for some reason that No-People wanted to stop him. But he had no idea of stopping, and I never even thought about it. This was a project, he was only half-way.

Once again, Francis's soulmate was backing him unquestioningly. In spite of their mutual hostility to the press, they understood necessary evils, signing a new contract with *The Sunday Times* for twice-weekly radio reports, the quirks of this newfangled long-range transmitting gadget permitting.

But there were amusing diversions. Their Excellencies the Governor-General and Lady Casey came up from Canberra to Sydney and invited the Chichesters to dinner at their residency, Admiralty House, still the most desirable property on the bay. Lord Casey, himself no slouch in the hero stakes, proposed a toast to Francis's voyage. Unfortunately the current Governor-General, Sir Peter Cosgrove, is in London when I am in Sydney or I would have bludged, as they say hereabouts, a visit to Admiralty House too. Sir Peter is an excellent sport and a Squadron member too, but his underlings start babbling about security; and anyway the archives I need are in Canberra. Annoying all the same.

On a return visit to Canberra Francis and Sheila were guests of Sir Charles Johnston, the High Commissioner to Australia, at Government House. The Chichesters and Johnstons were immediate and subsequently lifelong friends.

An even more amusing diversion came on New Year's Eve. At 10 pm Francis was just falling asleep when the Belevdere Hotel room phone rang.

'Oh, leave it', suggested a sleepy Sheila.

'Better not', said Francis.

It was Sir Charles Johnston from Canberra. A few moments later:

'Oh Charlie, it must be all your doing', laughed Francis.

'What happened?' asked Sheila.

Francis put back the phone and with a broad smile said: 'I've been knighted'.

Lady Sheila beamed right back at Sir Francis.

Of course the phone never stopped ringing after that. By 2 am Sheila had had enough and told the porter to stop putting through the calls. Later that day, New Years Day, while the Chichesters were lunching at the Royal Sydney Yacht Squadron, Lord and Lady Casey walked over to share their congratulations. From his pocket Lord Casey pulled out a telegram from the Queen:

IT GIVES ME GREAT PLEASURE TO BESTOW THE RANK AND TITLE KNIGHT BACHELOR TO OUR SERVANT: FRANCIS CHICHESTER STOP ELIZABETH R STOP

———⧞———

As we know Francis could be, in fact pretty much always was, a stubborn old cuss on a passage, and never more so than at his insistence on leaving on time. (It goes without saying that, onshore at least, he *always* arrived on time.) With the tiny Cape Horn summer in mind and working through the days and evenings and weekends of January, by the third week he could foresee and announce a time to leave: 11.00 am on Sunday 29 January, 1967.

Tropical cyclones are equally stubborn cusses and 500 miles north-east of Sydney Cyclone Tamara was busy gathering up her skirt for a merry dance across the Tasman Sea. Old Tasman hands implored Francis to let her blow through. He was having none of it: he said he was leaving at 11 am on Sunday 29 January 1967 regardless. Very well, said the Tasman hands, leave if you must but head south around New Zealand. As Francis later admitted, 'foolishly I disregarded this excellent advice'.

Lord Casey, entering into the clipper spirit of *Gipsy Moth IV*'s voyage, gave Francis three small bales of wool as cargo for London. Once clear of the well-wisher fleet, the Chichesters said their goodbyes. For Francis: 'Sheila and I parted as if for a day. She has an uncanny foresight in spiritual matters, and

The voyage continues, Gipsy Moth IV leaving Sydney Harbour

had no doubt but that we should meet again. I must confess that I wondered rather sadly if we would as I sailed away from the fleet'. For Sheila: 'Francis sailed away and I felt perfectly confident all would be well'.

Eight hours later Francis was becalmed. To the north the summer evening sky turned dark grey, then deep blue, then black. Zephyrs became breezes became gusts became winds became gales. Tamara was coming to find him.

When the capsize came Francis was lying on his bunk, trying to sleep. He had long since given up any hope of sailing the yacht. He later wrote:

> *That Monday night was as foul and black a night as you could meet at sea. Although it was pitch dark, the white breakers showed in the blackness like monstrous beasts charging down on the yacht. The sea was violently disturbed with winds gusting up to 80 knots. The breakers towered high in the sky. I wouldn't blame anyone for being terrified at the sight. There was nothing I could do about it. I did not worry over much, but just tried to exist until the storm passed.*

If Francis didn't suffer from fear, he also didn't suffer from imagination.

Down below he hung on as best he could. He felt seasick, which he put down to the Australian sparkling wine he had drunk so lustily the day before. As a remedy he made his favourite seasickness cure: warmed brandy, sugar and lemon. Giving up all hope of influencing events, he took to his bunk, trying to rest if not to sleep. Amidst the screaming noise and stomach-churning drops into troughs, Francis felt the rogue wave coming moments before it landed on top of him.

'Over she goes!' he remembered saying to himself in the upside-down pitch darkness. Moments later he was flying through the air; so was anything loose in the cabin: bottles, crockery, cutlery, books, boots. In the void and confusion he wondered if *Gipsy Moth IV* would roll over completely. When she righted herself she was on the same tack. Francis stumbled in the chaos for a light. Amazingly, it worked and some order was brought into the chaos.

One half of him desperately wanted to look outside to see how much damage the mast and rigging had taken; the wiser half knew a breaker would fill the cabin if invited in. It was bad enough inside:

> *The cabin was two foot deep all along with a jumbled-up pile of hundreds of tins, bottles, tools, shackles, blocks, sextants and oddments. Every settee locker, the whole starboard bunk, and the three starboard drop lockers had all emptied out when she was upside down. Water was swishing about on the cabin sole beside the chart table, but not much. I looked into the bilge, which is 5 feet deep, but it was not quite full, for which I thought, 'Thank God'.*

The next morning the worst of Tamara had passed and the gale had dropped to a regular Force 8. Francis was back in *mare cognitum*. The deck inspection showed that he had been lucky. One of the big genoas, a drogue [underwater parachute] and its 700 feet of rope had been washed overboard. The forehatch had been forced partially open. A piece of the cockpit had been torn off. She had shipped a lot of sea water and Francis had to spend exhausting hours on the pumps, counting 200 strokes at a time between breaks. Climbing below to report the damage in the log, he felt a mixture of fear and exhaustion, luck and dread. Francis-the-wise wished he could turn back; Francis-the-proud knew he never could. He feared rogue waves like never before but knew that more would be ready to ambush him as he neared Cape Horn.[17] He dreaded the Southern Ocean voyage ahead but knew his fate required him to be offered up to whatever the weather gods chose to throw at him.

It took a week to clear up the mess caused by the capsize and another six weeks to cross the 5,000 miles of wild ocean to reach Cape Horn. Francis would later recall that this was the most frightening and exhausting part of the circumnavigation and always for the same reason: the sheer unpredictability of the wild and windswept waves that he was crossing meant he could never relax, that he was always trying to stay ahead of the next turn in the weather and always trying to manage *Gipsy Moth IV's* unsuitability to the task.

It is easy to imagine him being fully preoccupied with just hanging in there, changing and trimming the sails, tuning the self-steering, navigating, feeding and watering himself, making radio calls and trying to stay as warm and dry as conditions allowed. But this was just the half of it. He had a long list of preventive maintenance jobs, which he called his 'agenda'. Every day this meant an inspection tour of the boat, checking on everything from the water tank connections to the alternator belts, all the lines and their connections; as they used to say in the Navy: if it moves, salute it; if it doesn't, paint it.

Then there were repairs tasks, some due to the capsize, others due to 'stuff happens', what insurers call 'inherent vice' – eggs break, chocolate melts, glass shatters. There was also a housekeeping agenda, anything from sowing wheatgerm to refilling meths containers to starting mustard and cress. If there was ever a calm day he had a calm day agenda, mostly repairing leaks and drying out clothes.

On top of this there was the occasional laundry day, such as midway to Cape Horn on Wednesday 15 February. His technique was to wash his clothes and sheets in warmed sea water, then rinse them over the side and finally rinse out the salt with fresh water. It worked well enough and saved fresh water. To celebrate he opened a bottle of Veuve Clicquot, only to find that 'as usual champagne brought me no luck, and only brought me rain and a backing wind. To try to defeat the influence of the champagne I had two glasses of Whitbread's beer from the keg, which was excellent'.

Reading his log now, it seems that the Southern Oceans crossing was a non-stop battle against vile weather in a semi-uncontrollable yacht, in constant discomfort pierced by moments of pure fear and the yearning for it all to be over. So I read this entry with as much pleasure as he must have had in writing it:

> There were good moments, though, when I would sit in the sun in the cockpit, drinking mugs of Whitbread. It amused me every time I drew off a half-pint from the keg in the bilge, and I would think, 'What a place to be sitting drinking beer, in glorious sunshine, with a deep blue sea and light blue sky'.
>
> It was never too hot, because of the southerly breeze coming up from the Antarctic. Once when I was sitting in the cockpit like this I tried to calculate whereabouts was the nearest human being to me. There might have been a ship somewhere in the vicinity, but unless there was, which was unlikely, the nearest living person would have been in the Chatham Islands, some 885 miles away.

One bad shock is duly timed and entered in the log, as befits its seriousness:

> Wednesday, 22 February. 19.25. I have just realised I have only four bottles of gin left, enough for four weeks. I reckon I have been pretty stupid not to have brought

plenty. I'll just have to ration it, and no hard drinks at lunch. It might be worse – I might have none.

A week of unremitting self-torture – and so indirect pleasure – defying the elements was to follow, up half the nights changing sail in the dark, on a bucking deck with freezing spray flying across the decks. Then came his wedding anniversary and Francis became human again:

> *I wish I was at home with my darling and feel sad to be away from her, but that is how life goes. I have only just finished breakfast, and will drink her health later. If this gale continues, I may wait until tomorrow for my celebration party.*

But he didn't wait. He decided that there was too much of a gale blowing to put on his smoking jacket, so he'd celebrate as best he could, given the circumstances:

> *I am drinking a toast to Sheila in the delicious Montrachet she brought out from England, and left on board for me. A long life, health and happiness, with grateful thanks for our happy thirty years together. A very remarkable, exceptional woman is Sheila. I did what is supposed to be un-British, shed a tear. Life seems such a slender thread in these circumstances here, and they make one see the true values in life, mostly things (or whatever you may call them) which one disregards, or brushes aside when with people. I must not get too sentimental. I will return to the Montrachet.*

Forty days after leaving Sydney he passed the 5,000 mile mark, leaving only 1,600 to the 'Old Ogre', Cape Horn. By then the sea, uninterrupted by land and stirred up by constant winds and gales, was always in swell. Outside the temperature was dropping and Francis dug out his winter warmies and had the stove on below more or less constantly. Here he warmed up his rum and lemon keep-warm panacea.

For non-Cape Horners I can report that the Cape itself is not a point at the end of a contiguous South American land mass; it is rather a 1,400-foot cliff on the southern tip of the most southerly island of an archipelago of a thousand islands and rocklets known as the 'Milky Way'. Friendly waters they are not. When Charles Darwin looked down from the deck of the *Beagle* he reported that 'Any landsman seeing the Milky Way would have nightmares for a week'. In his book *Along the Clipper Way*, written a year before he sailed around the Old Ogre, Francis noted:

Why has it such an evil reputation? The prevailing winds in the Forties and Fifties, are westerly and pretty fresh on the average. For instance, off the Horn there are gales of Force 8 or more on one day in four in the spring and one day in eight in the summer.

Winds have a lazy nature. They refuse to climb over a mountain range if they can sweep past the end of it. South America has one of the greatest mountain ranges of the world, the Andes, which blocks the westerlies along a front of 1,200 miles from 35° S. right down to Cape Horn. All this powerful wind is crowding through Drake's Strait between Cape Horn and the South Shetland Islands, 500 miles to the south.

The normal westerlies pouring through this gap are interfered with by the turbulent, vicious little cyclones rolling off the Andes. The same process occurs in reverse with the easterly winds, which though more rare than the westerlies, blow when a depression is passing north of the Horn.

As for the waves, the prevailing westerlies set up a current flowing eastwards round the world at a mean rate of 10 to 20 miles per day. This current flows in all directions at times due to the passing storms, but the result of all the different currents is this 10 to 20 miles per day flowing eastwards. As the easterly may check this current or even reverse it for a while, the prevailing stream flowing eastwards may sometimes amount to as much as 50 miles a day. As with the winds, this great ocean river is forced to pass between South America and the South Shetland Islands. This in itself tends to make the stream turbulent.

What size are these notorious waves? Recently one instrument with a 60-foot scale recorded a wave of which the trace went off the scale. This wave was estimated at 69 feet in height, higher than our five-storey house in London. An American steamship in the South Pacific is said to have encountered a wave 112 feet high.

Reading Francis's account of his Cape Horn day, one is immediately struck by the extraordinary confidence he had in his own navigation. Closing in on the archipelago, contact with any one of whose countless outlying members would have sunk him, he aimed to pass a mere 12 miles south of the nearest one in the middle of the night.

It was so dark that I did not think it worth keeping a watch, so I set the off-course alarm to warn me if there was a big wind shift, and I also set an alarm clock to wake me at daybreak. Then I put my trust in my navigation and turned in for a sleep. For a while I lay in the dark with the boat rushing into black night. In the end I slept, and soundly too.

He woke at 5 am and took stock. It was a cold, grey morning, wind merely Force 4 and now southerly and the sea state swelly but not violent. The barometer was steady. Dead reckoning put him 40 miles to the west of the Horn. He should round it by noon. It looked like he was going to be lucky, to catch the Old Ogre off guard. He decided to head directly for the Horn rather than pass 40 miles south of it, as usual conditions would have recommended. He treated himself to a fry-up special breakfast, excited about the next sail and change of course. For the first time in months he would have some north in his heading – and so a homeward heading. With a light heart, after breakfast he stepped on deck to change sails and set the new course. But then an unexpected, major annoyance, for Francis the ultimate spoiler. He was dumbfounded and furious:

> When I stepped into the cockpit I was astounded to see
> a ship nearby, about a half-mile off. I had a feeling that if
> there was one place in the world where I would not see
> a ship it was off Cape Horn. As soon as I recovered from
> the shock I realised that because of its drab overall colour
> it must be a warship, and therefore was likely to be HMS
> Protector.

She was on fishing patrol duty out of the Falklands and had picked up his radio reports to *The Sunday Times*. Working out his likely position, she had placed herself at the most likely choke-point between the islands and waited for him.

Francis's internal fury at having his finest hour, his pinnacle moment alone, witnessed by a whole ships' company was soon matched by the changing mood of the weather outside. By 9 am the wind had risen to 40 knots. Back on deck he took down the genoa and trysail, leaving only the storm jib to power him along. On his way back to the cockpit, hand-holding along the top of the cabin, from a wave crest he looked and saw the

Horn standing up from the sea 'like a black ice-cream cone'. A great wash of triumph and excitement swept over him. Then off the next crest he looked east and saw the still-lurking HMS *Protector*. Infuriating!

Two hours later it was gusting over 50 knots. He took a bearing and confirmed that he was east of the Cape Horn. He had rounded the old Ogre, alone! Or nearly alone. 'I cursed the *Protector* for hanging about. I just wanted to be left alone, by things and especially by people.'

But worse was to come. Much worse. 'Just then, I'm damned if an aircraft didn't buzz into sight. I cursed it. If there was one place in the world where I expected to be alone it was off Cape Horn. I was greatly relieved when it finally cleared off'. Soon HMS *Protector*, too, cleared off. Francis felt a forlorn, empty feeling of desolation at being alone again, as if the unwelcome company had not only spoiled his moment of triumph but left him even more alone than if he really had been all alone all along. He couldn't place the feeling: triumph and annoyance, loneliness and overcrowding. Something wasn't right when it should have been perfect.

—————⟨∞⟩—————

Infuriating though the intrusion on his ultimate hour of triumph had been for Francis, the correspondents on board the HMS *Protector* and the aeroplane did give us eyewitness accounts of that same ultimate hour.

On board the naval ship was a Reuter's stringer, Michael Hayes. He filed:

> *As I stood on the pitching and tossing deck of the Royal Navy Ice Patrol ship H.M.S. Protector 400 yards off, the sight was awesome. The translucent, bottle-green seas were moving mountains and valleys of water, rearing, rolling and subsiding with a fearful brute force. The 50-mile an hour wind slashed at the waves, slicing off*

foaming white crests and sending icy spume flying. Lead-grey clouds, blotting out the weak sun on the horizon, rolled across the sky, so low that it seemed I could reach up and touch them. The thermometer said the temperature was 43° F, but the numbing wind cut through my lined, Antarctic clothing like a knife, and salt spray swelled up and crashed against the face with stinging fury.

On board the battered old yellow Piper Apache was Murray Sayle of *The Sunday Times* and he filed for the 21 March 1967 edition:

The flight out to find and photograph him at the most dangerous point of his voyage was a magnificent and terrifying experience. I flew from Puerto Williams, the tiny Chilean naval base which is the southernmost inhabited spot in the Americas.

As my aircraft rose to find a cleft in the mountains of Hoste Island, the biggest of the Horn group, I was confronted with a superb sight. Green glaciers tumbling from the high snow-blanketed Darwin ranges into the Southern Ocean. As I flew by Cape Horn Island, its grey pyramid could be seen lashed by heavy seas and rimmed by breaking seas which appeared from time to time through the driving rain.

South of the Horn the waves were driving eastward in long ridges of white and grey-green. Overhead were black driving clouds driven by the gale and a mile or two ahead the clouds were joined to the sea by rain in a black, impenetrable barrier towards the south and the pole.

I picked up H.M.S. Protector first, wallowing in the heavy seas as she kept company with the yacht. Then I picked out the salt grimed hull of Gipsy Moth lurching forward as the seas passed under her. My Chilean pilot, Captain Rodolfo Fuenzalida, gamely took us down to

Rounding Cape Horn (Sunday Times)

60 ft. where spume torn from the seas lashed across the aircraft's windscreen. But I had time to pick out Chichester in his cockpit, apparently nonchalantly preparing for his change of course and the long voyage home.

When my pilot waggled his wings in salute we were rewarded by a wave of greeting. 'Muy hombre,' said the pilot, which I freely translate as 'What a man'.

On the flight home we had severe turbulence as we threaded our way back through the mountains, and we lost an engine over the Strait of Magellan. It was a flight I am not too anxious to repeat, but the sight of Gipsy Moth *ploughing bravely through this wilderness of rain and sea was well worth it.*

A week later Francis himself filed a report: 'Hot news! At noon today I passed half-way! I had sailed 7,673 miles from Sydney, and the distance along the Clipper Way to Plymouth was 7,634 miles by my measurement'.

Unbeknown to Francis, *The Sunday Times* had given Murray Sayle's piece the full works: two front-page columns and eight columns across pages 8 and 9. The splash had caused a stir and pretty soon a features editor was looking for some human interest – a quality, it has to be said, lacking from Francis's own despatches to the newspaper, which tended to be facts, facts and then more facts. One night over the long-distance radio came this question 'from a girl reporter working for the *Sunday Times*': 'What did you eat on your first meal after rounding the Horn?'

Francis could deal with facts but this was too personal. He radioed back:

I strongly urge you stop questioning and interviewing me, which poisons the romantic attraction of this voyage. I am beginning to dread transmitting nights, and I fear losing my enthusiasm for worthwhile dispatches. Maybe this is because I have been alone for 58 days; I do not feel the same as I would if leading an office life. I have my hands full driving this boat efficiently and maintaining the gear in good order. Difficult radio communication is a great strain anyway. Interviewing makes it intolerable. I do not want to hurt your feelings but hope you can sympathise with my state of mind.

As if to compensate for such trivialisation, Francis made himself the very meal the reporter – and of course all her readers – wanted to know about. Not many really cared about what he gave them: how he changed the genoa for a storm jib at 3.19 am with two hanks [sail to wire clips] missing – but everyone wanted to know what he ate, how he kept clean, tidied the boat, put up with himself, stuff they could all relate to on dry land. To drum home his 'mind your own business' bloody-mindedness, he shared the news they all wanted to hear only with his log:

To make up for these frustrations, I stood myself a notable lunch – I think it was the one I had enjoyed most on the passage. Here is the menu: A clove of garlic, with a hunk of Gruyère cheese and a glass of Whitbread; a tin of Australian peas, a tin of salmon, and three potatoes in their jackets with plenty of butter; a tin of pears.

Not for the first time, it seems that Francis thought PR stood for Privacy Removal and not Public Relations.

And so the passage home passed under the keel, mile by mile. One evening Francis noted that he had sailed out of the Forties, sharing that anyone who sailed there was bonkers – but that he knew that before he started, adding: 'It was one of life's great experiences, and I would feel unsatisfied if I had not done it'. A week later he was digging out his light clothes and washing in warmer, equatorial sea water.

Soon it was Sheila's birthday, 11 April, and Francis tried a long-range call to London, still 4,700 miles away. Messages had to be passed through a licensed operator and he heard that Sheila was having dinner with Edward and Belinda Montagu at Palace House in Beaulieu, helping them celebrate their wedding anniversary. 11 April was a bumper day: Sheila's birthday, the Montagus' anniversary and the completion of his circumnavigation – so inbound crossing his outbound track.

But of course these halcyon sailing days would have to come to an end. For Francis it was a double blow: the end of sailing and the start of people. The first sign of trouble came on 7 May, when he was hailed by the *Esso Winchester* oil tanker, heading for the Western Approaches. It was the first ship he had seen since Cape Horn. He had been alone for three months and the thought of having to deal with the world's pettiness and triviality after living not just in but with Nature, at one with her and himself, filled him with the dread of paradise lost.

His sense of foreboding was confirmed when a few days later he found that the *Sea Huntress* was bearing down on him. She had been chartered by *The Sunday Times* to hunt him down. There were still 1,500 miles to go but the newspaper had invested heavily in Francis's voyage and wanted to scoop as much as it could. The encounter confirmed all his worst fears about the outside world. Coming alongside to take photographs and ask questions, typical of which were not about the voyage or the boat or his health but to see if he wanted a bottle of gin. It was as if some features editor in London had already angled the story 'Old soak sails home' – as indeed they had. Francis declined the gin and waved cheerfully, his first pretence for months. Equally annoying, he needed to gybe, a long and complicated procedure with all the foresails flying and one that a photograph could easily make look clumsy and unseamanlike.

He knew that worse was to come – and come it did, from the sky. The RAF had decided to use finding *Gipsy Moth IV* as a training exercise; early on 13 May two Shackleton maritime patrol planes swept low overhead. Francis was deep in sleep and soon cursing. The Shackletons flew by low again. This time Francis was on deck. The pilot dipped his wings. The crew waved at him through the windows. Later that day one of them told the *Guardian*: 'He just sat there looking ahead as if we didn't exist, not waving back or anything'. If he knew Francis as we do, he would count himself lucky not to have been on the wrong end of a digital gesture.

View from the RAF Shackleton

It was just as well that Francis was not aware of the worldwide interest his voyage had generated. Ever since Murray Sayle's report and photographs from Cape Horn, the media appetite had grown and grown. Down below he composed himself for dealing with the relatively limited media interference that he was expecting, writing in his log:

> One soon forgets that there is not only the boat to worry about on this sort of long adventure; there are attitudes of mind, which one wishes to suppress by trying not to think of them, an obvious one being fear. At times one is attacked by the futility of making an effort incessantly, day and night for four months. It is difficult to keep up an effort incessantly by day and night.

A whole new incessant effort was about to need hoisting up the mast.

He also worried about habits formed in four months of being alone:

> What effect had four months of solitude had on me? What habits had I developed? One unsociable habit, which had become strong by then, was that of dropping asleep at any time of day. I never had enough sleep. I would eat huge breakfasts, and often have to stop in the middle of breakfast and sleep before the end of it. I reflected: 'If I am dining out in London in a few days' time, what will my hostess think if at the end of the soup I say I must sleep for ten minutes before the next course?'

The next morning two more Shackletons woke him again. This time, having already found him, they were using him as anti-submarine attack practice, perhaps in revenge for his unfriendliness the previous morning. By noon a BBC launch arrived, joined in the evening by one from ITV. There were still 200 miles to go and quite a media flotilla was forming to welcome him home. Francis counted thirteen ships escorting him in but they all gave way for the aircraft carrier HMS *Eagle*, her 2,500 strong crew lining the deck and giving Francis three cheers. He dipped his White Ensign in salute.

> *This was a great honour, which I found most moving. It must surely be unique in the history of the British Navy for a warship with a complement as big as the population of a small town to salute so ceremoniously a ship with a crew of one!*

I think it was at this point that Francis felt his voyage was complete.

Sunset arrival in Plymouth

Not so the rest of the world. Back in Plymouth, half a million people had gathered to welcome him home. With perfect sunset timing on a beautiful Devon evening, at 9.00 pm Francis sailed

Gipsy Moth IV past Rear-Commodore Colonel Jack Odling-Smee and the finishing guns of the Royal Western Yacht Club – guns plural because Smee feared that one would not be loud enough to be heard over the tumult. It seemed that everyone Francis had ever met was there to greet him: Geoffrey Goodwin had flown in from New Zealand, Tony Dulverton been chauffeured down from London – and, of course, Sheila. Francis tried to absorb every moment of the spectacular welcome, a different kind of solo endeavour – all directed towards him and him alone. Sheila and Giles climbed aboard *Gipsy Moth IV*. Francis was overwhelmed, bewildered at the other extreme he now faced.

'It's strange,' he said to Sheila, 'but I don't feel anything at all.'

'One can't', Sheila replied. 'There's too much to feel.'

The toll taken on his body by the months of vigour and fear, damp and cold, lack of sleep and square meals, and on his mind by the demands of media, trivia and celebrity soon laid Francis low. Already frail, after a week of being the focus of civic receptions and private parties in Plymouth, always on parade, always the star attraction at events he felt he couldn't decline, he collapsed. At the Royal Naval Hospital they demanded complete rest – and rest alone – for three weeks. As we saw in Chapter 1, this caused organisational problems in Buckingham Palace; but rest and recover he must.

Actually, Francis later revealed that he enjoyed the rest more than he cared to let on to Sheila at the time. He was meant to be ill, only he didn't feel ill, just deeply tired. While the doctors fretted about doing tests and Sheila did her best to keep them at bay, he knew that the original diagnosis and cure were correct: three months of exhaustion and three weeks' rest. Whenever he was feeling glum, he could always cheer himself up re-reading his Medical Officer's report:

The fact remains that apart from emphysema and bronchitis the lungs are at present moment free from any disease. If Sir Francis had been in the Navy he would have been invalided out on this account. On the other hand, had he been seen as a civilian his doctor would probably have recommended that he take a long sea voyage!

Three weeks later he was released but only into Sheila's care. She certainly wasn't going to put up with any unnecessary parting shenanigans. But even she could not keep Father Time at bay – and from now on Francis's health would be in decline. She was now tending a frailer husband than she had been used to.

And so they set sail for Greenwich and our opening chapter.

———— ❧ ————

Francis and *Gipsy Moth IV*'s voyage of 29,630 miles had taken just nine months and a day, beginning and ending in Plymouth. Of these, 226 were sailing days. Perhaps not equally amazingly, but still amazingly, Francis had logged more than 200,000 words during that time, for which I at least am immensely grateful.

———— ❧ ————

NOTES:

16. Claimed by Greenwich to be Francis's favourite tipple. It wasn't; he preferred whisky and soda but, like your author, if pushed would drink almost anything.

17. In Hong Kong Sheila had met Capt. Adie of the 28,000-ton liner *Himalaya*. He had been en route from Sydney to Hong Kong the same night as Tamara hit *Gipsy Moth IV*. He told Sheila about a rogue wave that had sent her over to 25 degrees; they reckoned that this was the one that capsized Francis. Adie told Sheila: 'Chichester can keep the bloody Tasman Sea!'

Nothing equals apprehension of the future for making one enjoy the unparalleled beauty and charm of the present.

CHAPTER 10

Gipsy Moth V

IT SEEMED TO SHEILA THAT IN THE MONTHS that followed Francis was the most famous man in the world. She cared nothing for fame, of course, with a Christian's eye for the perils of vanity and she considered fame's demands as a curse on Francis's delicate health. She was less dismissive about the newly found money, which was now pouring in. After all the years of being the sole source of their wealth, Francis was now in what she called the 'lovely lolly', a bestselling author with *Gipsy Moth Circles the World*, a top performer on the lecture circuit with newspaper fees and endorsements topping up the coffers.

In the days before the cult of celebrity, he was celebrated around the world. Rolex paid handsomely for them to fly to Switzerland to present him with a new Rolex watch to replace the one that had been his chronometric companion, getting him in and out of fixes across the oceans. Their hosts then laid on a short break for them at Survretta House in St Moritz, only to be greeted with full fanfare and municipal honours as they stepped off the famous mountain railway. Everywhere they went it was the same. At San Remo Francis was awarded the Polano Trophy, followed by a huge dinner. The Chichesters hid Francis's health concerns as best they could, he wishing that he was strong enough to stay later and join in with the boys, Sheila always keeping a wary eye on him and pushing him off to bed as soon as was polite.

Gipsy Moth IV's homecoming on the Beaulieu River

Of all the celebrations they particularly enjoyed the one given for *Gipsy Moth IV* and themselves at Buckler's Hard, a kind of nautical homecoming. On Francis's sixty-sixth birthday, 17 September 1967, he was presented with the Freedom of the Beaulieu River – so no more mooring fees – and driven from the dock up the Buckler's Hard Maritime Museum by Lord Montagu in his 1909 Rolls Royce Silver Ghost. There Francis presented the Museum with the charts he had used on his circumnavigation. They are still there, proudly displayed on the walls. At dusk the Soho Concertante played Handel's *Water Music*; *Gipsy Moth IV* was bathed in floodlight; the sky sparkled with spectacular fireworks. Francis loved it all (albeit feverishly, thanks to the flu), greeting and thanking his faithful friend the harbour master Bill Grindey, then Bill Martin, who had mended numerous mechanical breakages, and Mrs Martin, who had victualed many a *Gipsy Moth* from the village shop.

Barnstaple claimed him as their son too. His childhood friend – his only childhood friend – the gardener's son Bill Wilkie, was now an MBE and Mayor of Barnstaple. How well they had both done these past sixty years, these two boys who once played in the clerical tyrant's garden and ran free through the Devon woodlands. In his acceptance speech Francis said: 'I did love your father. If only he could see us both today.'

After finishing *Gipsy Moth Circles the World* in three months, Francis went on a nationwide lecture tour to promote the book, culminating in a talk to 3,000 people at Royal Festival Hall just before Christmas 1967. He and Sheila then left for a quick tour of New Zealand, another version of the triumphant

Arrival at Buckler's Hard with the Montagus, Francis carrying the charts he was to present to the Maritime Museum there

The 'Welcome Home' programme at Buckler's Hard

homecoming tour, and returned to find the book still top of the non-fiction bestseller list. Back in St James's Place lay a long pile of unopened invitations from yacht clubs, lecture halls and colleges from around the world. Francis did his best to answer, and if possible accept, them all; Sheila watched nervously lest his days in the sunlight of fame stretched his increasingly fragile health too far.

One invitation gave him particular pleasure: the *Yacht Club de France* had made him a *Membre d'Honneur*. Francis would never admit it except to himself, but the Tabarly defeat in the 1964 OSTAR still rankled – and this great honour was some sort of recompense. The British Embassy hosted his stay in Paris. The Chichesters sat with the self-exiled Duke and Duchess of Windsor for dinner: Francis had not seen HRH since the Duke had presented him with the Johnson Memorial Trophy for the Tasman Sea flight thirty years earlier. Comparing their lives as the centres of attention, the Duke commented dolefully to Francis: 'At least you have achieved something'.

The *Sunday Times*, too, noticed its circulation rising with Francis's fortunes, firstly as his media partner as he rounded Cape Horn and headed for home, then later reporting on the 'victor takes the spoils' angle of his new-found fame and comparative fortune. A year after Francis completed his circumnavigation, Sir Alec Rose on *Lively Lady* completed his. In many ways Sir Alec's voyage against all odds was more remarkable than Francis's. Either way, single-handed racing had caught the public's imagination and the *Sunday Times* made the next logical leap: in late 1967 it decided to sponsor a non-stop around the world single-handed yacht race.

Francis first heard about this in a telephone call from the newspaper when he was on his victory tour of New Zealand in early 1968. The race was to be called The Sunday Times Golden Globe Race. There would be no fixed starting date; instead all competitors could set off whenever they were ready, as long as it was between June and end October that year. There were to be no rules and no handicap. Given his distinguished record, they asked whether Francis would do them the honour of being Chairman of the Committee. Tired and a long way from home, and no doubt a little flattered, he said he would. 'Marry in haste, repent in leisure', as Sheila no doubt was soon reminding him.

By the time the Chichesters came home in March it was too late for him to quit, no matter how unsettling he found the lack of necessary qualifications or even basic experience among those who were entering the race. And of course history proved all his fears to be right. The tragedy of the resulting race has been well told in Peter Nichols's *A Voyage for Madmen* and movingly portrayed in *Deep Water*, Louise Osmond's drama documentary about Donald Crowhurst. Suffice to say here that of the nine runners at the start only one finished and therefore won: Sir Robin Knox-Johnston in *Suhaili*.

Actually, for many yachtsmen, romantics and poets, including Francis and the author, the real winner was the

Francis with Bernard Moitessier

Frenchman Bernard Moitessier, who was well ahead of the fleet as he rounded Cape Horn. Heading north to what seemed like certain victory, he contemplated all the brouhaha that would go with the victory, couldn't face the fuss and insincerity and instead turned east towards the Cape of Good Hope for the fun of going around again. He soon got bored of that too and eventually gave up his wanderings in Tahiti.

It is interesting to hear Sir Robin's memories of the dramas and shortcomings of the Golden Globe Race. Francis was on the BBC launch that came out to meet him off Falmouth on 22 April 1969 and later presented him with the Golden Globe. I ask Robin if that was the first time they had met. 'Yes, this was the first time I'd actually met him but not the first time I'd seen him. That was on the Thames when he was sailing up to Greenwich to be knighted. I was the first officer on SS *Kenya* in London Docks and saw it all. That was the day that spurred me on.

I thought "he's been around the world with one stop". The next challenge was obvious, no stops. I'd already committed to it by the time the *Sunday Times* came up with the Golden Globe Race idea. I was in the race before they'd thought of it.

'After the race, still in Falmouth, the *Sunday Times* decided to host us for dinner – the supposition being that we would not get on. He would resent the young upstart and I would think he was an old fart, that sort of thing. He was nearly seventy and I was thirty, so it wasn't an unreasonable angle. Of course the opposite happened and we hit it off.

'I had huge respect for him and he was very charming to me. We had the same literary agent, 'Gentleman' George Greenfield, who had charged the *Sunday Times* £500 for each of us to host and sit in on the dinner.'

'And did Francis know by then what had happened in the race?' I ask.

Robin Knox-Johnston finishing the Golden Globe; Francis is on the launch behind

'No. Of course there were no comms in those days. There were two still at sea, Tetley and Crowhurst. Then Francis said an interesting thing, he said "what are we going to do about Crowhurst?"'

'So he suspected something was wrong?'

'He was already onto it. In those days we used radio stations for directional fixes. Pre-satellite. Crowhurst was claiming to be off Australia with fixes from South American aerials Francis knew didn't reach where he said he was. Francis was already suspicious because Crowhurst was claiming he had beaten Francis's 200 miles a day target. OK, that's possible in a catamaran, but at that time Crowhurst should have been in the Doldrums.

'The *Sunday Times* didn't believe Francis, said he was just jealous. Then there were other radio comms mismatches. Francis spread his suspicions around and when Crowhurst came back there was going to be some very tight examination of his logbooks. Of course we now know he was running two of them. We all think this must have contributed to his suicide.'

'And then you won the Royal Yacht Squadron's Chichester Trophy?'

'In 1969. They named it after him of course and he had won it two years earlier.[20] I did and this shows you the quality of the man. He had been a member for a while and it's quite a daunting place if you haven't been there before. So he rang me up and asked if I knew my way around there. I said no I didn't and he said "let me buy you dinner and show you around before the award". That was very understanding of him – I'd only really lived at sea and never moved in those sorts of circles.'

But the reality was that by the time Francis welcomed Robin and *Suhaili* back to victory at Falmouth in April 1969, his attention was already on his own next great adventure. To reprise five years: when Francis came second to Tabarly in the 1964 OSTAR, his cousin Lord Dulverton had offered to pay for a boat that could win the next Transatlantic Solo, due in 1968.

Francis then persuaded him to finance – or so it seemed – *Gipsy Moth IV* and the 1966/67 circumnavigation instead. Meanwhile, transatlantic solo life continued and the 1968 OSTAR was won by Geoffrey Williams in *Sir Thomas Lipton*, a 57-footer designed by *Gipsy Moth III*'s designer, Robert Clark. Clark's *Gipsy Moth III* had always been Francis's favourite yacht and he saw a bigger, better version of her in the *Sir Thomas Lipton*. For his new venture, still an evolving secret plan kept even from Sheila, Francis would need a bigger *Gipsy Moth III*; he would actually need a bigger *Sir Thomas Lipton*. He would also need to mend some fences with Robert Clark after unfairly highlighting some of *Gipsy Moth III*'s few shortcomings.

In any event, Francis had burnt his *Gipsy Moth IV* bridges by constantly belittling her, which was partly justified and partly self-aggrandisement. Either way, it was not good PR; it was Francis PR. She had been the star of the 1969 London Boat Show and Tony Dulverton, as the owner, had then given her to the nation to lie alongside *Cutty Sark* at Greenwich. While the boat was being lauded by the nation she was being endlessly criticised by Francis, with, *inter alia*, a long diatribe against her, her designers and builders in the opening chapters of *Gipsy Moth Circles the World*. In his talks he would say, for example: '*Gipsy Moth IV* has no sentimental value for me at all. She is cantankerous and difficult and needs a crew of three: a man to navigate, an elephant to move the tiller and a three and a half foot chimpanzee with arms eight feet long to get about below and work some of the gear'.

As Francis had done twice with *Gipsy Moth III*, Geoffrey Williams sailed *Sir Thomas Lipton* back from New York to the Solent in the late summer after the Golden Globe Race. Francis made himself known to Geoffrey once he had arrived and one dim day in November 1968 the two solo yachtsmen were joined on board by their shared designer, Robert Clark. The three of them sailed from Buckler's Hard over to Cowes, where Francis stood them dinner at the Royal Yacht Squadron. It was Francis's first time at the helm of a yacht for well over a year but he knew instantly that *Sir Thomas Lipton* was inherently 'hands-off', well balanced in a way that *Gipsy Moth IV* never was.

Over dinner Francis told them of his latest plan. On his circumnavigation he had enjoyed a very fast run home from the Azores to the Western Approaches. In ideal wind conditions and a smooth sea he had made a run of 1,408 miles in eight days, averaging 176 miles per day. With a truer-running yacht that didn't veer off course whenever he napped, he felt that his average could have been nearer 200 miles per day. This, he told them, was his plan: a record-breaking run from A to B averaging 200 miles a day. Then and later they discussed routes and tactics, and all questions came up with the same answer: 200 miles a day would only be possible sailing down the north-east trade winds, which blow across the North Atlantic from North Africa to Central America in winter and spring.

This trade wind transatlantic crossing is now quite routine, made both by solo sailors and yachtsmen joining rallies, but the vast majority make the crossing too early for the trade winds to have set in properly. The allure of Christmas in the Caribbean means that they leave the Canary Islands, the main jumping-off point, in early November. While a November crossing shouldn't run into any bad weather, it can hardly guarantee the 'milk run' of a trade wind crossing. Better wait till spring, when a sound and steady 20 or so knots of wind should blow you across without having to adjust the sails or steering with any great frequency. I can see Francis considering this 'set it and forget it' approach to a transatlantic crossing as a bit of a mixed blessing: he liked a good struggle against impossible odds. No doubt the thought of endless trimming to squeeze the last fraction of a knot out of his yacht cheered him up somewhat.

So back to the dinner at the Royal Yacht Squadron and Francis's plans. He would need Robert Clark to design him a 'Trade Winds

Special' version of *Sir Thomas Lipton*. They discussed her pros and cons, her downwind balance and her general demeanour. On the back of a menu Robert sketched a design built for running fast in the trades: the design that would become *Gipsy Moth V*.

Unfortunately the menu page no longer exists, so we will never know what they had for dinner or how Clark's first sketches looked. Luckily his son Adrian still has the menu-plus level drawings and tells me his father said that the final *Gipsy Moth V* was very much as first sketched over dinner. Her distinguishing feature is what Robert called a 'staysail ketch rig'. Instead of a mainsail she would fly two staysails [small fore-and-aft triangular sails], one running forward from the top of the mizzen mast and the other aft from midway up the main mast, the idea being to leave no gaps in the rig through which the wind could blow without pushing her along at a goodly rate. Adrian says the deal was done within a week with Francis footing the bill. Like their previous collaboration on *Gipsy Moth III* she would be built in Ireland, this time as Crosshaven. The build went smoothly, starting in early 1970 and finishing at the end of June.

Robin Knox-Johnston remembers meeting Francis then. 'I was on the Round Britain Race in *Ocean Spirit* and we'd stopped at Crosshaven. Francis knew I was on board, he rowed over, knocked on the hull and said "let's have lunch". So we did.

'The place was full of yachting journalists covering the race and one of them came over and asked if he could join us if he paid for lunch. Francis said no, it was private. Very typical of him. What was said to Francis stayed with Francis. I'm the same, one of the reasons we hit it off.

'I asked him what he was going to do with *Gipsy Moth V*. He was being a bit coy I thought. I said "Francis don't worry, I'm just trying to find out what I'm going to be doing next after you've set another record!"'

Gipsy Moth V in full flow (Chichester Archive/PPL)

While the build was going on, Francis studied his route options. Originally he wanted to attempt 1,000 miles in five days between two points in the ocean. His literary agent, 'Gentleman' George Greenfield, persuaded him that box office demanded two points on the shore. With the only trade wind option being to head east to west, this meant crossing the Atlantic, thus upping the distance considerably. The standard transatlantic route from the Canary Islands to the Windward Islands is 2,700 miles. There's no trade wind reason to start further north than the Canary Islands, so to stretch his course to the more headline-friendly 3,000 miles in fifteen days Francis would have to start in Africa and end in Central America. Dakar was just about in the trade wind zone and there was the intriguing Chichesteresque-sounding port Chichi on the coat of Venezuela. But by now Francis was into the swing of it and aiming for 4,000 miles in twenty days. This led him to Bissau, then the capital of Portuguese Guinea, now the capital of the hell-hole of Guinea-Bissau, at the eastern end of the route, and San Juan del Norte in Nicaragua at the western end.

Sometimes really bright people, experts in their field, do some really dumb things. With all Francis's experience and expertise in the art and science of long-distance yachting, adding this extra 1,000 miles and so putting himself outside the trade wind route and at the mercy of African hospitality was one of them. I'm surprised Sheila didn't put her foot down, especially as Francis had just done something almost as silly on *Gipsy Moth V*'s shake-down cruise. For some reason he thought a run from Beaulieu to Mallorca, leaving in early August, would give him steady winds to prove out her rig. Crewed by the BBC film-maker Christopher Doll on the way out and by Giles on the way home, it was, in Francis's own words, a waste of time: 'I never seemed to have good luck on this voyage, which probably means that I did not plan or carry it out skilfully.' Quite. Everyone who has sailed there knows there's no wind in the western Med in

August and that the high pressure that sits over the Azores all summer long guarantees a headwind on the way home up the Portuguese coast, the opposite of the fast running before the wind that Francis wanted for the sea trials. He did not arrive arrived back at Buckler's Hard until 22 October 1970, having proved nothing and not even having had an enjoyable outing. Worse, he had left himself only six weeks before his planned departure down the coast of Africa.

Francis wasn't one to believe in omens and portents; but if he had been, they were stacking up against him. After the own goal of the wasted voyage to Mallorca and back, he had finally set sail for Plymouth with Giles as crew on 12 December. All sailors will tell of near misses with illegally unwatched freighters, and Francis's came off Exmouth:

> *She had such a near escape from being smashed by a steamer that my blood still runs cold when I think of it. On a fine sunny morning in perfect visibility I saw a steamer 3 or 4 miles to Starboard. Gipsy Moth, under sail, had right of way. I made a note of our closing angle, checked our course, was satisfied all was well and went below to cook some breakfast.*
>
> *It seemed only minutes later that suddenly looking up, I saw through the rust-speckled side of the steamer a few feet away. I don't think I will ever again reach the cockpit as quickly as I did then. Gipsy Moth's bow was just about to hit the side of the big steamer. I grabbed the helm, overriding the self-steering gear by force and turned onto a parallel heading. The great iron hulk was now eighteen inches or so from the side of Gipsy Moth. I had to keep her sailing almost parallel to the side of the ship and between one or two feet off it. Giles was lying in his berth hard against the starboard side and I dreaded our side being torn away with Giles trapped in his bunk. One*

of the crew on the steamer looked down over the side and I told him what I thought of Crystal Kobos, *registered in Panama.*

Francis sailed alone from Plymouth, bound for Bissau, on 18 December. Not surprisingly, the midwinter Bay of Biscay dished the dirt on him. These were the gales that would prove out *Gipsy Moth V*'s rig and his ability to handle it. His account fairly brims with the fun he is having in conditions that most yachtsmen would dread, even with a crew. But she was consistently covering over 200 miles a day and that was its own reward.

Down the Portuguese coast the wind slowed to merely strong and gusty, but off Morocco all hell broke loose. Even Francis was impressed:

At 3.00 am I had to take down the staysail, the last sail set. Gipsy Moth *had been crashing through the night at 9 knots under sail alone out of control of the self-steering gear. I could hardly keep from being thrown out of my bunk. It seemed the outskirts of a hurricane.*

The wind pressed my clothes to my body and my vision was limited because the peak of my cap was being blown hard against my nose. I saw great sheets of spray in the air, scattered like giant bucketfuls of water. The ordinary spray burst as if it were smoke from a cannon. If only the boat could have stayed unmoving, the force of the blows from the waves would've been that much less. I was soon soaked. The wind blew the water up under my oilskin smock top, even though I had fastened it tightly round the waist.

When I returned to the cockpit I spent what seemed like a long time trying to coax her downwind under her bare poles, but an extra fierce blast of wind with a slewing wave would broach her across the wind. Broadside-on seemed to be the natural stance for her racing lines and nothing less than a man at the helm would keep headed elsewhere.

By 0400 the next day the wind had increased to 60 knots. At 1000 a big wave came aboard and there was a great crashing of crockery and gear as she was flung viciously on her side. I felt lucky that I had been forced back into my bunk rather than being flung out of it. As she righted herself I clambered out but I could not see any damage except to the spinnaker pole, which had been well and truly kyboshed by the waves.

By midday the wind had eased to less than 50 knots. More importantly, it had not got the same savage shriek. I have often noticed the difference between two winds of the same speed. One may have a powerful, urgent, impatient note. The other, of the same speed, will not. It is some extra quality which I have never heard or read about.

North of the Canary Islands Francis entered the north-east trade wind zone and the sea's fury abated. He logged good news and bad: *Gipsy Moth V* was certainly capable of 200 miles per day, pleasurably so, but some of the rig was too lightweight and so under-strength. Fixable, Francis presumed correctly, by the under-stressed and Anglo-friendly Portuguese Navy in Guinea-Bissau.

───── ❧ ─────

On 12 January 1971 Francis was sent off ceremoniously by Tiago Fidalgo Bastos, Commodore of the Portuguese Navy and Vice-Governor of Guinea-Bissau, and so started what he called 'the Romantic Challenge': the 4,000-mile dash across the Atlantic at 200 miles a day, a voyage of twenty days. Twenty-two days and six hours later the British Ambassador to Nicaragua and his wife, Ivor and Patricia Vincent, welcomed him off San Juan del Norte. Francis had lost his main bet with himself but won his side-bet of sailing 1,000 miles in five days. He had also won something more important: for the first time he had enjoyed rather than endured a whole ocean passage.

When it was all over and he was safely back in London, he wrote *The Romantic Challenge*, a book about his adventures in *Gipsy Moth V*. Actually, it's by far the best of his six books; in general he wrote as he socialised, awkwardly. For this, his last book, he wrote as he now sailed, freely. The book is partly retrospective, partly political and partly philosophical; and tucked away in the middle of a paragraph is what could be Francis's defining philosophy: 'Nothing equals apprehension of the future for making one enjoy the unparalleled beauty and charm of the present.'

In fact the only poor part of the book is Chapter 4, 'The 4,000-Mile Race', which describes his Atlantic crossing. It's poor because it's boring and it's boring because nothing Franciscan happens. It's a most un-Francis-like ocean passage, a lovely, smooth tropical sail with a following wind, starry nights and pour-a-bucket-over-me-to-keep-cool days: no death-defying dramas, no if-it-wasn't-for-me-I'd-be-dead episodes, not even any catastrophic gear failures. In fact, for the first time his account of an ocean voyage reads much like one of ours:

> *The balmy air flowing over my naked body was deliciously cooling after the heat of the cabin. The diamond-bright stars were set in a black sky. Occasionally I shrank from the side of the cockpit when a wave broke over the counter but nothing came over the combing and I gave myself over to the romantic pleasure of sliding fast through the seas into the night in my slim, powerful craft.*

He even rose to the challenge, pathos abounding, of knowing from day one that his attempt was doomed by his decision to start up a tidal estuary out of the trade wind zone, just to round up the Romantic Challenge to 4,000 miles. Why he didn't start in the Canaries and throw in a Caribbean island dog-leg on the way to, say, Panama is a mystery that, writing later, he didn't even attempt to answer:

> *I knew I had blundered badly in starting from Bissau. With at least twenty days and twenty nights of continuous hard racing ahead I had had the stupidity to lumber myself at the start with navigating a long, tricky estuary, with at best light tropical winds and at worst calms. But I had said that I was going to start from Bissau to make up the distance across the Atlantic to 4,000 miles and start from Bissau I would.*

At the end of the first day he had only made 72 miles and then the 200-mile a day challenge was already 206 miles. By the end of third day it had risen to 210 miles per day for seventeen days. He didn't enter into the trade wind belt until the sixth day, when he made over 200 miles for the first time – but by then it was too late to worry about the averages: 'It was no use getting depressed; it was my own fault for letting myself be trapped by a romantic notion.'

On he sped, across the Atlantic. But on the tenth day, after another day's run of over 200 miles and just as the first thought of succeeding after all was reviving, the spinnaker pole broke and shattered with it all hope of success: apart from the obvious loss of sail area, the time taken off flat-out sailing over the next two days while he was splicing up an alternative pole meant losing any chance of the record attempt.

Rather than mope about lost opportunities and bent spinnaker poles, Francis cracked on with breaking his original, pre-grandiose Romantic Challenge plan, of sailing 1,000 miles in five days. This remarkable achievement has these days been overshadowed by technology and design. Today's solo adventurers sail carbon fibre multihulls, eat specially developed hybrid space food and are fit to levels that poor old – actually slowly dying – Francis could only imagine, and are guided along their routes by amazingly sophisticated weather-forecasting software. Two hundred miles a day now is for sissies: the likes of Thomas Coville and Francis Joyon regularly sail over 600 miles a day, the current record being held by Coville at 718 miles.

At the other end of the spectrum, when I'm passage-planning on *Vasco da Gama*, I reckon we cruise along at an average of 5 knots, so 120 miles a day. This puts Francis's prowess into better perspective. The difference in effort on board between 120 and 200 miles a day is immense. Francis drove himself constantly, sleeping fitfully at best, always tweaking and trimming the sails for the last zephyr of a knot. We set sails, bung on the autopilot, kettle up a brew and watch the seas go by in their own time. At night, and only when it's all quiet out there, we set the radar alarm to 12 miles, have a final stab at the autopilot and final trim of the sails, and turn in for a good night's sleep. But don't tell anyone: it's really no more legal than Francis napping around the world.

Francis's new lashed-up spinnaker pole was strong enough itself but it caused problems to all parts of the yacht to which it was connected. He rather enjoyed his fixing forays:

> *I am suffering from a complaint quite new to me tonight. My bottom is sore from sunburn. I was working for an hour or two on the clew of the big runner and I must have got burnt then. But I am not moaning about it because it is such a wonderful thing for a Briton to be able to get a burnt bottom in January.*

There were always wildlife diversions on Francis's voyages. In Africa a particularly aggressive-looking spider had stowed away.

It was impervious to Francis's spray-gun attacks. On another occasion he noticed that *Gipsy Moth V* suddenly felt draggy and had slowed by 2 knots. Leaning over the side, he saw that a detached fishing net had wrapped itself around the hull. Hauling it in with a grappling hook, he discovered a turtle caught in the net, its head through one square and its paddles through others. Francis carefully unravelled him, noticing how the ungrateful turtle kept trying to bite him for his kindness. Later he mused:

> *Finally I slid him back into the ocean where he flipped off gaily, as if he regularly made year-long voyages across the Atlantic imprisoned in a net.*
>
> *I wondered what the cumulative odds must be against his being released. First of all there were the odds against his being caught in the net; then the longer odds against the net breaking away. Then there were the further odds against the net being swept out to sea, even further odds against it entering the Guinea current and being carried out into the Atlantic.*
>
> *Now add incredibly long odds against the net being caught in the keel of a yacht 2,300 miles out in the Atlantic, almost as long odds against the net been hauled on board – and finally I would think it was a pretty lone chance that the skipper of said yacht would be vegetarian by preference.*

Francis approached the coast of Nicaragua on 3 February 1971. It had never been his intention to land at San Juan del Norte but to cross an imaginary line 8 miles offshore, 4,000 miles from the estuary at Bissau. From there he was planning to sail 250 miles down to Panama in order to affect the inevitable repairs that a hard-driving transatlantic crossing will demand. However, unbeknownst to him, while he was scudding across the Mid-Atlantic, a flurry of Anglo-Nicaraguan diplomatic activity was scudding across the North Atlantic.

Nicaragua then was a classic banana republic, a hereditary military dictatorship ruled by the Somoza family.[21] The Director-General of Tourism was the President's first cousin, a Dr Luis Correa, who saw Francis's arrival as a wonderful opportunity to bring his country to the world's attention. (He later suggested to Francis that he should organise the 4,000-mile crossing as a yearly race; Francis, who warmed to Dr Correa for his enthusiasm, made his excuses.) The Somoza family's more distant relative, the Nicaraguan Ambassador to the Court of St James's, petitioned the Foreign and Commonwealth Secretary, the Rt. Hon. Sir Alec Douglas-Home, that Francis should not only be a guest of honour in his country but the personal guest of President Anastasio Somoza DeBayle in the capital, Managua.

Despatches flew back and forth between Whitehall and the embassy in Managua:

> *Very substantial efforts have been made here to look after Chichester ... His non-arrival at the Presidential Palace in Managua could have serious consequences ... If the embassy does not do everything in their power to get Chichester to do this ... Anglo-Nicaraguan relations, for what they are worth, would suffer.*

The Ambassador, Ivor Vincent, added wryly: 'I studied such of Chichester's books as were available, and began to realise what we were letting ourselves in for, in trying to bring him ashore.'

In the meantime the Ambassador Ivor had to humour the Director-General of Tourism. He reported to the Foreign and Commonwealth Secretary:

> *Dr Correa was obviously indulging in dreams of glory, a ceremonial landing at San Juan del Norte, presentation of the keys of the town and of a gold medal commemorating the Indian Chief Nicarao after whom the country is*

named, a flight by helicopter to Managua and a reception by President Somoza. I should explain that San Juan del Norte, which had been a prosperous township of 20,000 inhabitants in the 19th and early 20th century in Gold Rush times, has by now dwindled into a marshy, ruined and hopeless village of three hundred families completely cut off from the outer world.

Realising that San Juan was a non-starter, Dr Correa then arrived at a much more sensible suggestion, the fishing-fleet port of El Bluff, only 60 miles north of Francis's self-imposed finishing line. The first Francis heard of it was when an ungainly fishing boat came out to greet him. On board were the British Ambassador and his wife Patricia, Christopher Doll and his BBC film crew, and Dr Correa.

The Ambassador did his best to make a speech; Francis felt sorry for him, and even sorrier for his wife as the top-heavy boat rolled around in the swell. Dr Correa then suggested his better plan than Panama: why not head 60 miles north to El Bluff? El Bluff? Yes, El Bluff, there a *gringo capitan* runs a yard with eighty-five shrimp trawlers under his care; he can fix your boat, easy.

Francis had already heard the *gringo capitan* over the radio – and had liked what he had heard. Captain Bartlett, 'Bart', or 'El Capitan de Connecticut', was as sound in person as he was on the airwaves. Francis and Bart were instant soul buddies, fixing buddies, yarning buddies and drinking buddies. Francis reckoned that Bart 'would have needed no make-up at all to play the part of a pirate captain of two centuries or more ago. His tremendous personality alone would, surely have made him the most successful – and certainly the most efficient – privateer on the Spanish Main.' He never did find out Bart's age – 'whenever I asked him, he dodged the question' – and reckoned he could be anywhere between fifty and seventy.

There were more blessings in store: Donata, Bart's head maid, was a terrific cook and with the bounty of the sea at her disposal, every lunch turned into a magnificent seafood *extravaganza*. Every lunch also turned into a kind of meeting of the local *meros merors*, the big bosses who plied their various trades around Bart's enormous dining table. On one occasion Francis counted no fewer than five ambassadors from neighbouring countries, which he recorded as a useful geography lesson, if nothing else.

It went without saying that the lunches were liquid and that every afternoon Francis went *troppo* with the others, enjoying a good siesta to sleep things off. An early evening work spurt on the boats was followed by a visit by Bart to *Gipsy Moth V*:

> *At nightfall he used to come back and have supper with me on board. We would settle down to yarning, but towards the end of a bottle of brandy or gin, the talking would give way to Bart's stentorian sea songs. When he was in full song he made the welkin ring and it felt as if Gipsy Moth's hull were quivering, the warehouses along the wharf shaking as if in an earthquake.*

All the while the Ambassador was in full swing arranging Francis's VIP visit to President Somoza in Managua. A special gold medal had been struck in his honour and the Ambassador suggested that Frances should give the President a gift in return. All he had on board to spare was his Royal Cork Yacht Club burgee, of significance to sailors as the Royal Cork is the oldest yacht club in the world, older even than the Royal Yacht Squadron (albeit a gift of less significance to banana republic dictators). A small plane was sent to pick Francis up and that night the Vincents threw a cocktail party at the Embassy in his honour. He remarked he had never seen so many ambassadors in one place at a time; well, he wouldn't have. Ambassador Vincent reported back to London that 'Over 300 people attended this reception, though less than 24 hours' notice had been possible. Chichester made a very favourable impression indeed, talking to well over half the guests personally.'

Later that evening Vincent and Francis were presented to the President. Francis handed over the burgee but noticed that the gold medal was not forthcoming; maybe later. They chatted and drank *Flor de Caña*, the local rum. Somoza was 'most amiable and said he would hang the burgee on his bedroom wall'. They repaired to the enormous balcony, where Francis noted Cerro Negro, an active volcano that was spreading its pall of dust 50 miles in all directions. Somoza revisited the subject of Correa's transatlantic yacht race idea; Francis promised to mention it to the Duke of Edinburgh, with whom he was in touch. Suitably sozzled, he and Somoza hugged and slapped their farewells. Francis never did get his gold medal and Somoza never did get his yacht race.

I do believe that the twelve days Francis spent in El Bluff and Managua, surrounded by boats and boatmen – proper hands-on boatmen with not a blazer in sight – lunching with ambassadors and eccentrics, being hosted by his own embassy and a president, repairing *Gipsy Moth V* by day and rekindling her captain with his soul chum Bart by night were among the happiest of Francis's life.

And diplomatic honour was satisfied too. Ambassador Vincent reported back to Sir Alec Douglas-Home: 'From a local point of view the visit was a great boon for Anglo-Nicaraguan relations, and I am sure we shall benefit for some time to come. Chichester proved himself a flexible and friendly person, quite unlike the dour, misanthropic portrait painted for us by the BBC. The whole comedy was in the best film tradition, and I think that everybody who took part or watched it would have enjoyed it.'

The Nicaraguan press certainly did, dubbing Francis 'El Viejo Lobo del Mar'; Francis rather liked being 'The Old Wolf of the Sea'.

◦◦◦

Inspired by his sojourn in El Bluff, he then began what would become his swansong, what he himself called 'The Great Amble Eastwards', his own kind of 'No Direction Home': three months in which to sail as he liked it best – alone – in his favourite ocean, the North Atlantic.

After freeing himself from the contrary winds and tides of the Caribbean, he escaped into the Atlantic between Cuba and Haiti. A few days later he wrote:

> *I am lying in my berth, relaxed. It seems an age since I could rest or let go the tension and allow myself to have a deep sleep. Caribbean sailing woes were in the past; I was at large on the edge of the ocean, in calm seas under the sunshine, and with a light, pleasant breeze. I stood looking at the clumps of Sargasso weed, pale yellowy brown, the size of a lily pond, drifting past and let me briefly cut a straight path for Gipsy Moth to pass through. There followed a delightful sail such as yachtsmen all hope for but in most cases only experience in their dreams. Smooth seas, moderate winds, sunshine and mostly fine weather.*

It's a funny thing, but all yachtsmen sailing in the Bounty advertisement seas of the tropical islands experience what is known as 'paradise fatigue'. So there they are, off yet another swaying palm tree-fringed, grass-skirted, potentially topless island, just back up on deck after the early morning wake-up swim, scooping out the last of the local papaya, fresh coffee aroma wafting up from the galley, and they look all around and say to themselves: 'Not another effing day in Paradise'.

After a week of the Great Amble, Francis reverted to type and set himself a challenge. I can almost see the thought bubble: 'I have an ocean greyhound and well found one too. I'm on the edge of the north-east trades. I'm fit and relaxed. Let's set a fresh speed record.' He then spent two days down below on another favourite pastime, plotting himself a course. The finishing line would be the Equator, the starting gate a point 1,600 miles upwind of it, Point X, a notional islet in the mid-Atlantic.

Calculations behind him, he was in fine spirits as he sailed towards Point X:

At a meeting of the Ship's Company this morning, the Medical Officer and Chaplain in attendance, Captain presiding, it was unanimously agreed to sail down the 40th Meridian from 20° North to the Equator. The Medical Officer said he was very relieved the Captain had come out of his mental purdah, and finished his cerebral ordeal with some result, whatever it may be, and apparently without loosing his sanity. Some of the less understanding of the crew had wondered if the master was doing his nut or, in scientific medical language, going crackers. The captain ordered an extra round of brandy for all hands and grunted his way below to the security of his cabin.

Truth to tell, it wasn't one of his more successful dashes across the oceans blue. The trade winds were playing up, and not just wimpishly. They breezed rather than blew, this way and that, stopping only for the occasional deluge. After 1,200 miles Francis gave up the hopeless quest and at 1420 on 27 March, he logged: 'Tacked for home and loved ones (I hope)'.

Reading all this now, I think it was during the unfulfilled record run to the Equator that his cancer returned, noticeably. He wrote of pains in his legs, jolts from his remaining kidney, lethargy and exhaustion. He became morose and maudlin in his reflections:

I do not know if all kinds of solitary living have the same affect. Solitary sea life makes me think and feel more than is comfortable for my peace of mind. I have dreadful attacks of remorse. My chief remorse is for unkind acts to friends in the past. Maybe something deeply wounding that I have said or done. Then I find myself stuck with such things forever: they cannot be undone and the awful thing is that often they did not mean that much to me, or were even seriously believed.

This life makes one so sympathetic with others in trouble with their conscience, or unable to cope with the overwhelming difficulties of their lives.

I often think of Donald Crowhurst with great sympathy. For me, to be nine months alone without aim, project, objective, challenge, would mean exposing myself far too much. I can understand his soul being damaged or destroyed by continuous considering of it, relentless probing of it. I can only stand a very little peep of it now and then. Thank God for activity of body and mind to keep you away from my soul.

On Sheila's birthday, 11 April, south of the Azores, he opened a bottle of champagne and toasted her and

Edward and Belinda Montagu, who were married on the same date. We four have a tradition of holding a party together. It was wonderful thinking of them and Gipsy Moth's home in Edward's Beaulieu River.

This is the most lovely part of the ocean that I know: it has a peaceful, happy, relaxed atmosphere which is unique and would be an ideal place for one soul to take off if it wished to leave the earth.

And on he sailed to Horta in the Azores for his final pit stop there.

—∞∞∞—

Francis saved his best storm until last. He also saved his greatest act of heroism until last. Three hundred miles north of the Azores, en route to Plymouth, at just after midnight on a moonless night he was hit by what to him seemed like a mini-hurricane from out of the blue. Just when he needed all his strength to clamber up onto the gale-swept deck, crawl through the stinging spray and lower the sails, as he had done dozens of times before, time caught up with his old body and its remaining strength would not let him leave his bunk.

Lying there helplessly as *Gipsy Moth V* was careening dizzily through the storm, he could only wait for the inevitable: within five minutes he was upside down and being poured onto the cabin ceiling now beneath him. All around, the contents of the cabin were flying this way and that. He landed badly on an edge and was soon in fresh agony from what he thought was a burst kidney. ('Having only one kidney, I was concerned. If that one burst I would be poorly placed in an hour or two's time'.)

Events now moved quickly. *Gipsy Moth V* was out of control, sailing far too fast and soon to capsize, twice, again. Down below, in agony and helpless, in near-darkness and surrounded by the detritus of the capsizes. Francis decided to send out an SOS. For him of all people, the exemplar of self-reliance, it must have been a desperate decision. But again events conspired against him: the knockdown had let sea water into the bilges, some sloshes of which had flooded the batteries.

There was nothing to do but hang on and hope. In the early light he could write:

The seas are the danger: they are terrific. Like Cape Horn, but steeper and shorter with more frequent breakers. I feel depressed and frightened. How many hours of this before Gipsy Moth *sank? I was deeply sad. There is so much in Life. It is dreadful for death to tear me away from all the people I love. But it looks as if this is it. I*

reckon this was one of the tightest jams I've been in: I was
deadbeat with sheer fatigue, fear, tension and depression.

Then it got a whole lot worse. By now in daylight, he noticed
that she was leaking – and seriously. The water in the hull
was a storm in itself, washing around the cabin floor, making
finding the source of the leak below the waterline impossible.
Desperately, he summoned up the strength to fill a bucket, walk
it over to the cockpit, pour it onto the cockpit floor and let it
drain through the scuppers. It seemed hopeless, yet it was his
only hope. Bending down hurt enough, hauling a bucket of water
across the heaving cabin hurt twice as much, then pouring it into
the storm-bound cockpit twice as much again. After two dozen
buckets, his spirit broke: he saw that the source of the leak was
not below the waterline but in the corner of the cockpit, where
he had been pouring the water. All those buckets, all that agony,
had been spent on sending the water around in circles.

There are many instances in Francis's life that could be
called heroic but what follows, for me, tops the list. Cold, wet,
frightened, in deep pain – and, in fact, dying – he cut out a piece
of Tupperware, of all mundane life-savers, and nailed it over the
leak. He could for now ignore sailing; the yacht's sails had been
torn asunder by the hurricane winds and three capsizes; she
was out of his control and now in her own control, a floating,
crippled piece of wood with nowhere to go and nothing to do.
Down below, bucket by bucket, shards of pain coursing through
his every movement, Francis emptied the hull. He would later
write: 'I carried 341 buckets of water. It may not sound much,
but carrying a full bucket 20 feet in a boat is a long way in a
rough seaway…', He had saved his boat and his own life, for
now.

But storms go from whence they came and hour by hour,
then day by day, the seas died down just as Francis was dying
down. Amid the tidying up he found a bottle of champagne.

The brandy had survived too; he made himself a champagne cocktail. His spirits rose. Ten days later he wrote:

> *I passed the great breakwater across Plymouth Sound just as my beloveds, Sheila and Giles, came to meet me in the Flag Officer's launch. Soon after midnight we were all eating scrambled eggs at the Royal Western Yacht Club while I was telling my tale.*

Five months after the knockdowns in the Western Approaches and the scrambled eggs in Plymouth, on 17 September 1971, Francis was in Greyshott Hall health farm celebrating his seventieth birthday and reflecting on his life. He had just finished his best and last book, *The Romantic Challenge*, about his adventures on *Gipsy Moth V*. Being Francis, he had made heavy weather of it, rewriting through the night, driving himself as hard at the desk as he did on deck. He was constantly exhausted, so much so that a month earlier he was admitted to King Edward VII's hospital in London for an enforced three-week rest. Greyshott Hall followed, on doctor's orders.

The 'Romantic Challenge' started with the words: 'I love Life; this great, exciting, absorbing, puzzling, adventurous Life'. He now had all the trappings of a successful life: a long and happy marriage; a beautiful yacht on a beautiful mooring; money to pay for it all; a successful business; and a knighthood, bestowed on him by his Queen, with Drake's sword on his shoulder, for being a hero. No schoolboy could dream of more. But family aside, he saw the trappings for what they were: traps, detracting from his lodestar to life: happiness lies in striving for perfection.

For Francis the striving for perfection didn't always mean breaking records or pushing oneself to the limits. Perfection could equally be the way he stroked a cat, talked with the milkman, helped a friend in need. His single-mindedness when pursuing a goal was all-absorbing, to the point of sometimes appearing rude or uncaring to those on the periphery or not involved at all in his expeditions. Like all monomaniacs on a mission, he had a switch that blanked out all distractions from the task in hand. When not on a monomaniac's mission, he made the seemingly mundane, day-to-day dealings with life and its protagonists missions in themselves, to be carried out with meticulous care. Mission Francis was selfish and self-absorbed, stonehearted; mundane Francis was warm and generous, open- and warm-hearted.

He took the news of his final, spinal cancer stoically, as one would expect. Diagnosed in Reading Hospital a month later, he didn't mope or moan. It was inoperable; with steady rounds of blood transfusions he could expect to live for two more years if he slowed down and took life easy.

Of course it was hopeless advice. Francis didn't do 'easy'. Life for him was a series of heartbeats: one was allotted that number and then had the responsibility to make each one chime. A chimeless heartbeat was a wasted heartbeat and he only had so many left. Luckily for him, the perfect final challenge, really the last hurrah, was just around the corner.

———✖✖✖———

Quite why Sheila let him race in the 1972 OSTAR we will never know. Previously, when he was recovering from cancer courtesy of her nature cures, she felt a solo sail against his own odds would be the final part of the cure. And she was right; it had been. But this time he was clearly in seriously bad shape.

He had been reacting poorly to the blood transfusions, to the point of crying off from the last one before leaving Buckler's Hard in June 1972. Sometimes he was barely able to stand; always he was heavily dosed with painkillers. But as usual, his determination overrode all objections.

The race and life afloat had changed beyond imagination since he and Blondie Hasler had rounded up two other

Corinthians to enter the first OSTAR eight years ago. There were now fifty-two entrants and most of them, like the French 128-foot schooner and race favourite *Vendredi 13*, not Corinthians at all. Technology, especially communications technology, was upgrading so rapidly that Francis was signed up by the *Sunday Times* to file daily reports of his voyage – and in the expectation that they would reach home.

Students of disasters know that it is seldom a catastrophic failure that causes trouble but a series of small, seemingly unimportant and unrelated incidents that conspire to cause the calamity. On *Gipsy Moth V* it was the radio. It would receive but not transmit, with calamitous consequences; and calamity is the only way to describe Francis's 1972 OSTAR.

He was never really in the race in his own terms. In constant pain, he would lie in his bunk rather than tend to the boat and, as he knew better than anyone, the only way to win was by continuously maximising the sail trim. What had finally brought him to his senses and convinced him to retire was regaining consciousness after anaesthetising himself with a near-overdose of morphine. The pain was no longer localised but spread agonisingly through every bone and marrow of his body, surpassing his oral tablets' ability to cope. Unable to bear the pain any longer, he had resorted to the strongest solution in his emergency medical bag, the hypodermic needle and its morphine solution. He passed out peacefully, slept and slept, but for how long had he been gone? It was still daylight, but which day?[22] His mind befuddled by meds, his body anaemic to the point of uselessness, he made the only sensible decision he had made in weeks. He headed *Gipsy Moth V* back to Plymouth; he had retired honourably.

When he was later criticised for taking part in the race at all, he wrote a letter to *The Times* from his Royal Naval Hospital bed, from which:

Unfortunately the cancer presented two particular problems. It made me become anaemic because the bones which were involved with the tumour could no longer do their normal job of making blood: and secondly, as the bones were increasingly affected they became increasingly painful.

I had been given painkillers to use as necessary and I had to take them at times in order to get some sleep. In spite of their help, continued buffeting during the first part of the race made the pain more and more intense and I feared that if I did not get some sleep I would be unable to go on. So I gave myself an injection of one of the emergency painkillers. It certainly stopped the pain but I soon realised that, under its influence, my mind was no longer functioning normally. I could not think clearly and in particular could not rely on my calculations. There was a danger that my navigation would become inaccurate, and I was heading towards the Azores, a difficult area of currents and variable winds.

It was then that I decided to give up, not because of hazard to myself, but because of the risks to others if I passed out, which seemed probable, so I put about heading for home.

I did not want any help then and I certainly did not ask for any.

Meanwhile, back on land, the lack of radio contact was setting its own hares running. Francis was the most famous yachtsman in the race and the race was now the most famous yachting race in the world. All the other competitors were reporting their positions except Francis, who couldn't, and the skipper of the favourite, *Vendredi 13*, who wouldn't. No-one knew where Francis was or how he was doing. Into this news vacuum the newspaper headlines stirred up *Daily Mail*-style fear and loathing. Worse still for Francis, he could hear all these rumours and conjectures perfectly – the receiving half of the radio was working, he just couldn't reply or report.

If the semi-redundant radio was the first of the conspiring incidents, the second soon hove into view over the horizon. SS *Barrister*, a merchant ship, happened across Francis half-way between the Azores and Land's End. While not specifically searching for *Gipsy Moth V*, her crew were aware of the mystery caused by the radio silence. They duly reported *Gipsy Moth V*'s position to the world, adding that she was in fine shape, that they had seen Francis waving from the stern and that they were both heading north-west towards New York, albeit with reduced sail. Of course they weren't; Francis had put her on a starboard tack, which temporarily put him on a northerly heading when SS *Barrister* happened to pass close by. The reduced sail was merely the result of Francis deciding to cruise rather than race home. The radio operator on *SS Barrister* took Francis's northing to be north-westing and the reduced sail to be a sign of gear failure.

This set the headlines wagging with fresh frenzy. His reported position and heading were interpreted as meaning that he was last in the race to New York, by hundreds of miles, as a result of sail problems, rather than the reality: that he was cruising all the way back to Plymouth. On board, Francis was becoming increasingly distressed by all these wrong conclusions, which he could hear all too clearly but do nothing about. Francis never appreciated doing nothing about something.

Now that the world knew where he was, thanks to the SS *Barrister*, it wasn't long before the third conspirator hove into view, this time a Nimrod from the sky. The RAF routinely carried search and rescue exercises over the Atlantic and now had the added fun of having a real live target on which to practise. Buzzing Francis several times, they mistook his vigorous waves for greetings rather than annoyance; but at least they knew about navigation and reported that he was, in fact, heading home. Cue more overwrought headlines and misplaced speculation.

By now it was clear to everyone that *Gipsy Moth V*'s radio could not transmit; what was not clear was whether it could receive. Ever ingenious, the RAF sent in its next Nimrod with an Aldis lamp. This was a powerful spotlight used by the Navy to signal Morse code from ship to ship, or ship to shore, when radio silence was needed. Being of that era, Francis knew his Morse code and had an Aldis lamp on board. *Gipsy Moth V* and the Shackleton tried to signal to each other but only with partial success; the Aldis is intended for slow-moving or stationary vessels, not low-flying aircraft with views hindered by a yacht's swaying masts and rigging. After an hour Francis grew tired and signalled: 'Weak and cold. Want rest'. In a kind of tragicomic Morse version of Chinese whispers, the RAF reported that he was 'weak and cold and going to Brest'.

So the watching world thought he was now heading for Brest and therefore must be in trouble; enter sea right our next troublemaker, and – as it later transpired – the real villain, the French weather ship *France II*. When Francis first saw her he was mildly annoyed at yet another intrusion and flashed a message: 'No aid needed. Thank you. Go away.' But *France II* came closer and closer on to him and he started to worry: the captain seemed not to know the basic rules – or even courtesy – of the sea. Far too close already, her captain swung her round to starboard and Francis watched, horrified, as *Gipsy Moth V*, still on autopilot, headed straight for her amidships. Frantically and in piercing pain, he kicked off the self-steering and swung the tiller over. But it was too late; the mizzen mast and rigging had fouled on *France II*'s superstructure. Even now the crew could see nothing amiss, shouting offers of help at Francis; the air turned as blue as the sea as Francis hurled abuse back at them.

Fortunately sanity was about to enter the story in the shape of the Royal Navy frigate HMS *Salisbury*. She was sailing past Brest on her way home to Plymouth and was tasked with seeing if Francis needed help. Harold Evans, then Editor of the *Sunday*

Times and in charge of Francis's media contracts, decided that Giles should be part of any rescue attempt. He arranged for him to be helicoptered out to HMS *Salisbury* as part of the 'rescue' story.

Soon the crew on HMS *Salisbury* were joined by three volunteer seamen from the nearby HMS *Ark Royal*. Commander McQueen hailed Francis: 'Good morning Sir Francis. Can we send a launch across to see how you are?' Already impressed by the complete contrast with his previous encounter with the French weather-ship, Francis was delighted to accept. Soon the expert crew of five had *Gipsy Moth V* sailing as well as her broken mizzen would allow and they were back to Plymouth so quickly that the press missed their arrival, much to Francis's delight and *schadenfreude*.

The sorry tale had its comic moments but was to end in drama and tragedy. On her way back to Brest, *France II* ran into and sank the yacht *Lefteria*. Of the eleven souls on board, seven were drowned. The press already knew that *France II* had been involved in the 'rescue' of *Gipsy Moth V*. Now someone at *Agence France Presse* put out a bulletin that *Lefteria* was searching for *Gipsy Moth V* too and drew the conclusion that the mission to search for and rescue Francis had led to the death of eight fellow yachtsmen. Other outlets picked up the story and it became common currency around the world within days that Francis's foolhardiness and poor seamanship had caused this terrible tragedy.

Francis, of course, was totally distraught at the mere thought of the misinterpretations. He had never needed 'rescuing'; he had never asked to be 'rescued'; the whole 'rescue' operation was imposed on him, often by nincompoops. Predictably, a completely witless Labour MP, William Price, asked in Parliament how much the whole 'rescue' operation had cost the taxpayer. The answer was practically nothing, as the Nimrods were out there anyway, but now the press had a new angle: not only did Francis's poor seamanship cause the death of eight fellow seaman but it cost the hard-pressed British taxpayer £3,000.

Clearing up all this misinformation became a consuming part of Francis's dying days. Yes, we are at that part of his life. After disembarking at Plymouth he was readmitted to the Royal Naval Hospital there and, for once, needed no persuasion to take a complete mental and physical rest. He knew he was unwell; he knew, of course, that he was dying. After a month he was released to spend more recovery time at the Meudon Hotel on the Helford River in Cornwall. What he really needed was a hospice, not a hotel. A week later he was back at the Royal Naval Hospital.

While Sheila was nursing him as comfortably as she could, Giles was working successfully to clear up the misapprehensions over the *France II* sinking the *Lefteria* being related in any way to his father's actions.

They were both by his side when he died, on 26 August 1972. When the end came it came decisively, as if Francis had shrugged and smiled and said, 'Enough!'

For his family and the world his body may have died but his spirit lived on through dozens of obituaries and three church services. On 31 August, Devon's finest attended the funeral at St Andrew's Church in Plymouth, his coffin carried by Giles and the flag officers of the Royal Western Yacht Club. Outside thousands lined the streets for the cortège. Later he was buried at St Peter's Church at Shirwell, the churchyard overflowing with well-wishers for their most famous son. Villagers still remember the church bell tolling, not doleful and sad but triumphant and homecoming. For those who were not there, BBC News broadcast the service around the world.

The memorial service at Westminster Abbey was, of course, a much grander affair. Everybody who was anybody from the seafaring world was there. He may have been the worst Prime Minister until Gordon Brown, but Edward Heath gave a moving and powerful address, part yachtsman to yachtsman, part underdog to underdog. It fitted the new meritocratic age perfectly.

Sir Francis was never content with second-best, he strove for ever greater achievements. That he succeeded is his finest testimony ... All through his life Sir Francis had tested himself against the strongest forces he knew: the wind, the air and the ever-shifting sea ... Those who sail alone acquire characteristics of their own, in their movements, reactions and timing. Solitude sometimes breeds remoteness. But Sir Francis was a kind, warm-hearted man, who always maintained his own integrity and perfectionism ... When he visited me at Chequers a week or two before his last voyage, I wondered how he could ever survive it. Or did he too perhaps realise that his long series of voyages might end in his own boat, in which he had triumphed so often? ... Above all, he always respected his adversary, the sea ... Sir Francis was unsurpassed as a navigator, an indomitable sailor and a superb example to the youth of this country ... He was one of our country's great men.

Looking back from here, it seems that it was when the mourners left the Abbey that tough old Francis, cussed old Francis, faithful old Francis, mission accomplished old Francis really died. He was a man's man, a twentieth century man, a particular breed

REMEMBER
SIR FRANCIS CHICHESTER KBE
17 SEPTEMBER 1901 · 26 AUGUST 1972
They that go down to the sea in ships and occupy their business in great waters
These men see the works of the Lord and his wonders in the deep

Navigator of the skies and seas. Inspirer of the hearts of men

Remember also SHEILA MARY CHICHESTER (née Craven)
1905 · 1989
Dedicated wife, mother, friend and artist. A woman of great faith and one ahead of her time

of Empire Englishman, the last page of the last edition of Boy's Own heroism man. The untried world he conquered is no more. He was lucky enough to be born into a world with feats still left unclaimed and we are lucky enough to have him as the last link into that disappearing world.

It's been exhausting keeping up with Francis these last three years. I will miss him and his madcap dreams and schemes; I will miss Sheila too, even though I can hear her telling me not to be so silly.

———— ✺ ————

NOTES:

20. Sir Robin Knox-Johnston has won the Chichester Trophy twice since, in 1994 and 2007.

21. When they were deposed by the Sandinistas in 1979 the Somozas were judged to be worth US$1billion.

22. Funnily enough, I am writing these words at 40,000 feet over the International Date Line from San Francisco to Auckland to research Chapter 3, thereby losing a Tuesday.

INDEX

Locators with '*n.*' refer to information in the notes, those in italics relate to photos and illustrations. Subheadings for entries of major races and voyages, and for aircraft and vessels used are in chronological order.